SEEDS OF AMARANTH

BOOK ONE

RECOVERING THE CASKETS

Heather Charnley

Seeds of Amaranth
Recovering the Caskets

**Copyright ©
Heather Charnley
Purple Spirit
Press 2016
ISBN 978-1-907042-24-9**

This book is dedicated to those who believe in the constructive freedom of spiritual understanding and expression to contribute to our world.

**Book cover photography and design
Copyright © Sam L. Rollinson 2016**

THE SEEDS OF AMARANTH TRILOGY

HEATHER'S FOREWORD

I began the trilogy purely through channelled inspiration, when I was walking through Prudhoe, Northumberland. I wasn't thinking of anything in particular when some thoughts came out of the blue, 'you will write a trilogy about Atlantis', and as succinctly as that! This was mildly surprising, as I had not even considered anything about Atlantis. I took note of this revelation and continued with my daily activities.

Some months later, once I began to write book one of The Seeds of Amaranth. I wrote as if I were channelling the book, for I would await inspiration, and often go to sacred sites or near our local ley lines to help the input.

I wished to capture some elements of Atlantean ways of living within the writing, so as to discover the best of their culture to bring into our own time period. It is a bit hard to define, for many books working around possibilities, and old legendary information. There is, of course some inspirational written information on the shelves, but I felt that consultation of Akashic records would be the only option, having read some of the former references. I do know that I have lived in such cultures of the past, and was around in the final cataclysm that I have described in the first chapter of this book one.

<u>These words below describe how the storyline begins!</u>
Two young women, Karin and Alyssia are spending some time in Cornwall. They find a hexagonal casket on a beach, and it has crystals embedded on it. They take it to their friend Sarah, who lives near Zennor. During meditation the lid of the box flies open and a holographic image comes out of a large crystal inside. They realise they are viewing imagery from the last days of Atlantis; one scene is from the final cataclysm, and another from an oppressive society in the latter days with their escaping population.

Although these books will be classed as fiction, which implies a story that is made up, it is much more than that, and should be classified under 'channelled inspiration drawn from the Akashic Records, and formed into a story'.

LIST OF PEOPLE IN THE STORY

Sarah Blenheim – healer and craftsperson, initially based in Zennor
Alyssia Lacey – artist from Kendal
Karin Sloane – runs Plas Myrddin, Oswestry
Kenny Kenton – Karin's partner, runs Plas Myrddin
Maraya – tarot reader, and one of Moroccan group, who now lives locally
Costillo – doorkeeper of Moroccan group
Sagario – crystal holder, Moroccan group
Danuel – crystal holder, Moroccan group
Bertha – shop assistant, Plas Myrddin
Geraldine – healer and friend of Sarah
Peter – grocery deliverer at St Ives
Andy Pearson – bookshop owner in Penzance
Vince – lorry driver

Anchorin – high priest in Atlantis – 12,000 BC
Jadeir – elf, who comes to help the Oswestry group
Pireus, Galen, Calani and Derien – elves, Jadeir's friends in Atlantis
Saliera – undine in Atlantis, contemporary to Jadeir and others
Ganus - gnome
Hudlath – high priest from a time period 200 years later than Anchorin
Rhianah – high priestess from 11,659 BC
'Allegiance of Lethe' Men & renegades - from 11,659 BC
Azorca, Tolega, Majoc and Sornel – warrior priests from last moments
of Atlantis' final destruction in 10,000 BC
Alessa, Lucia, Lydia, Styrios, Atellan, Gregarios and Ossias –
escapees from latter days in Atlantis in 10,000 BC

The Council of Twelve
Zanadar – from Cassiopeia
Gelsior – from Pollux
Aurion – from Sirius
Siral – from Andromeda
Maeron – from the Hyades
Golan – from Arcturus
Gillan – from Antares
Talar – from Betelgeuse
Sikaron – from Castor
Melkior – from Lyra

Salaron – from the Pleiades
Kelaré – Ursa Major

Garalph, Ganor, Staloph & Gemalion – gnomes from Pistyl Rhaeadr
Leannah, Philone, Phairos & Alynda – fairies from Pistyl Rhaeadr
Gadair, Cyaphon, Seilon & Kanas – elves from Pistyl Rhaeadr
Kavanos and Kyphos – fauns from Pistyl Rhaeadr
(**Garalph, Leannah, Gadair & Kavanos** – join the group going to Colony Y)
Guyanah – high priestess and friend of Rhianah
Golilio, Kenalph, Gario, Petros, Stephano, Feredino, Elania, Kalaph, Salena, Ellaia and Kyrian – escapees from Colony Y

Arwena – gatekeeper to the Garden of Eden
The Sentinel group – who tend the Garden of Eden
Anui, Deanu, & Giana – guardian priestesses of the essence in the alabaster pot
Uyindin – monk in Anchorin's temple

CONTENTS

<u>SEEDS OF AMARANTH</u>
<u>RECOVERING THE CASKETS</u>

<u>CHAPTER 1 – A CASKET DISCOVERED</u>

Alyssia walked across the sands in a carefree manner. Her features had a refinement about them. Although she had an easygoing smile, there was an air of discernment in her eyes. Her long auburn hair was tied in a ponytail to one side. She was walking along with her friend Karin who was jovial and outgoing, with short dark hair to just below the ear, and she had a merry twinkle in her eyes.

"Ooh look at that, glinting in the sun!" said Karin.
"Let's go and see," said Alyssia, "I knew it was best to come early".
They almost ran to the water's edge. Although it was late summer there had been a bit of a storm in the night and a variety of things had been washed up. The women bent over to look.

"It's a crystal I think," said Alyssia, reaching her hand to it, and glancing at Karin with an excited half-expectant look.
"Oh! It's a box with crystals encrusted over it. Help me dig it out", said Alyssia.
"Gosh, what a splendid box, just a bit more sand away and we'll be able to get it out. Hey! I didn't know we'd come to Treasure Island," laughed Karin, "It maybe was dropped by mistake by 'em smugglers at high tide," she chortled.
"Let's get back to our hideaway and examine it, arr!" said Alyssia.

The box was put in a carrier bag, and they sauntered back across the sands, with the rugged rocks of the Cornish coastline around them. The mellow sunlight at dawn cast a pale yellow-orange light over cliff edges, the crests of waves and the backs of the women's legs as they eagerly walked up a steep pathway back to their car. Karin's eyes were twinkling especially as she talked animatedly, and they were both laughing about something as they got into the car.

Back at the hotel they got the box out of the carrier bag and rested it on a towel to dry it off and clean off the sand. The box had tiny quartz crystals on it and five larger polished ones. It was firmly sealed up and the

women could not prise it open. Karin looked at it and with a puzzled look turned to Alyssia and said.
"I thought the box was made of wood but it seems to be something else. Is it metal or plastic and I can hardly see any joins. I mean, how do you open it?" she gave a little shrug and a thoughtful look came into her eyes.

"How about asking Sarah, she may know what to do. I'm sure this box has something valuable inside, I'm really intrigued."
"Ok," said Alyssia, "let's get down to breakfast; I hope they might be starting up now, then we can ring her, good idea."

"Describe it to me," asked Sarah on the other end of the phone, "yes, hexagonal with quartz crystals on, and what else? No join where the lid meets the box, and it's eight inches in diameter. Is it wood or metal, oh you don't know! Well, bring it over and I'll try and figure out something. It will be nice to see you again after all this time and catch up on news. See you later."

Sarah looked at her phone with a quizzical air. She was sitting in line with the door to her veranda, which overlooked the sea, near a tiny hamlet not far from Zennor. The morning sun filtered through, cascading into her bright airy lounge and illuminated half of her face. It was quite a weathered face, of a person who loved to be outdoors. Her eyes, quite deep-set, were often animated and held a wisdom and kindly air, which was sometimes belied by her pertinent manner. She wore an old roll neck navy sweater and had a headscarf on. She got up and went out onto her veranda, and then tended to some plants in her garden, becoming absorbed in what she was doing.

The two women meanwhile had the strange box in the car and were driving down the narrow Cornish roads to Sarah's cottage. The high banks down the lanes were covered in flowers.

"Oh there's Lanyon Quoit!" said Alyssia, "the men-an-tol should be further along here; it's a while since I was last here."
"Yes, I went years ago, poor Herb nearly got stuck in the hole," said Karin and they both laughed. She added, "well we can laugh about it now but at the time he pulled his back just as he bent and put his head through, though not seriously."
"Oh no!" responded Alyssia, "I didn't realise it was as unpleasant."

"Yes, and he couldn't back out because his shoulders were through the hole too, so we had to somehow tease him through," said Karin.
"How awful and it's supposed to be healing," said Alyssia.
"Yes, I didn't dare suggest going through again for a healing experience," said Karin with a wince.

Karin looked at the map again and said "Hey we should have taken the other road, it would have been more direct to Zennor." They both groaned.

Sarah heard a car pull up and two car doors slamming; it broke her concentration on gardening work and she looked up to see the two smiling young women and went to greet them.

They hugged and Sarah said, "come on in and I'll get something to drink." She stepped in beckoning them to follow. She put the kettle on swiftly and scattered snacks on her small lounge table with an adroit gesture.

"Well? Where's this box then? Let's see it!" said Sarah as she pushed items on the table aside gently to allow room for it. "My! It's an impressive thing." Sarah looked at it from all angles then gently picked it up. "I see what you mean, there seems to be no opening at all, it's watertight!" She looked closely at the base.

"Look, there's a hollow underneath in the centre about the size of an Allen key, I've got one in the kitchen in my bag of tools," she said, then rushed into the kitchen, returning with the key. "I've brought some oil too in case it's rusting, although it doesn't appear to be, surprising after being so long underwater. In fact, I don't know if it is wood, plastic or metal, or perhaps all three combined."
Sarah tweaked with the Allen key to no avail.

"Perhaps it needs some inner guidance, let's have our break and then we can consider the next step," Sarah added.
"That's what we thought," said Karin, "about the material the box is made from, we can't work out what it is."
"Perhaps it came from outer space," said Alyssia in a bemused tone.
They all looked at one another and cautiously nodded, with raised eyebrows.

The box was sitting on the table, still with the late morning sun catching it. The three women had been deep in conversation, catching up. It had been a few years since they had met Sarah, for Karin and Alyssia lived further north.

"Look at the box," said Sarah in a startled voice, "it's beginning to glow."
 "Crumbs, I thought it was the light on it, but it is glowing," said Karin.
"Yeah," said Alyssia, "the light's coming out of the box."
"I wonder if we should move it," said Sarah, "as we don't know the mechanics of it at this stage." She got up to move it and then started back.
"Oh! It feels hot to touch, well actually it's the energy inside, it's radiating out so strongly I just can't touch it," said Sarah. "I'll try tuning in on it and see if I can pick up on what is happening, you join in too." She added with a concerned look.
All three of them sat back in their chairs, attuned, and then Sarah started speaking.

"I think I'm getting something now, I can see the box in my vision, and it has a large crystal inside. There are also three small ones, but it is the large one, which is sending out the light and energy, it has things to tell us. It also says that the box will open if you chant the same note as the crystal gives out. This chant resonates with the structure of the box and it will unseal itself by becoming pliant. Also, we must send out our thoughts into the crystals on the lid one by one in a clockwise direction. It concerns the five inner ones, one in the centre and the other four equidistant. Right, are you ready?"

They all chanted the relevant notes Sarah had intuited as being relevant; then they focused their attention on the lid crystals.
"We'll start with this one here," Sarah had pointed to one particular one," and go round clockwise until something happens."

They focused on the crystals one by one and slowly went round. Nothing happened. Suddenly Sarah said, "I know, let's gather around the box and hold hands to add some compassionate energy to it."
They did this several times and then a strange sound like a vibrating hum, echoing the chant with a sound of voices faintly singing. A beautiful pearly light came around the box, also a reddish hue, which turned to

deepest purple. Then, it seemed, without warning that the box lid flew open and everyone jumped.

"What's that smell?" said Alyssia looking at everyone with a puzzled expression, "it's a bit like smoke."
Sarah looked puzzled, "perhaps it was present when whoever put this crystal in the box, and I somehow think we're going to find out."
"Let's look at the crystals," said Karin, "and get acquainted with them before we start." They got up and looked in the box.
"Well, it looks like a cylinder or seal, we'll have to examine it later," concluded Sarah.
"But there must be a layer underneath," added Alyssia, "it's deep enough. These flanges must be used to lift it with; shall I?"
The other nodded and she carefully lifted the top layer off and placed it onto the table.
"It's amazing, look at that crystal," remarked Karin.
They all stared in disbelief, for the crystal was a large clear quartz. It was very distinctive looking and it was still glowing. There were the other three smaller quartz crystals, also glowing a little. The big crystal attracted their attention.
"Look, there seems to be markings on its side," said Sarah, "let's see; there's an upward triangle, then a downward triangle, a sun image, then an eye, a mouth and an image of the earth."
"What does that mean?" asked Karin.
"I think it means what we have encountered, the two triangles make up a six pointed star, but separately one points to heaven and the other points to earth. When the energies of both come together, i.e. a spiritual gathering. The eye means seeing and seeking understanding, the mouth maybe our chanting, but the earth? Well, maybe we should meditate on this crystal and find out," said Sarah.
The crystal seemed to flicker a moment, then it started glowing brightly again. It sat, along with the three crystals in a neatly moulded case. Whoever had made it was doing it especially for these crystals and to have such a sealing capacity on the box against being immersed in the sea was certainly impressive.

"Let's meet up later, we'll have an early meal and see what this crystal holds," added Sarah, "I've got to go out and see someone in St Ives this afternoon."

Suddenly the lid of the crystal box slammed shut and everyone jumped. They all looked at one another momentarily.

"Wow!" said Karin, "that's really weird!"

"Yeah," said Alyssia, with a hesitant tone in her voice.

"Indeed," said Sarah, "but don't worry too much, it seems as if the box has its own self-programming mechanism built into it, perhaps via the crystals on top of the box and automatically shuts when people have stopped working with it, just like some of our automatically programmed things like thermostats, electric eyes although this is much more sophisticated in its own way".

Sarah examined the closed box again. "You know, there is a fine line along the bottom edge of the box, but it's so fine it really isn't very visible," added Sarah.

"Well, we had better do our sightseeing while we can, I can see we're going to be busy," laughed Alyssia.

"Perhaps I could get a notepad while we're out?" asked Karin.

"Yes, that might be a good idea, don't worry, I'll get a few as I know the bargain shops in town," answered Sarah. Then she added, "Well, I do have a tape recorder that's working, I could get a bunch of tapes also. I don't know what we're going to find and I usually find the unexpected when I start looking! When you live as far out from town as me, I always get prepared, usually over-prepared, but it saves a lot of petrol in the long run!"

The two women then went off. Sarah watched them leave and they sauntered along the coast road towards Land's End. Sarah returned to pottering around her garden for a while longer. As she worked away she could sense something, and looked up with a concerned expression.

'What was that!' thought Sarah. 'It seemed like a roaring sound, no, exploding. I thought they weren't going to do any more mining around here. I can hear voices now like cries… I wonder, the crystals!' and Sarah dashed into the house.

The sun was still gleaming on the crystal box and she thought best to wrap it with a dark shawl, so she hurried to her bedroom for it and then placed the wrapped box into a cupboard in the lounge.

'There, I think that seems to have calmed it now, it really wants to tell a story!' She gave the box a little reassuring pat and closed the cupboard door firmly and returned to her garden before having lunch and departing off to see a friend of hers in St Ives.

Later on near 5pm Sarah wended her way back to her home, the sea a calm deep blue, which reflected in her eyes as she looked out to sea with the faraway look of a mariner. Only the faintest of wispy clouds lingered above. On arrival she unloaded her car. She was still doing this when Alyssia and Karin returned, smiling broadly.
"Hi! Had a good day?" asked Sarah, squinting a little into the late afternoon sun.
"Yeah," said Karin, "we walked a part of the coastal path near Pendeen and pottered around some ancient sites as well as some viewing point stops. The weather has been lovely and the flowers are beautiful around here".
"Oh, I bet you had some long viewing point stops!" quipped Sarah.
"Karin did while I did the walking!" added Alyssia.
"Oi, that's not entirely true!" emphasised Karin and they all laughed.
"Sarah, let's help you with all that stuff," responded Karin, rushing to grab some bags.
Alyssia picked up a large bag and pretended to stagger.
"Boy! What's in here, St Ives' winter stocks," she added.

Once inside they prepared tea and sat down to eat.
"You know, just after you left I heard this bang and some voices, and at first I thought it was someone re-working the mine down the coast or discovered a new site around here. Then, I heard the voices, which came just after that bang. I suddenly thought of the crystal box and immediately wrapped it up and put it away. I think the sun was somehow activating it. Maybe if we get it out and put it in the sun again it will get ready for action while we finish off our tea," said Sarah.
"Whereabouts did you put it, I'll get it?" asked Alyssia.
Sarah pointed to the relevant cupboard and Alyssia retrieved the box and unwrapped it. The late afternoon sun began to warm it and the crystals on the top started to sparkle brightly.

"Let's get prepared then," announced Sarah, and she began to clear things away from the area and re-arranged the table for the approaching ceremony. She closed the curtains, but just left a gap so that the light shone through onto the box. The curtains were thick royal blue velvet, which contrasted with the deep terra cotta coloured carpet. Here and there around the room the terra cotta re-appeared with diamond pattern designs, reminding one of South America.

The box was glowing strongly, giving out its sound.

"Let's sound the chant," said Sarah and they all did it a few times. They then focused their attention on the lid crystals each in turn, starting with the central one and working clockwise. The pearly light re-appeared, also the reddish hue, which turned to purple again and then the lid flew open. Although everyone expected the lid to open suddenly, they still jumped involuntarily once more!

Sarah reached for the crystal underneath the top layer. She whispered, "We have to find out about this too," pointing to the cylindrical seal on the top layer. Everyone was silently expectant. Sarah took the crystal and was going to sit down with it in her hand when she started.

"Oh! I think the crystal wants to stay here on the table. Right, I'll put it on top of the table, but I'll just slip this mat underneath in case it gets very active," said Sarah.

She re-arranged everything so everyone had a good view of the crystal. Everything was very silent for a moment, and then they noticed the crystal getting increasingly brighter until it was too brilliant to look at. There was a rushing sound and a bright filmy energy emanated from out of the crystal and hung above the table. Everyone drew back a little, not daring to speak.

The bright energy formed into a roughly spherical shape. There was a loud bang and everyone looked at each other. They all understood it was what Sarah had heard earlier. There were swirls of colour forming in the sphere and it went very misty, and then all of a sudden they all saw a face. Strangely, when they remarked on it afterwards, it seemed that everyone had seen the same face and scenes at the same angle as each other, since they were sitting in a circle, so that was remarkable.

The face was fair skinned, the eyes were deep set and although they looked as if they could have been cruel, they now held a deeply troubled air. The hair was long and flaxen, and would have hung in braids, but it was very matted and unkempt. There were small cuts all over his head and he kept on glancing around. On his head was a strange looking hat a bit like a helmet, maybe made from the substance the box was manufactured. It had crystals decorating its surface and its refinement looked a little incongruous on the head of this dishevelled person.

He began to speak; he had a commanding voice and spoke in a language that was unfamiliar.
"Oh no, what is he saying?" asked Karin in slight disappointment.
Immediately there was a stirring from within the crystal and the face disappeared and then re-appeared again.

He began to speak again. "I, Azorca, the leader of the people have this to say to you, if you can hear it. Our land is in desolation; we are in the outer lands away from the city and the earthquake's epicentre, yet we are trapped. We forage day and night for food and water. The earthquakes are coming in greater frequency. There are a few of us here, Tolega, Majoc and Sornel also. When the earthquakes die down we will resume control and wish the rest of the world to know it. So, I am talking into this crystal and will send it out over the churning seas to the eastern lands in a hover disk, for that is where many of the others went. There are still many here in these outer lands".
The women could see a crowd of people around the main figure. "We had seen many people emigrating periodically, going west to explore the lands there. We had seen those lands too; and the native people had been here to Huanca, one of our great cities, on many occasions to trade with us".

There was another ear-splitting rumble, and all the people staggered with the blast and cried out, and the faces disappeared from view for a moment. Once again the crystal stirred and the images returned.
"We have to face it," said Azorca with a very pained expression, "we may not live, we may not survive, so this record is a testament to what happened. Several days ago we were in Huanca in comfort with our things around us. Now, we have nothing and nowhere to go", he paused.

"A number of us were very angry. The present day elders promised us a safe and good life, yet some of us felt deprived. They felt we were left out of ceremonies, privileges and decided to change things for themselves. We took the temple of Isis on the south-western slopes, and told the elders that we wished to serve the people of the outer reaches, and so we built another temple from the ruined one. We did not know how it would all turn out. We all strongly believed in ourselves, our ways though ended up as a seeking of power. I had been drawn into being one of the power seekers, yet I regret it now, and wish solemnly to warn you who listen what to avoid if you don't want the world to end up like this!"

Azorca gave a penetrating look and turned to his men. Some were badly wounded. The women could see them lying on the ground and Azorca and his compatriots surrounded them and simply looked at them. With a touch of their hands on the wounded areas they were healed. They didn't need to speak to one another. It was as if they could hear each other's thoughts.

"We realised afterwards," said Azorca, "that the masters who were in control of our temple and our people did not have our best interests at heart. They tricked us for their own convenience and they were so cunning we believed them, until there was little we could do to avoid what was happening. The genuine elders had been right after all and sensibly departed this land of treachery when it was expedient, and now we may die for our folly".

Just then an enormous shudder sent everyone flying sideways. The crystal refocused on Azorca again.
"We shall focus on this crystal to ensure the history of our land shall be preserved. There is little time now," he said with almost a tremor in his voice, we must input our thoughts. Gather around everyone and send your thoughts to this crystal now".
There was a pause as everyone intently focused on the crystal.
"Now, build up a connection between the crystal and the halls of history consider the section in the library to the western side of the entrance".

The women could see beams of light emanating from each person towards the crystal.
"Now think of the halls of wisdom, go around all the walls in a clockwise direction from the door," said Azorca. They all concentrated and a beam of light went to the crystal, from beyond them as well as from the group itself.
A strange wind stirred; the women could hear it whining in the background, gathering in momentum.
"The sea! It's crashing against the shore hard," uttered Tolgan, and a look of contained fear swept through his eyes and across his features. His face was thin and his eyes were wide, and he had to use all his willpower to stop fear taking hold entirely.

There was a huge, almighty bang and everyone looked over to the mountains in the north. The sky was black and acrid although it was midday.
"Look the mountain is spewing lava! This is it now!" said Azorca, "I'm sending the crystal out now, quickly".
He placed it in the box, and although it was inside, the women could still see what was going on despite it being concealed somewhat by the lid.
"Everyone pray to Isis. Dear Isis give us comfort we pray, help us all now at this time....." Azorca's voice trailed off.

The women could see all the people with their arms over their heads from a bird's eye view. The massive mountains were spewing out lava and smoke. The black churning waters, which were getting more turbulent threatened ever closer. The bangs became more frequent, then the mountain in the epicentre of the volcanic activity seemed to lift up, pouring out lava and it broke apart like segments of an orange being pulled outwards. The people huddled together were slowly being engulfed by fumes, showers of sparks and the earthquakes themselves.

The crystal's view from high up showed that there were other groups of people that were scattered everywhere. All unable to move due to a combination of fear, jostled constantly by earthquakes and an inner certainty that there was nowhere to go.

The terrible scene gradually faded, yet the women sensed that the crystal was still travelling. It seemed to move increasingly faster through the dark air, which gradually got a little lighter, then there was a sense that the crystal was on a descending arc and it plummeted downwards landing into the sea and gently lowered itself to the seabed. By then the images had faded considerably until the three women realised that they were sitting in a darkened room, the sun having set, and they reflected on what they had seen. Would there be more episodes like this to see?

Sarah got up and gently turned on a small table lamp in the corner of the room.
"I almost can't believe what we've seen", said Karin slowly.
"It's like we've possibly stumbled upon something truly unique and worth knowing about", added Alyssia.
"You don't think someone's playing some kind of outlandish trick on us", responded Karin, "yet it seems very plausible".

"I know it seems hard to take in, so it is best to reflect on what we've seen. Yet the way the box opened and how the images emanated from the crystal, it is both believable and unbelievable!" said Sarah, adding, "Let's get a good night's sleep and have another meeting soon. See how we feel eh!"

"Yes, let's take a day off to think it all over then", responded Alyssia.

"Perhaps it might help if we each write up what we witnessed while it's fresh in our minds", added Karin.

"Well, I did take a recording, but I'll take notes too of what I saw", agreed Sarah.

They all agreed on that, and to take a day off and meet up on the following day. The two younger women said goodbye and went back to their hotel near Penzance area.

Two days later there was a knock on the hotel door to Alyssia and Karin's room. "Telephone message from a Sarah Blenheim for you?" said the room service man at the door with a questioning air. "She says please come around to her house as soon as you can. If you can't make it tonight then tomorrow will have to do. It sounded as though it was urgent," finalised the man.

"Thank you very much," responded Karin smiling to him. "Maybe we should get around there tonight," she said turning to Alyssia, before turning back to the man, smiled again and thanked him before shutting the door.

"Yeah, we could pick up some take-away stuff on the way," added Alyssia with a slight look of animation in her eyes.

They tidied up their room after their day out on the sands and walking along country routes. They had also visited a smattering of gift shops to collect a few souvenirs for the 'folks back home routine' as they called it! They picked up their jackets and set off.

"Let's get something to eat at that place across the road," said Alyssia viewing it with her hand over her eyes, then turned to Karin, her eyes narrowed a little against the evening sun, "it seems to have some vegetarian items." They went in and obtained three portions and returned to the car. They soon found themselves along the familiar lanes, which took them to Zennor.

Once at Sarah's they saw her opening the door as they arrived. She looked anxious but a look of relief came over her face as soon as she saw them "Come inside, come inside," she said.
"What's up Sarah?" asked Karin anxiously.
"I'll tell you once we are seated," said Sarah rushing to her kitchen. The sound of a kettle being boiled came to their ears as they entered the lounge. "Would the same tea do?" came a voice from the kitchen.
"Yes," said the women in unison, as they stood waiting.
"I'll take the meals through," said Alyssia to Karin.

Immediately Sarah came into the lounge with her tray and she distributed the drinks around and put out a plate of biscuits.
"Sarah, we've brought a meal for us all," said Alyssia proffering the take-away carrier bag.
"Oh great, I hadn't really got around to preparing anything much as yet. I'll put it in the oven and we can have it later. Are either of you hungry yet or can it wait for half an hour?"
They looked at each other and shook their heads.
 "No we don't mind waiting," replied Karin, "but you'll have to tell us what this is all about, we can't stand the suspense any longer!"

"Well," said Sarah thoughtfully and paused looking up at the others. "I don't quite know where to begin. It happened the other night after you left. All was peaceful and I felt most intrigued, like yourselves about what we had witnessed during that session with the crystal like a hologram. Well, I wrote up what I had seen, did you do yours?"
Alyssia and Karin nodded.
"Then I was just going to bed," said Sarah pensively, "I switched off the lights when I heard something strange." She looked up with a worried look.
"Go on," said Karin, "please tell us. We can see you are very upset."
The women almost motioned to come over to Sarah but she gestured that it was ok and that she would carry on.

"I could hear sounds, ones that I would be unable to describe, quite intriguing, but not sure how to express what they were. Perhaps like chants one minute, like many voices at another time, sometimes like dolphins singing, it's like everything you could think of that is to do with Atlantis, that's all I could describe it as, but I'm not sure how to react to it, so I am finding that I am feeling quite worried about experiencing it alone. If you both could help to interpret it, I would feel better about it". She turned and looked at the others and added, "this is an area of the psychic which I am not familiar with. It seems as if this crystal is active now, whether we have the box open or not".

"Perhaps it would be better if we stayed with you Sarah," responded Karin at once.
"Yes," added Alyssia, "under the circumstances we must be supportive, and perhaps we should meditate on what we can do with these experiences, the three of us?"
"Well, it is a relief that you understand," said Sarah immediately looking less anxious, "I'd be most grateful if you stayed here. However, don't you have to return northwards quite soon though?"

"I'm sure we could stay another two weeks," responded Alyssia, "for I'm just waiting for another job to come through and could let them know I'm here".
"And I'm not needed at present at work, but I could ring my boyfriend, I'm sure he won't mind and could manage the workload without me," added Karin.
"Anyway, would you be alright tonight?" asked Alyssia.
"Yes, I'll manage knowing you'll be over in the morning," said Sarah.
"Here!" said Alyssia in an exclamatory tone, "I bought it earlier!" She smiled and handed a little package to Sarah.
"Oh!" Sarah said in surprise. She hurriedly opened it, revealing a little glass dolphin skimming the surf. "It's lovely, you know how I like dolphins and anything like that".
"It's a good luck charm," chirped Karin, and they all laughed.
"Well, that meal should be ready now," smiled Sarah, and she got up to bring the necessary crockery and cutlery through. Alyssia followed her into the kitchen.

"Can I get something Sarah?" asked Alyssia.
"Actually, I'll just put everything on the plates directly after all, it saves messing about, what do you think?" asked Sarah.
Alyssia agreed and the two of them brought everything through and sat down.
"By the way, there's a nice bottle of Aqua Libra in the fridge," added Sarah.

"I'll get it!" announced Karin, with an animated look of glee. She whizzed into the kitchen and returned almost instantly with a handful of glasses. They sat, talking and eating happily.
Later they said their goodbyes and the two women returned to the hotel for their last night.

The sea was rough on their return to Zennor next morning. A storm was brewing and they could feel the headwind catching their car in sudden gusts. They pulled up to Sarah's, and the curtains were still drawn. The women looked at each other in concern.
"Let's get out quick and see what's happening to Sarah," said Karin.
They both rushed to the door and banged on it as well as ring the bell. It seemed a while before Sarah appeared at her window and peered out. They both waved and Sarah disappeared to re-appear at her front door.
"Hello girls, sorry I wasn't up and dressed for your arrival, I had quite a sleepless night. Do come in, don't mind me pottering around sleepily," she said with a smile.
The two women brought in their things and plonked them down in the spare room Sarah had offered to them and then returned to the lounge.
"Cor! It's getting wild out there now," observed Alyssia.
"Yes, when it starts, those storms can be really strong here, and this is a summertime number!" answered Sarah, "I had my roof re-upholstered last year just to make sure it would be A1!" she added, "I'll just get myself shipshape and Zennor-fashion now. Help yourself to drinks". Sarah departed and the last sentence was louder since she was down the corridor by then.

Sarah returned after half-an-hour looking a bit fresher and came into the lounge to sit with Alyssia and Karin, happily drinking some fresher tea they'd made for her.
"How was last night?" Karin and Alyssia asked quizzically.
"Well," said Sarah, "I'm still trying to work out what happened. I kept on seeing that seal in front of my eyes. It was like the crystal was empowering the image of the seal into my mind. Strange. I was so tired, but it was very insistent until I mentally promised that I would look at it in the morning and then the whole thing stopped. If only I'd thought of promising sooner, I would have had a better night's sleep!" she concluded with a long yawn.
"Ok, we can look at it once you've had some breakfast," said Alyssia.

"Did either of you meditate on the things I had experienced?" asked
Sarah.
"Yes we did," the girls replied, "I think it is the whole of the experiences of
the box wanting to be heard simultaneously, and we think that if the
stories are told, the pressure of this will begin to fade."
"That sounds plausible, thank you, both of you!" cried Sarah.

They got the box out and glanced up to hear the rain beating against the
window. It was placed with a reverential air on the table in the centre of
the room. Candles were lit to give an extra warm atmosphere to the
room.
They all focused on the chanting and also concentrated upon the crystals
on the top of the box and then the lid flew open. Sarah hesitated and
then reached for the seal lying on the top layer. She returned to her chair
and held it.
"I've just received the words 'put ink on it and roll onto paper' in my
mind. There's some paper on my desk, and an ink pad just inside it,"
uttered Sarah.
Alyssia brought the things and placed them on the table. They all
gathered round and kneeled on the floor as Sarah applied the ink and then
slowly rolled it onto the paper.

The following symbols appeared from off the seal. First there was a sheaf
of corn, then a flail, an image of the sun followed that, then a flowing
image symbolising the current of a river, then a wise man who was
carrying a staff. Sarah implied that it could have been a flail or sheaf, but
ideally it should have been a staff. Next came an image of someone with
energy coming from the hands denoting healing energy and finally a huge
star.

They all pondered a moment on seeing the images on the paper.
"It seems like a ceremony or way of life. If you reap the benefits of all the
riches, you have the potential to learn, and the wisdom of life will instil
into you," said Alyssia thoughtfully.
"Then there will be a flow, like 'going with the flow', which will make you a
wise person," added Karin.
"And you will become a healer, for those who can heal and nurture
themselves effectively, can in turn heal others. Then they can reach to
the cosmic universal forces at large," finalised Sarah.
"Well that sounds about right," said Alyssia.

With that there was a strange crackling sound and energy started emanating from the crystal again. They all looked at each other in anticipation!
"Well, it looks like our crystal wants to talk with us again," said Sarah, and she removed the top layer of the box and placed the crystal on the tablemat again.
Suddenly the holographic type of imagery format arose again and a big surge of energy filled the space directly over the crystal, which glowed and sparkled. The area was filmy. No one could see anything as yet.

"I wonder what is happening," whispered Sarah, as she was concerned about the images she had encountered the other night. The other two women looked over wondering what would appear.
There was a voice calling, "over here, over here, come to us. Don't go, don't go.."

An image started to appear. It was a young girl. She looked sad and the view panned over to a group of people moving reluctantly. The expression in their eyes was of confused pain. In the centre of each of their foreheads was a strange little disc. The little girl didn't have a disc, but another girl who was a little older had one. They all moved without any sense of animation. The little girl was calling to her family and crying. Someone came up to her and took her by the hand and gently led her away. It was a lady with a cloak and a hood drawn over her head.

The crystal's energy focused on this lady. Her eyes were penetrating, both sad and resolute. She didn't have a disc on her forehead. The women could see her talking to the girl.
"Now, we must be brave. I have to take you to the safe grounds. I'm sorry about your people. They are in the great God's hands now."

They hurried down a few streets until they came near an entrance to a particular building.
"Let's get inside," whispered the lady to the little girl.
Once inside, she took her up the stairs into an apartment on the first floor.
"Now, my name is Lucia, what's yours?" asked Lucia.
"It's Alessanara," replied the girl, taking time over pronouncing her name, "but everyone calls me Alessa."
"Well, Alessa it is then!" added Lucia, smiling.

The room was in a round building, so the room they were in had a curved outer wall and one straight inner wall. The room was filled with plants and crystals. The little girl froze when she saw the crystals.

"Don't worry," said Lucia, "they won't harm us. I have re-programmed them, after being very persistent, so they are now on our side." Lucia nodded encouragingly.

"But," cried Alessa, and her eyes filled with tears. "But all our crystals talked to the greycloaks."

"I know," responded Lucia sympathetically, putting an arm around her. "I managed to intercept the various crystals embedded into walls, floors, ceilings and larger ones under the ground. As well as others in the neighbourhood, which had been well programmed too. There was a very intricate code we found out that the greycloaks had placed on the crystals, and a few friends and I sorted it out and changed it. We are all communicating this to others as best we can. Though we must work carefully or else we'll be noticed."

This information was a bit too much for the little girl to take in entirely. She looked up at Lucia sadly and imploringly, and Lucia gave her another hug.

"Just wait here a moment and I'll get you something to eat from the kitchen, Alessa," she added, giving her a backward glance as she sprinted into the small functional sized kitchen. After a brief moment or two, she returned with a plateful of buttered bread and bits of fruit and vegetables in slices beside it.

"Here," said Lucia, smiling, "this is just a snack to keep you going. We can have something more later."

"Oh!" said Alessa, her face beaming a little, "where did you get this from? Our food doesn't grow. Stocks near us are always low."

"Well, it's to do with the crystals," explained Lucia, "without all that bad programming they allow plants to grow instead of stunting them."

"Why do the people in charge want us to be hungry?" asked Alessa.

"I think they don't want us to be too fit or happy and healthy. If you are hungry all the time it is hard to concentrate on what we wish to and our lives are not as rich, and we get run down and tired, and don't have the will to escape," said Lucia.

"They are horrid, and now they have my mum and dad, and Sarana and Jesha too," said Alessa, and big tears rolled down her face. "Will they return? Will I ever see them again?" She burst into tears. Lucia quickly went to her side and tried to comfort her.

Alessa became tired and fell asleep on Lucia's lap, her thick head of fair curly hair cascading around her. Lucia sat quietly for a while and then placed some cushions around Alessa and carefully placed Alessa's head onto one of the cushions, so that Lucia could get up. She found a rug to place over her. Lucia went to the window and saw a group of men supporting those Gestapo-like greycloaks who took the others away. She didn't like to think where they had gone, but just knew that their time in this strangely unpleasant regime was now over. No one ever knew what exactly happened to them, but they could guess a variety of possibilities. It was no good thinking about it all, as it was too depressing, and the crystals always picked up on your state of mind, for even though they were safe indoors, there would be crystals outside that might do so.

Lucia closed the shutters in the rooms as the light faded and lit a crystal lamp. The bulb shone its mellow light upon the two of them, giving welcome warmth into the room. Lucia watched Alessa sleeping, and her face was relaxed, free for a while of the concerns of the day. Lucia gathered up her belongings and the sought after foods to keep them going, for they would leave that night. Once she had finished she gently roused Alessa from her sleep.

"Alessa, we must rise and leave here now, come on, get up now," urged Lucia.
Alessa stirred and gradually opened her eyes, stretching herself a little.
"Why? Can't I stay here to sleep, I'm tired," murmured Alessa, with very sleepy eyes.
"No, this is the best time to go. I thought I'd let you sleep a little, but now we must go. I have a friend we can stay with on the way!" added Lucia.

Alessa was about to ask more questions when Lucia smiled, "okay! So you want to know everything. I'll tell you once we are out of town and in a safer area."
Lucia did a last minute check to see she had everything required and then they were both out of the door.

"It was good to have the use of this flat," smiled Lucia with a gleam in her eye. Alessa just looked at her as she lowered the hood of her coat over her head. They both moved very silently along the back lanes of the city.

"Wait, we must be very careful here," whispered Lucia with an air of urgent warning in her voice. "There are guards around at this point and so we have to get across this square without being spotted. Usually they don't turn the crystal network on at night, so we can move easier. You walk closely by me, so they cannot see you." Lucia put her finger to her mouth indicating to Alessa to be silent.
"Now! The guards are in the process of changing over. They are relaxing a little and not looking our way. Quick! Round that corner!"

They hurried as fast as they could across the road and round the corner and then into another back lane on tiptoe and as noiselessly as they could. "Thank the Great Mother! They didn't see us," smiled Lucia. "I've crossed that place many a time."
"Have you ever been spotted?" asked Alessa.
"Yes once. A guard came up to me and I told him I was going to a doctor, as my mother was very ill. He relented and let me go," said Lucia. "I was worried in case I was ever caught again, they might not believe me at all the next time!"

They moved up the back lanes and began to relax a little more.
"Why don't you have a disk on your brow?" asked Alessa.
"I had it removed by a surgeon who was on our side a little while ago. That disk is a monitoring device so that the greycloaks can detect our whereabouts, and now they can't detect me!" responded Lucia.
"Where does the surgeon put the disks?" asked Alessa again.
"Ah! I think he buries them in churchyards and places like that; which is ideal for the damp soil renders them inactive within a short space of time and so they are undetectable," replied Lucia, adding, "do you know that he actually removes about twelve disks every week, so that's very encouraging." Alessa smiled.

Their route took them uphill until the evening mists on the brow of that hill obscured their view.
"It's not much further until we are free of this town," said Lucia.

Before them the last houses stood bleakly. Their shuttered windows reflected the closed minds of their occupants, sadly unable to free themselves from their regime. Lucia ushered Alessa to one side.

"Watch now! This last house has been given to a greycloak. He sometimes looks out for anyone passing. There's a light on, we'd best be careful. Follow me quietly until we are out of sight of the house," she whispered.

They could hear voices as they ducked below the window and crept past as soundlessly as they could. The window burst open and they crouched down, hugging each other, hoping a small bank of earth nearby would hide them.
"Bah! That food's wretched, why can't I get anything decent round here!" rasped an angry male voice, followed by a torrent of cooked food, bread and other items ejected out of the window. The window was slammed shut immediately, and more shouting ensued demanding something else to replace the rejected food.
"Quick," whispered Lucia, "run along this pathway now."

They both rushed along it nimbly. They could hardly see where they were going, but the mists were comforting, blanketing them from being seen. Once finally over the summit they clambered down to a little ledge and sat down.
"Ha! That's better," said Lucia, relaxing in relief. "It won't be long now before we get to the woods, and then it isn't much further."
"I don't like this mist, it's scary," said Alessa hugging her coat around herself more tightly and looking around with big frightened eyes.
 "Oh, don't worry!" smiled Lucia, "there are no crystals here that would bother us. The greycloaks don't go for strolls in the countryside. Come on, let's get going now!"

They got to their feet, gently and gradually made their tentative way down the slope, which was still fairly obscured by the mist.
"There's the wood," said Lucia, "we must go through it. There are others expecting us, so don't be frightened when we meet them at the other end."

There was a stirring of small creatures rustling about, and then an owl hooted. In the middle distance the sound of a howling wolf.

"Oh! I don't want to be chased by a wolf," cried Alessa.
"Quick, let's run along this way and then down this cutting and it's not far away now!" said Lucia, her tall figure silhouetted in amongst the dark branches, and her cape billowing a little behind her. Alessa kept close beside her.
"Ah! Got you!" cried a man lurching forwards to grab Alessa. Another took Lucia.
"Thought you could escape us did you?" Both the greycloaks laughed vociferously. Alessa screamed loudly and Lucia struggled.
"Don't hurt us please, we wanted to visit my poor sick mother who is by herself," cried Lucia, trying not to allow a hint of desperation enter her voice.
"Oh dear, and why can't she find someone local to get her a physician then!" snapped the greycloak holding Lucia.
"Because she is infirm and doesn't know many people. I have to visit her and get help for her," explained Lucia.
"And who is this little girl?" demanded the greycloak.
"My little daughter," answered Lucia.

The greycloak eyed Lucia closely for a moment, lifting her hood back for a better look. Lucia's eyes caught a slight gleam of the moonlight, her face pale and almost gaunt.
"We've seen your face before without the girl, and where's your disk?" he said angrily, "I think it's time you came along with us. Come and see the commandant, he likes visitors," he said, grimacing unpleasantly.
"Please let my girl go. If it's me you want. She's too young to be taken to the counsellors, she's only eight," cried Lucia with desperation in her voice.
"Well, I think I can make my own decisions on the matter, not you!" shouted the greycloak striking her over the face.

Just then figures appeared out of the shadowy edges of the wood and struck at the greycloaks, knocking them out.
"Thank goodness you've arrived!" cried Lucia with relief. "Where shall we put these greycloaks?"
"They'll soon be found," said one voice, "we'd better bury them."
"What! Are they dead?" cried Lucia sounding alarmed.
"I think so," cried another, "come on, remove their clothing, we can use it."
The sound of wolves drew closer.

"We can leave the bodies in a spot where the wolves can find them now," cried another.

They pulled off the outer clothes leaving the two bodies within reach of the wolves. One of the party of men gave a wolf-like howl, making Alessa jump a little. It seemed to attract the wolves closer. The group quickened their pace, crossing the valley and over the next hill. Within a little hollow obscured by trees stood a small cottage. They entered it.

Lucia was struck by the cosiness of the atmosphere there. There was also food on the table.
"Come," said a kindly smiling woman, "come and sit yourselves down."
"Hello Lydia," said Lucia, "I'm so glad to see you again, I can't tell you how much!"
They hugged each other briefly.
"Come along dear, come and sit down and eat," said Lydia to Alessa and she asked her name and took everyone's cloaks away into another room. Alessa sat down with Lucia and they began to sample the food. The little girl's face became more relaxed and she began to smile and look more contented.

"This is getting serious, we'll have to have an embarkation," remarked one of the men in a serious tone.
"Yes, I'm not sure we can let the rescuers continue their missions any longer, it's too risky," said another. Lydia nodded sadly and beckoned them over to the table.
"Let's all eat," she said, "who knows when we will find more food now, besides we need all of the stock for the journey."

They all tucked into their food, their usual preoccupation of survival was given a respite at that moment, for they just concentrated on their meal.
"Ah!" said Lydia, "we are all so hungry and tired; we haven't introduced ourselves. This is Greganos, Styrios and Atellan." She pointed around the table as she spoke.
"I'm sorry also," said Lucia, "for I haven't even said thank you for rescuing us. You know Lydia, we were seized by those greycloaks, we could have been..." and her voice trailed off. Lydia held Lucia's hand firmly.

To the men Lydia said, "This is Lucia, and Alessa."
"Alessa's been through quite a lot recently," added Lucia.

Lydia reached out to Alessa, "we'll take care of you now dear, don't worry. I'll find a nice warm bed for you in a minute." Alessa looked up with a glow in her eyes.

They finished off the meal and Lydia ushered Alessa upstairs to a tiny room. It had a small bed in it. A crystal lamp gave a mellow light to the room. A rare sight for most children at that time, a few books and toys lay in a box on the floor.
"Here you are Alessa, this is our children's room. It's your room while you are here, so make yourself at home. I have some spare clothing in that drawer there that you can use in the morning," said Lucia with a motherly smile.
"Where will Lucia be?" asked Alessa with a note of concern.
"Don't worry, she'll be in the next room. I'll get her to look in on you. I don't think any of us will be up for long now. We're all tired out just like you. When you hear the knock on the door, it will be the time for breakfast, alright!" said Lydia.
Alessa smiled a little, "yes," she said.

Downstairs, Lucia and the three men were talking.
"You mean we could be able to go soon? How soon?" asked Lucia.
"In the next day or two," said Greganos, "we have supplies ready, stowed in nearby places." His dark features were strong and emphatic.
"How do you obtain a ship these days? I mean the ports are so well guarded. The greycloaks don't want anyone to escape!" asked Lucia.
"Aha!" said Styrios in his heavily accented voice. "We have a secret hiding place, smugglers cove, as you say!" he winked jovially, trying to lighten the spirits of everyone.
"Bah! You know what we have to do. Steal the ship, board it and put everything and everyone before the greycloaks know another ship is being stolen in front of their noses!" said Atellan with a straight face.
"But how can you manage that?" exclaimed Lucia.
"We become greycloaks of course, telling the port authorities we are taking trade to wherever we choose to mention, on a date of choice and then stow everyone on board, inside the cargo hold until we've embarked," explained Atellan.
"Haven't they ever suspected anything?" asked Lucia.
"Yes, often. They go over every piece of cargo. We have to be legitimate in our operations and several of the other men work at the ports so they

know a thing or two! If all the stowaways keep very quiet, all will be fine," added Atellan.

Lucia looked doubtful. There was a silence produced more by tiredness than anything else. As the discussion was over everyone began to relax. Lydia returned downstairs.
"Look at you all! Get up to bed, you're all half asleep!" said Lydia chiding them with a hint of joviality.
"Alright mother!" said Styrios, putting an arm around Lydia's shoulder. "We go quietly as mouses now."
"Mice!" said someone, correcting. And they all went upstairs.

Next morning there was a feverish knocking on all doors. People were clambering and rushing around in a chaotic state. Lucia rushed to Alessa's door.
"Alessa! Alessa!" she cried. Once Alessa came to open her door she added, "Alessa, get ready quickly, I think we must go! I mean, we are all going, on a ship!"
Alessa nodded and quickly closed the door and sounds of activity ensued. Once downstairs the lure of cooking smells brought their tired faces into a better state of wakefulness.

"Ah Lydia, magnificent!" cried Styrios with a broad grin as a huge plate of appetising food landed in front of him.
"It might be the last decent meal you'll all see for a bit, so make the most of it!" said Lydia, darting off to get more platefuls for the others.

"So, who got the green light call?" asked Lydia.
"It was Atellan with his crystal interceptor, word from one of the port boys," said Greganos.
"Good, the less time we have to think about it, the better," concluded Lydia.
Lydia and Lucia looked as if they were about to ask what would happen next and Greganos observed their expression and responded. "Don't worry, we will explain what happens on the way."

They all cleared up carefully so that there was no trace of their presence left behind. The men all dressed themselves in greycloak clothing, and they set off. It was still dark outside and the fresh cool air made them brace themselves a little.

"Are the greycloaks detectible in any way?" asked Lucia with a direct look towards Greganos.

"Yes, there is a little console in the cloak that gives off a signal to the main headquarters, so they know where each one lives and operates, the greycloaks can switch the signals off, but the headquarters would get suspicious if they were switched off for more than an hour or so. So, we must work quickly, for we don't want to be identified right now do we!" answered Greganos with a kindly look to Alessa.

One of the port boys came around to collect them.

"Wow! It's a long time since I've seen a crystal car!" said Lucia with an amazed look.

The vehicle hovered about a foot above the ground.

"How does the car work?" Alessa asked Greganos.

Yes, it is powered by a fair sized crystal, which is able to empower a system creating a type of magnetic energy which causes weightlessness," he said.

 "Not when you've got on!" chided Styrios with a gleam in his eye looking at Greganos. Greganos gave him a jovial punch on his arm.

They set off; the crystal car bobbed slightly as it silently glided along.

After a while Greganos caught the women's attention. "Now, you three must all get off when we stop a while to prepare to be checked at the office."

They nodded and soon enough they came near the port. Greganos escorted the women off the car and took them to one of the port boys he knew.

"Ossios, here they are, can you take over?" said Greganos in a low voice. "See you later!" he added to Lydia, Lucia and Alessa.

Ossios wrapped a strange garment around each of them, and he indicated for them to cover over their heads too. With that each one became invisible. Lydia and Lucia knew this material, it was made from crystal that had been crushed and embedded into material and then energised so that it could reach a level of invisibility. It had originally been used for healing purposes in the ancient healing temples. It was very unusual for some of this material to still be around.

They followed Ossios to the ship's side and alighted one of the cargo caskets being prepared for lifting onto the ship at any minute. Ossios was used to escorting invisible people to cargo caskets and just lifted his hand in such a way to acknowledge their departure without drawing attention to his movements.

They found themselves suddenly feeling cramped without seeing anyone else in there! They knew then that there were many others in there too. After what seemed like a long time they heard the restraints being released and the vibration of the engines, as well as the characteristic sideways movement of a ship pulling out of the harbour. The three of them touched each other with a growing sense of excitement and relief that they were at last setting off. Though they had been warned not to make a murmur until the ship was well out of port.

Just when they all thought that their moment to relax had come, the cargo hold passengers got a surprise call from one of the crew.
"Watch out everyone! A greycloak prowler ship has come over to give us an inspection. All quietly now!"
No one would have to make a murmur, not even a movement when the inspection happened. To be prepared, someone coughed quickly however, and one or two people changed position.

In the ensuing silence everyone could hear the approach of the prowler ship and the people getting on board. The usual snarling voices of the greycloaks could be heard, and getting increasingly louder, which meant that they were approaching the cargo hold.

"I want to see what type of cargo you have," yelled one greycloak, "open up this casket!"
Obligingly, the casket was opened. Daylight flooded in.
"What's in those boxes?" he asked.
"Paper and card," answered the crewman and he reached forward to open up a carton. The greycloak peered in and gave a nod of approval. The people lying on top of the cartons had not been disturbed.

"Right!" that casket over there!" he beckoned over to another at random. It was duly opened up and luckily it wasn't one with people inside. The goods were checked and then the greycloak left.
After a while the crewman returned to the cargo hold to say that all was well and that the prowler ship had gone.

"I'll let you out soon. Once we've crossed the 'non-signal line' we'll be safe from invasion," said the crewman.

The three of them dozed gently, in a more relaxed state now. The others in there slept also. Later the crewman returned with others for they were talking together and this woke the occupants of the caskets.
"Rise and shine everybody now!" said a voice with a cheerful air.
"Oh that's Styrios!" said Lucia with excitement.

The doorway opened letting in the light once more and the three of them unfurled themselves from the crystal shawls and crawled a little stiffly out of their hiding place.
They all hugged Styrios and Lydia said to him, "I hope you've got lunch ready!" and he laughed.
They all went up on deck delighted to see the sky again and take in a deep breath or two. All the stowaways looked at each other, shook hands and smiled.

"Come!" said one of the crewmen, "Ossios here! Come down here, there is some food for you all," he said with a welcoming air. They all followed eagerly and climbed down the steep stairs into the crewmen's eating area. Lucia was moved to see that they had arranged everything to look more homely, putting tablecloths on and a few refinements for them.
"This is lovely," said Lydia, "where did you manage to get hold of these tablecloths and such nice cutlery?"
"Ah, well," said Greganos with a nonchalant scratch of his nose and shrug of his shoulders, "Just a few presents from a greycloak, eh boys?" and turned his head to the others with folded arms, and laughed.
"Yes," added Atellan, "some goodies we took when we raided a few greycloaks' houses in search of useful equipment."

Styrios picked up a bag and swiftly picked out some of its contents, "and for the ladies, some lovely underwear! Taken from one of the married quarters!" He grinned mischievously and Lydia nearly threw a bread roll at him, but mentioned that she'd rather eat it!
They all sat down to eat and then there was a message from another crewman who came into the eating area.
"It's plain sailing from here everyone. We shall see the port of Tartessos tomorrow. No need to worry now, we've long since left the non-signal line and Atlantis behind!" he winked and departed with a smile.

Everyone looked at each other and a rousing cheer went up all round.
There was a fading of the images then, and the whole scene clouded over and then vanished, leaving the three women in the cottage able to see each other again. They sat in silence a moment re-adjusting their eyes and began to stretch.

"If that was an instance of people escaping from Atlantis, do you think that this happened before the first instance we saw, and related to the same time period?" asked Alyssia.
"It seems possible," pondered Karin.

"What do you think if we all did some research on Atlantis, I don't know anything about it at all, what do you think?" asked Sarah.
"Good idea, are there any good bookshops around here?" asked Alyssia.
"Yes, there are some second hand ones in St Ives and even more in Penzance," said Sarah, "I think we shall go for an excursion tomorrow!" she concluded, and everyone agreed.
"I'll just fix us something to eat, I think some good hot soup would be in order," said Sarah who was now in the kitchen.

Meanwhile, outside the stormy weather was gathering momentum, so they all decided to hibernate for the day, hoping that the next day would be an improvement for their bookshops outing.
"I can look up some sources for books or information on the internet via my laptop," said Alyssia.
"Great! Something we can do this afternoon," agreed Sarah, "the soup'll be ready in a minute!"

<u>CHAPTER 2 – LINKS TO THE PAST</u>

Next morning saw a marked improvement in the weather. After breakfast Sarah tramped around the garden inspecting her plants and her new roof. Giving the thumbs up sign to the other two who were still inside when no damage was found.

Sarah entered the door, "phew! I'm so glad nothing has been harmed at all. My old roof wouldn't have lasted five minutes in that. The only thing that is different is I found an old hat in one of the bushes," Sarah paused thoughtfully, "you know, I think that's old Dan's gardening hat, he must have left it lying around." She laughed and added, "I'll take it up to him sometime, don't think he'll be missing it right now!"

There was a sound of washing up as Karin obliged dutifully and the other two scurried around gathering bags and sorting out all the errand requirements in preparation for their outing to Penzance. "Always good to get as much as we can, there's no such thing as a casual shop for me out here!" commented Sarah.

Before long they were out on the road making their way to Penzance with the sunlight ahead of them. It caught the edge of farmhouses, stonewalls and Alyssia looked over to where Mulfra Quoit would be on a small hill as they were passing.
"Oh I expect the light will be beautiful on Mulfra Quoit! I've got to get a picture of it. I bet it's etched with that rosy tint!" she said.
"Like the archetypal artist that she is!" said Karin laughing, "that's lovely. You always come up with inspiring descriptions. What was that one you told me about concerning that lovely stone circle?"

Alyssia paused thoughtfully a moment, "Well, I don't usually remember unless I write things down. Wait! Here's my notebook." Alyssia delved into her shoulder bag that held her camera and sketchbooks. "Yes," as she thumbed through a few pages, "here it is. 'Into the recesses of the innermost mind-sight. Governed from afar, the light of the cosmos shone fairly upon this site and the activated power linked earth and heaven in an immutably stable light, giving new life and soul and spirit there.' " Alyssia looked up with an expectant air, waiting for comments.

"That is interesting Alyssia," said Sarah, "sounds like something straight from Atlantis."
"Or Lemuria too!" added Karin, and the others nodded.
"Well, don't let us stop your artistic flow Alyssia!" laughed Sarah and Karin chuckled.

They watched Alyssia lightly clamber over a fence and go up the hill to the quoit, clicking eagerly, reappearing every so often at the brow of the hill as she looked around with a meditative air while reaching for her notebook and writing profusely every so often.

"Have you heard from your boyfriend yet Karin?" asked Sarah.
"Yes, Kenny's left me text messages recently, asking me how things are progressing etc., and I've replied to say I don't know exactly how long things will take. He talked of coming down sometime soon if we intend to stay a while longer. However, I don't know how he'll get away because of the shop," she said with a slight shrug.
"What kind of shop is it?" asked Sarah.
"Sorry! I haven't told you yet. It's a bookshop, with some crafts too, some of it is ethnic, traidcraft and new age orientated. He's hoping to expand and have other things like new age music; clothes and crystals as the shop next door has become empty, possibly might have a small café too! He says if he gets more trade and staff, he won't be tied to the shop as much. I've told Alyssia as her artwork would be useful, she said she'd help out with the fitting out, that is, the painting and design work, as we want the shop to have an intriguing mystical air," said Karin with a slight flourish, which made Sarah smile.

Alyssia returned to the car and they sped off again.
"Got some great shots!" said Alyssia excitedly, bundling her bag to one side and throwing her seatbelt on speedily. Karin smiled appreciatively saying she couldn't wait to see them later.

Once in Penzance they found one of Sarah's special side-street freebie parking spots, and wandered down the hill to the main shopping area. Alyssia was looking over to St Michael's Mount eagerly once it was in view.
"Look at the light on St Michael's Mount, it's like an etching!" she cried.
"Yes, lovely," responded Karin.
"Look at the sunlight catching the icing on that cake!" said Sarah eagerly eyeing something tempting in a bakery window.

"Oh really!" said Karin, "one satisfies the eye, and the other the stomach!" Alyssia looked round, "what a philosophy!" and she shook her head a little in disapproval and then smiled, "are we going to get something to satisfy our bodies then?"
The others didn't need much persuading and were into the shop before Alyssia finished her sentence.
"Look! This one looks like strawberry icing on top of it!" said Sarah.
"Yummy then!" responded the other two.
An assistant came up and Sarah asked, "Is this a strawberry icing?"
"Yes madam it is," came the reply.
"Well, three of them please," looking round, she asked, "how about some pasties for lunch?" The others agreed. Sarah quickly continued the conversation with the assistant, "yes, also three vegetarian pasties please."

Once out of the shop, Sarah indicated with a point where they could go next, and they sped off down the street, the sunlight catching their faces.
"Here's the first shop I had in mind, Second-Handy Andy's I call it!" Sarah said with a smile.
"Why do you call it that when the shop front says "Pearson's Books"?" asked Karin.
"Because the shop owner is called Andy, Andy Pearson in fact," said Sarah.
"Ah!" the other two said.

In they went and Sarah went up to the counter. A large genial looking man sat behind the counter, and on seeing Sarah a broad grin spread over his face, making him look a little like the Cheshire cat.
"Hello, hello there Sarah, and who are your friends?" he asked.
"This is Alyssia and this is Karin," she responded with gestures.
"What can I do you for?" he asked with a look of animation.
"Do you have anything on Atlantis?" asked Sarah.
"Hmm, let me see. You may be in luck, for a whole pile of books came into the mind, body and spirit section the other day. Go and see, they are in the usual place near the left side," said Andy.

They wandered off over to the left side of the shop and immediately spotted about six books on the subject.
"Wow! Great! We are lucky, let's get them all!" said Alyssia.

"Well, we didn't need to look far there.   I'll pay for them with the understanding that we share them as need be, eh?" said Sarah.

They went to the counter and Sarah paid, "Do let me know if you have any more on the subject will you Andy," said Sarah.
"Yes Sarah.   My!   You're all keen, what's the big attraction then?" asked Andy, looking intrigued.

Not wanting to give much away Sarah tried to sound casual, "It's just that all three of us are interested in knowing more about the subject at the same time, so this will give each of us a chance to read up, and Karin's boyfriend is interested too, so I said we'd just get whatever we could and we can share the books together.   I also have other friends who I know are interested in the subject too."
Andy nodded with a look of acceptance and a smile, and they all departed.

Once down the street a little, Sarah said, "Phew!   Glad I managed to convince him with that line, I wouldn't want any strange stories spreading around here, blossoming on anyone's grapevine."
"Definitely not!" agreed Karin.
"Do you think we'd better look round the other bookshops, and you can do your errands meanwhile, just in case?" asked Alyssia.

"Oh it's alright, the folk round here know I'm not a conventional type, so a few intriguing books shouldn't make much difference.   However, it may save some time, as I've got to go to Grumpy's Electricals and the shop next door, both of which are miles away the other end of town," said Sarah.

"Who's Grumpy?" asked Alyssia quizzically.
"Granby is the name, and grumpy is his mien.   I put off going there as much as poss, but he's the only choice in Penzance for my requirements. Never a chance available to get some new equipment at a different stockist," said Sarah, "well, when the hoover expires hopefully I'll have saved up enough to go elsewhere.   He's the cheapest, probably that's why he's grumpy!"

"Well, when I've got another job I'll help you out financially," smiled Alyssia.

Sarah smiled comically and then added, "if you go up to Hobson Street and turn left, there's the other second hand shop, and the third is on a parallel street behind. See you as soon as possible. We could meet at a café nearby. I think it has a yellow frontage with tables and chairs outside. In half and hour then!" and she sped off. The other two strode up the hill pointing in shop windows as they went.

Half an hour later Alyssia and Karin converged on the café that fitted the description, and waited a moment.
"Let's get a table out here and we can be waiting for her and be doing some reading too!" said Alyssia.
"Ok, you sit there and I'll go in and ask for some tea and that Sarah will be coming," said Karin with a smile.

Sarah came up to the table a little later to where they were sitting and plonked herself down.
"Boy! I'm not going back there in a hurry! What have you ordered?" asked Sarah.
"A pot of herbie!" said Karin.
"Lovely!" replied Sarah, "peppermint?"
"Liquorice!" answered Alyssia, and Sarah murmured with appreciation.
"Did you find much?" asked Sarah.
"Yes we got another four books. I think we've cleaned Penzance out on the subject!" smiled Karin.

"I'm just reading that sun worship was used widely in Mu and Atlantis, and the winged disk was used in both cultures. It fits in with the Egyptian traditions. Also, the Mayans were contemporary with at least Atlantis," said Alyssia, adding, "here it says that info taken from tablets in India and Mexico talk of the age of Mu going back as far as 45-50,000bc and the Mayans who were one of the two sources, it is mentioned that their last Can king, (Can is a period), was around 16,000 years ago, and the Can period lasted 18,000 years," said Alyssia.

"Hey! Save a book for me!" said Sarah grabbing one, "if I don't get one quick, you'll have digested them all before lunch!"
"Well," said Karin, emerging from another book, "I think I'm quite happy to have a cup of tea and look at the view at present, and save this book for later digestion!"

They had their pot of tea, watching people going past.
"I've just got to call over there at the watch shop there, battery's gone," said Sarah examining her watch face with resignation, "then grab some groceries from the supermarket, and then we can escape!"

Once achieved, they were happily returning towards Sarah's home and speedily unloaded the car in the driveway.
"I'll put the pasties in the oven to warm," said Karin, "how about another pot of tea?"
"Great!" came the chorus in response as they brought in more provisions from the boot.
"Lovely! This lot should keep us going quite well for at least a fortnight. Now we can concentrate more on our investigations!"

Once settled with food and drink, their books opened, they all began to read avidly.
There was a sudden spell of bright sunlight, emerging from the bleak post-stormy weather in shafts, which caught the edges of chairs, faces and curtains. Its warm glow seemed to activate a response in the women and they looked up one by one, glancing every so often out through the window.

"Well?" asked Sarah, "this looks like a moment to perhaps stop and share what we've all discovered."
 "Ok," said Alyssia, "I've come across something very precise which explains the demise of their civilisation – it says here that nations degenerate when a civilisation's facilities are denied, and knowledge of higher aspects such as humanities, art and science have slipped into myth and legend."
"That sounds very apt," said Karin, "it puts it in a nutshell doesn't it. Well, I've been reading of the demise of Lemuria being the waxing time for Atlantean culture. The first Lemurians to emigrate were blond-white and were driven from Lemuria by a race of brunettes."

"And I've found here that the Atlantean races had high cheekbones and were of a Mongolian appearance with slanted eyes, in both the red hairs and blond strains. There were two white races here. The Atlanteans weren't corpulent and were very tall, seven feet plus, and had a healthy diet. The more ruling classes of the Atlanteans had violet or blue eyes as they had brought the culture to Atlantis. Other races with coloured skins came over in later times, but without the racial tensions of today," said Sarah.

"Well, everything is in tension today due to a true lack of spiritual leadership isn't it?" said Alyssia.

"I know and it isn't really meant for only certain people to fix the world, but for every single person to be invited into a worldwide team of care, sharing and cooperation, so that all work together in harmony and peace," added Karin.

"Definitely," chipped in Sarah, "but everyone to the degree in which they are capable of doing, and not to feel pressurised, and especially not to feel outcast or worthless, but to be praised for their efforts. It's time that old competitiveness stopped and cooperation, care and sharing took over."

"Yes, I'm sure it will catch on at some point, it's so much nicer," said Alyssia.

"Oh, I've found something here about the origins of the Atlantean culture from another angle," said Karin, "about Poseidon, though the original names have long since been forgotten now and there are Grecian substitutes, who came from another climate of Godly nature, being able to create food in abundance and make springs rise. He married a native called Cleito, and created a series of concentric islands where they lived, and had five pairs of twins, who became very rich rulers of the land. Everything they owned, i.e. buildings, temples and the like were adorned with a special metal unobtainable now, called orichalcum, which was more precious than gold and had a reddish light," said Karin, adding, "though they did have laws written on tablets for the common people to follow, they were quite strict, ruled directly by the blue robed priesthood."

"Sounds rather intense, that tablet business," said Alyssia, "wouldn't have liked to swallow them!"

"It certainly doesn't sound like a golden age," added Sarah, "but that bit about the metal sounds interesting, for that box had a reddish light when the crystal glowed, giving it a kind of translucence, whilst remaining opaque, if that doesn't sound too crazy!"

"I know! But the light did give it that sort of appearance, but without being able to see what was on the other side of the lid," agreed Karin.

"Hey!   I've found out something else folks!" cried Alyssia, "it's about Poseidon, that he was considered an extra-terrestrial, and came from the Pleiades, which is in the constellation of Taurus, and accounts for the bull worshipping and names of places etc., with Taurus in them. He started the culture of Atlantis via Pleiadean instruction and it says on this page that the Pleiadeans eventually stopped the culture also, via Zeus.

The Pleiades have about 250 stars, but the seven sisters are some of the brightest ones, and they are younger than our sun. Some say that the seven chambers in the Great Pyramid relate to the seven stars.

Many native peoples know of the Pleiades: on the Society & Tonga islands, the Abipones of the Paraguay River, those in South America as well as Mayans. Arabs, Berbers, Dyaks of Borneo, Aborigines, the Tuaregs of the Sahara (like Taurus) and also the Maoris."

Alyssia finished reading and looked up, and added, "Do you know that these native people still have been keeping that knowledge alive, while Copernicus had to try and convince the so-called cultured Western world that the earth wasn't the centre of the universe as well as not being a flat disc!"

"Yeah, so much for Western culture!" answered Sarah, "culture born of wisdom and deep understanding are the only premises for a truly valuable culture."

"Yes, I've found out that there are also some other natives living in Northern Colombia called the Kogi who live on the higher slopes of a mountain, where the nearest town is Santa Mata. Their elders wanted to give a message to the rest of the world (younger brothers), to appeal to them to care for the earth environmentally, and are a highly spiritual people who believe in equality of all living things, which deserve respect. They have a legacy of city ruins and its culture from a long time ago. They link this to the philosophies in connection with this culture, though much has been forgotten."
"I must say that I'd prefer a loving and kind culture with simple lifestyle, to one like ours which is very sparse on love and wisdom," mused Karin.
"..and so would I!" chorused Sarah and Alyssia.
With that they all decided on another pot of tea and to get the chairs in order to sit outside, for the sun was beginning to shine cheerfully, contrasting with the past day or two of very overcast and windy weather.

I haven't seen Geraldine for quite some time," said Sarah, "do you remember me ever mentioning her. She's very much into the spiritual scene, she does healing work, that is, of the psyche rather than just a spot of aromatherapy and that's it!"
"Does she live far away?" asked Karin.
"No, just down at Land's End area near St Just. If she's not doing some healing though, her second home is at a stone circle on the moors nearby!" said Sarah with a chuckle.
"Well, I've got a second home like that!" responded Alyssia, "it helps me get my artistic work flowing."
"I'm sure it gets everything flowing right!" added Karin animatedly.
"What was that sound?" asked Sarah.
"What? I didn't hear anything except a fly scratching itself," responded Alyssia.
"Really!" said Sarah with a sudden look directed at Alyssia, "it was like…"
"Like what?" asked Karin sounding concerned, "I thought I felt a vibration or a kind of half noise, half resonance if you know what I mean."
"I don't think either of us know to be honest! But we'll go along with you for the moment and see," said Sarah.
"Do you think it's that box again?" asked Alyssia looking serious now. The others just looked and then they all glanced out of the window at the sunlight, as if gleaning some reassurance before taking any action.
"Looks like we've got to find out," said Sarah almost apprehensively.
"It should be an adventure! Let's not get so anxious about it," said Alyssia, trying to lighten the atmosphere.

Sarah was worried in case those Auschwitz-type faces might come to the surface again, and their reading had portrayed the Atlantean culture as experiencing many changes from both ends of the spectrum of cultural and spiritual progression and regression. So they all felt that they could expect anything to happen!

They all rose from their chairs now as the sun was beginning to approach the horizon a little, and a nearby bush was casting a shadow over their chairs. Once inside the lounge again, the feeling came upon them again and a little stronger.

"I feel a little light-headed," said Karin quickly sitting down.
"I can see pearly-toned lights in front of me," said Alyssia.

"And I have a strange vibration running through me," said Sarah, continuing after a momentary pause, "well, we'll just have to find out what's going on, whatever is affecting us all right now."
Sarah got the box out and set it respectfully on the central table. The three of them instinctively sat more closely together than the other times, Alyssia and Karin on the sofa and Sarah on an adjacent chair.

They opened the ceremony with candles and a strong prayer, and their chanting sequence whilst concentrating on the crystals on the top of the box, in order to open it. It flew open and the central crystal threw up an image, which startled the girls.
"Can you see those three women?" asked Sarah in a barely audible whisper.
"Yes, look! The images keep changing, it's like the figures are men and women in all kinds of cultures. Look!" said Alyssia, and the last word was almost shouted.
Suddenly the last image that each of the figures changed to was how they looked in much more recent times. Each of them gasped as they had recognised themselves.
"My!" said Sarah, her mouth still open.
All they could do initially was look at each other.
"I wonder what the significance of this is?" ventured Karin. With that a pulsating light came out of the box.
"I've got that light-headed feeling again," said Karin.
Sarah leant forwards and peered into the box.
"There's one of the three crystals throbbing," said Sarah and she looked pensive a moment, "I wonder if you are meant to take it?" she added with a glance over to Karin.
Karin gave a look of half amazement, "yes, you may be right, ok."
She took the crystal and sat down.

Then there was the pulsating light again and Sarah felt her feeling of vibrations again, and she got up and took hers. They both looked over to Alyssia who somehow waited for the lights to re-appear before she got up and took her crystal also.
"I wonder what we are supposed to do with them?" asked Karin.
"Perhaps we should just carry them around with us until we get re-acquainted with them," said Sarah, with a somewhat penetrating look at the others, as if echoing how her mind was searching for the answer.

"Yes, perhaps, but maybe we could meditate with them also, and find out more about those people," said Karin.
"Yes, that sounds good," agreed Alyssia.
"Right then!" concluded Sarah, "let's get started."

They shut their eyes and concentrated, and the crystals began to pulsate a little meanwhile. Their faces hinted their past, looking a little graver, yet wiser but also with the serenity of a Buddhist statue. Finally they stirred and slowly moved, looking at each other and smiled.

Karin spoke first, "I saw an image of myself as a priestess conducting ceremonies and linking strongly to the light. We could use our power of thought to heal, could lift things with our minds with ease and much was healed every day, which would be called miracles by today's standards."

"I knew myself to be a priestess too, but one who could see into other realms and give guidance and understanding to all people who came. I could sing too, and those who didn't understand very much, we put on plays or life stories, so that they could relate to a type of lesson life could teach them, but use that lesson to teach useful lessons generally, and not to disregard instances in life as simply 'bad luck'," said Alyssia.

"I could see myself as another priestess whose main skill was linking with the earth and bringing that energy to bear in the everyday world. I could see images of wells and holy sites with the energy emanating out of them like white fountains and of drawing that energy into the healing temples, so that others could use it for healing. I saw images of earth spirits, you know, fairies, elves and the like," said Sarah.

"Do you know, that seems like the reason why we each got a different reaction, because of our skills being different," said Alyssia.
"To think that these skills could have been learnt so long ago, and that they are still here now!" mused Karin.
"Well, that turned out to be a very good session!" said Sarah, almost laughing with relief.
"Yes very, have you got some means of carrying your crystal around with you?" Karin asked Sarah.
"Hmm, I may have a bag that's kicking around in a cupboard," said Sarah with a twinkle in her eye, "but if you don't I can whizz stitches round some material and create some bags pretty pronto!"

"Yes please!" came the chorus as Sarah nodded and smiled, then dashed off to her cupboard in one of the spare rooms. After some sounds of tussling and a few bangs and crashes, at which Alyssia and Karin both gave half grimaces and shouted, "Are you alright in there, Sarah?"

Sarah re-emerged with her material and workbox.
"I've always been a bit of a hoarder, it comes with living in remote places for so long. One day I'll have to get it all shipshape and Bristol sometime. Everything tries to escape from that cupboard before you can say Jack Robinson!" she said.

They carried on talking together cheerfully as Sarah created some nicely padded crystal bags for them all, and Alyssia thoughtfully painted a motif on each of them.

CHAPTER 3 – PLAS MYRDDIN

A few days later Karin was back up in Oswestry as Kenny was so busy in their shop that he needed her help again. Alyssia came up too saying to Sarah, "I'm sure the crystals will call us all back together when the time is right." This had reassured her and she smiled and waved enthusiastically as they left.

It was mid August and Alyssia decided to explore the area.
"Why don't I take you to a beautiful waterfall at the weekend, on Sunday?" said Karin, "right now we have the shop fitters in readjusting the basics until Saturday."
"I just feel I'd like to go today, you know that feeling when you are impressed to do something," explained Alyssia, putting her hand on Karin's shoulder.
"Yes I know, I'll give you a map of the area, one we show tourists," said Karin rushing off, with a look over her shoulder to Alyssia with the last words.
"Oh yes, here it is, look! You go due west along the B4580 through Llansilin to Llanrhaeadr and it's signposted from there!" said Karin, and added with a stage whisper, "Wish I was coming with you!"
"Thanks," said Alyssia and they gave each other a hug, she added, "I'll show you the photos etc. when I return!"
"You'd better!" said Karin smiling, and then called out to Kenny, "Kenny! Alyssia's just going out to the waterfall!"
"Oh good, it's great out there today, might as well keep away from the chaos," said Kenny, emerging from behind a doorway looking a bit dishevelled with the sawdust and radio blasts in the air.

Alyssia set off with her usual artistic gear in her shoulder bag and the crystal in its bag of green velvet.
"It's not a colour I would have chosen," Alyssia had said to Sarah, "but this emerald green colour is rather lovely and very fitting somehow. You were lucky getting such a colour, I've never seen it to buy." Sarah had intimated that she knew some craft workers' outlets and so managed to obtain the necessary.

The sunlight was irradiating the countryside ahead of her as she drove along the quiet country road; the rolling hills around were green and lush. It wasn't long before she reached Llanrhaeadr and the entrance to the

valley up to the waterfall. There were many trees and Alyssia looked around her as she noticed the hillside skirting the sides of the valley.
"It's a bit like a canyon," she said to herself as she approached the end where the hillsides turned craggier, grander and more scenic. She drove up to where she could just see the waterfall and found a car park there with a small café and caravan site beside it.
A man in the car park greeted her.
"I've just come to view the waterfall," said Alyssia, "can I park here?"
"That's fine, just pay me that sum stated on the sign if you are happy to stay here." Alyssia parked her car and paid.

Alyssia got out her bag and wandered off to the waterfall, taking photos and jotting impressions in her notebook. Later she returned to the car and the man was there again.
"The waterfall has a great sense of presence, a bit like some of the ancient sites I've often visited," said Alyssia.
"Ah yes," he said with a look of animation, "come into the café and I can show you a picture in there, for there is a living spirit in the waterfall, a lady or feminine energy."

"Really, that's lovely," she said as they wandered through the restaurant and over to pictures on the wall near the back. "I'll take a postcard of the waterfall in the snow, as well as this one of the curious rocks. They remind me of the tufa rock I came across in Arizona, which formed into curious shapes, one was called the stone mother," said Alyssia.

"Whereabouts in Arizona did you see that?" asked the man.
"By the side of Pyramid Lake, so called because there was a huge rock shaped like a pyramid, and the tufa was on the shoreline," explained Alyssia, continuing, "The whole area had been and still is, covered in hot springs and the level of the lake used to be twenty feet higher in ancient times, so that explains why the tufa was sitting around on the land."

"These rocks are indigenous to the area, no hot springs have been doing anything exotic round here, maybe in the Carboniferous period things were a bit different though!" and he shrugged and smiled.
Alyssia paid for the two cards and then added, "actually I'll be generous and get another copy of each for my friends in Oswestry."
The man gave a swift look, "Oswestry! Have you seen the old hill fort, Guinevere's castle?"

"No, not yet, we only just returned from a trip and it's actually the first time I've stayed in Oswestry," said Alyssia.
"I'd go there, it's worth a visit," he said emphatically.

They said goodbye to each other and Alyssia spent a bit more time going to see the curious rocks, he'd called them the Giant and Giantess, and there was a story behind them, in that the Giantess was supposed to have been fought over by her suitor and a rival, and there was an image of the rival to be seen on the side of the Giant from a certain angle. Alyssia found the Giantess on the far side of the pair, and she sensed that if they really had existed, they could well have been buried right there.

Once back in Oswestry territory, Alyssia managed to find the circuitous back road to the hill fort. As she was walking around the perimeter of the fort, she became aware of a face. The figure accompanying her was from the spirit realms. As she entered the fort properly by going over a stile she thought to herself "its Merlin!"

"Yes indeed, it is Myrddin!" came the response.
Alyssia proceeded straight to the centre of the area as if guided there.
Myrddin said, "Where is the castle? Find exactly where it is."
She moved onwards more slowly and felt she had got there.
"Go over to a spot you feel drawn to from here," said Myrddin.
Alyssia moved forwards a little more to the south-east.
"This is where Guinevere slept," came the reply and Alyssia looked curious and surprised.
"Try another place you feel drawn to," said Myrddin again.
Alyssia moved a small way forward again and stopped.
"This is where she used to contemplate as a 17-18 year old, and the time when she was told that she would marry Arthur," said Myrddin.
Alyssia began to feel emotion welling up, "then it all went pear-shaped," she said and tears began to well up into her eyes.

Myrddin stayed, accompanying Alyssia until she reached the car. She had to hurry as a wall of rain cloud was fast approaching Oswestry. By the time Alyssia returned to Karin and Kenny's shop, she had regained her composure.
"We're still up to the ceiling in sawdust, fumes and Radio One!" said Kenny, ever cheerful despite the chaos, manoeuvring amongst several workmen working vigorously around him. "I'd better return to the other

half of the shop that's still intact!" He rushed off with a smile and before long Karin returned and greeting Alyssia.

"Let's have something to eat upstairs," said Karin, "I'll want to know all about your trip, I'm jealous!" she said with a wide grin. Alyssia followed having proffered a nice loaf she'd bought on her travels and other goodies. "That waterfall was splendid, with that lady energy, there is also supposed to be the energy of a monk and dragon there too, look! There's two postcards for you both!" said Alyssia.
"Oh they're really nice, I'll look forward to visiting the waterfall. We've never made enough time to get there you know, though we have been to other places however," said Karin, "now have some of this soup."
"Lovely!" said Alyssia with a Welsh intonation, "will we have enough time to talk at length?"
"Yes, we have an assistant in the shop some afternoons and she'll be arriving anytime now, she's called Bertha," said Karin.

"I had a profound experience at the hill fort as the man at Pistyll Rhaeadr mentioned that it was Guinevere's Castle, and it seemed that spirit was working through him acting as a catalyst to ensure that I went!" explained Alyssia.
"Go on," said Karin, "so what happened at the fort?"
"I heard from Merlin or Myrddin as he prefers, and he told me to go to various places of my choosing at the fort, and sure enough, I came to where Guinevere slept, and also to a garden spot where she had been told that Arthur and she would be married and I felt quite emotional," said Alyssia.
"That usually means that you are connected on some way. Do you think you were Guinevere or someone else present at the time?" asked Karin.
"I feel drawn to Guinevere and I felt and sensed whatever was around there beforehand, and Myrddin confirmed it afterwards, but I feel I need to mull it over a little for a day or two to really know it," said Alyssia.

They continued to eat and talk, when they heard the sound of footsteps and Kenny appeared at the door.
"Phew!" he said, rubbing a hand through his tousled hair, "I'm really looking forward to some of that soup!"
"Hold on!" said Karin, "I'll just reheat it and make some toast. Did you know Alyssia has had some really interesting experiences today?"

Kenny looked enquiringly at Alyssia, his well defined eyebrows seemed to lower a little adding an intensity to his look, but with his shock of curly hair and a broad moustache he looked more comical than anything else.

Alyssia smiled, "Yes Kenny, after going to Pistyll Rhaeadr I was directed to go to Guinevere's Castle and I saw Myrddin and all sorts. I'll tell you the story!"

"Do!" replied Kenny as he leant on his hand listening intently as Alyssia retold the day's occurrences.

"That's intriguing," said Kenny eventually, "do you feel that you were Guinevere?"

"That's what Karin asked, but I said that I'd have to think it all over for a day or two and see how everything comes together," said Alyssia.

"I think you were Isolde," said Kenny earnestly to Karin, "and I was Tristan," he added dramatically putting his hands to his heart and half collapsing in the chair. Karin and Alyssia chuckled.

"Ah well, duty calls!" said Kenny standing to attention having gulped down his soup and toast, then he departed off down the stairs, the others smiling after him.

"I've just got some washing to pop in the machine as we need some clean clothes tomorrow!" said Karin.

"What's happening tomorrow then?" asked Alyssia.

"Well nothing really, except that we won't have anything clean available!" said Karin, "with all this building work, Kenny said there was something funny with the plumbing, as it went off for quite a bit before we returned, I think the men did some alterations to the pipes accidentally, so Kenny resorted to some hand washing."

"Oh I see!" Alyssia responded, "Carry on the good work!"

Karin disappeared into the adjacent room to fill up the machine. Alyssia looked out of the window over the rooftops, the clear sky had a few clouds gliding past very slowly. Slowly one cloud began to change shape with increasing rapidity, then suddenly it was a man's profile with a helmet on, Alyssia knew it was Lancelot and she continued to look at it and reflect on everything. Just then an image came into her minds eye, it was a cross with arms of equal length and it was a pendant, and there was a pattern along the centre of each arm and also a pearl at each end, with a fifth at the centre.

Karin came back into the room and Alyssia half jumped out of her reverie.

"You look miles away Alyssia, are you okay?" asked Karin.

"Fine really, I was just given two confirmations about Guinevere just now, and I had been told that I would see two signs later when I was at the Castle," said Alyssia.

"Is it all right to ask, I'm not prying Alyssia, am I?" said Karin concernedly.

"No it's fine," and Alyssia told Karin what she saw.

"You know, that is interesting," explained Karin, "Do you think that there could be a connection between the five crystals on the box and those five pearls on the pendant?"

"Wow! I hadn't thought of that! That's quite an intriguing thought," mused Alyssia, the number five links to the earth."

"Was your crystal glowing while you were on the hill fort?" asked Karin.

"I don't recall anything happening actually, I was too busy concentrating on Myrddin and what I was seeing," said Alyssia, "you know, I think I'm going to have to consider making a journal or something. I feel I'll have to write about Guinevere I think," said Alyssia with an inquiring air, turning to look at Karin.

"That's good, perhaps that will help to resolve the situation or bring things to light, and there may well be something there in connection with the crystal and so Atlantis, we'll have to see," said Karin.

"Well, it's your turn next!" said Alyssia with a smile.

"For what?" asked Karin.

"Your inner experience in connection with your crystal," explained Alyssia.

"Oh, of course, but I hope that it can wait until the workmen have been! I don't think I've got spare energy for both!" answered Karin.

A few days later Alyssia arose and looked out of the window. It was quite a fair day, yet a pensive looking cloud hung over to the north west, reminding her of a sad looking woman, with head bowed and supported by her hand. Alyssia's expression showed a slight puzzled frown, though she was not feeling unduly sad in any way herself. She got ready and went to the kitchen and saw Karin preparing breakfast.

"Have you seen that cloud out there Karin?" asked Alyssia.

Karin looked where Alyssia pointed, and her expression held a look of dismay.

"Why are you showing me such a sad looking image Alyssia?" she asked.

"I don't know, but felt it was relevant somehow," Alyssia replied thoughtfully.

"It is actually," Karin said, giving Alyssia a fleeting glance, "but I'm trying not to think about it, Alyssia".
Although Karin looked calm, Alyssia sensed she was keeping her feelings in check.
"Well Karin, I don't want to pry, yet if there is something bothering you, you know I am here and sympathetic," said Alyssia gently.
"Thank you Alyssia. It is as you said the other day, it's my turn and I will try to make sense of it and deal with it when I can, either today or tomorrow. I'm still not sure of what it is aiming at yet, but something is emerging."
Karin spoke in measured tones as if pondering on the issue as she spoke and then looked at Alyssia afterwards.
Alyssia smiled and reassured Karin, helping her cook the meal.

"I think I will return home soon, but will stay until you have uncovered your experience," said Alyssia.
Kenny came in at that moment.
"Ha! What's for breakfast ladies? Poached eggs on fried bread with parsley garnish, followed by vegetarian sausages and fried tomatoes and lashings of toast," he said, looking at them with an expectant expression.
"Here you are Kenny dear, porridge!" answered Karin, "that's made with love, it's special," she emphasised.
"Oh, that makes all the difference!" he responded, carrying the bowl to the table as if it were extremely precious.

The other two took theirs to the table and they all started eating.
"Hey! It could be the last day of the workmen today, fingers crossed," Kenny announced suddenly, looking happy.
"Alyssia's thinking of returning home soon Kenny," said Karin.
"Oh well, I guess you need to return at some point eh!" he responded, looking at Alyssia.
"Yes, I'm supposed to be starting another job soon and don't want to outstay my welcome here," Alyssia replied.
"What job is it?" asked Kenny.
"It's a pottery job in Kendal. I've been waiting because the owners have been in the process of setting it up. I'll check my emails today and see how things are going," she said.

Kenny looked at his watch, "Uh oh, time to open the shop, chaps!"

The doorbell went and Kenny started. "The workmen, and they're on time too!"
He had finished eating and took some gulps of tea and then carried his mug to the door, and gave a quick wave to the others before going downstairs.
"You know that if things don't work out in Kendal you could stay here Alyssia," said Karin, with a cheerful look in her eyes.
"Ok! Then I could help in the shop with those signs and not have to rush the job," she replied.
"Yes, you could advertise your services as a sign writer from here too," said Karin.
"I like the idea," smiled Alyssia.

Later in the day Alyssia got an email from the pottery.
"Due to unforeseen circumstances, we will have to postpone setting up the pottery any further, Alan had an accident while at work, so will have to leave matters until further notice. Very sorry Alyssia."
"Somehow I thought it wouldn't happen Karin," remarked Alyssia, "the pottery job's off for the time being. So that means I can stay here after all. I'll have to go to Kendal and gather my things."
"You don't have much do you?" asked Karin.
"Probably a couple of suitcases worth, a few boxes and a pile of paintings," answered Alyssia.
"Paintings! You could put them up in our new extension!" said Karin excitedly, "I'll tell Kenny. How many do you have?"
"About ten A2 sized ones, a couple of A1's and several A4's," said Alyssia.
"We'll be able to get a number of them up and keep circulating them around. Do you have transport to bring everything down in?" asked Karin.
"I know a friend with a van who travels regularly to Chester. I could get everything down to there, and then get a hire van from there, or perhaps use a little persuasion and a bit more money to come further!" laughed Alyssia, "I know he'd come to Oswestry if I produced a yummy chocolate cake!"
Kenny came in at that moment.
"Chocolate cake! I'll go for that!" he said with a gleam in his eyes, "the boys have finished downstairs, so it's all hands on deck to clear up the mess!"
He beckoned them both downstairs. Alyssia said she'd just email her man with a van friend first.

After sweeping and clearing up, Kenny got out the paint.
"Guess what? I got some extra of the shop carpet at the time I bought it, Alyssia," he said, pointing to it, "It was going as a job lot at the time, and there's enough for the extension."
They all set to with the painting until more customers came in and Karin went to the customer desk.
"I'm going to stay here Kenny as my pottery job hasn't come off," explained Alyssia, "the owner had an accident, so the pottery setting up process has been put on hold."
"Oh great! Glad to have you aboard the good ship Plas Myrddin. When will you get your clutter?" he asked, looking especially comical as he had some pink paint on the end of his nose!
"I'd just sent an email off before we started sweeping up and will go up north once I hear from the van man," answered Alyssia, "by the way, do you know that you have a blob of pink paint on the end of your nose?"
Alyssia lowered her voice for the latter statement as some customers had come into the shop and were wandering nearer the extension area. Kenny wiped it off swiftly, and raised an eyebrow.
"Back to my usual attractive self again!" he stated.
They both finished off the walls and the woodwork was painted in a shade of lavender.
"How about a spot of lunch?" enquired Karin from the counter, "Bertha's just arrived so we can go upstairs."

Kenny didn't need a prompt and speedily left. Alyssia moved the paint tins and brushes into the store cupboard and left the brushes to soak. Upstairs, they sat down to soup and toast. Kenny said that he'd get the second coat of paint over the walls and woodwork after lunch, and that Alyssia could come down to help when she could.
After lunch Kenny returned downstairs and Alyssia looked at her emails.
"My pal Vince is free in a couple of days time, that means going up fairly promptly," said Alyssia thinking things through, and looked at Karin, "perhaps I'd better get up there today."
"I think you had Alyssia," replied Karin emphatically, "I'll just dig out a train timetable from the local info collection we have. The T.I.C. have timetables if I can't find ours in time," she said while rummaging through a pile of the shelves by the table, and finally found it. "Here! There's a train in just over an hour's time and it stops at Lancaster and Oxenholme."

"Oh good, Oxenholme would be fine, I could just walk into Kendal from there," responded Alyssia, "I'll just gather my things together."
Alyssia went out of the kitchen, through the utility room to her bedroom and gathered up her belongings she would need over the time up north and brought them through to the kitchen in an overnight bag.

Karin looked a little pensive as Alyssia entered, and looked up slightly when she entered, a slightly apprehensive look fleetingly crossed her eyes.
"Are you okay Karin, is it the past life thing that's bothering you?" asked Alyssia.
Karin nodded and paused, formulating the words in her mind.
"You see, I've just been having glimpses," she paused and looked at Alyssia in consternation, "I see myself in long robes, running with a group. I realise that they all have robes too. We seem to be in a mountainous area somewhere, but I know it's not Britain. I see the others around me are all anxious, some are crying. I heard a deep sobbing, and then I realise that it was me. Then I came out of the glimpse into that life."
Karin looked at Alyssia intently. "I don't know who they were and why they are running and unhappy."

"They sound as if they were being pursued," said Alyssia after a moments thought, "perhaps a religious sect...the Cathars?"
Karin looked at Alyssia intently, then she turned aside and tears started trickling down her face.
"Yes, I think so. Don't worry about my tears; I'm relieved to have pinpointed the answer. It's like a weight off my mind, despite the emotions that are being released," she said with a tremor in her voice.
Alyssia sat beside Karin and offered a tissue from the table. "It must have been the time when the Cathars were being expelled," said Alyssia.
"Yes, that explains the sense of fear and sadness in the air. I heard screams in the background, perhaps they were being..."
Karin trailed off with a sad look, but they both knew the last word. They sat quietly a while, then Alyssia made them a pot of tea and gradually Karin looked more relieved.

"I think I'd better hurry! That train, Karin!" announced Alyssia, suddenly remembering.

"Oh yes, of course, you'd better go," exclaimed Karin, "I feel okay now," she said smiling at Alyssia, then reached for a handful of snacks and handed them to Alyssia.

Alyssia smiled and took them, putting them in her holdall. She put her jacket on, hugged Karin and left. She told Kenny downstairs as he was painting the top coat and he cheerily waved and said, "see you soon again!"

The next morning a letter came amongst the pile that arrived every morning in the interior letterbox of Plas Myrddin. Kenny usually went to collect the post and bring it upstairs for Karin to sort out.

"This one's postmarked Cornwall," announced Kenny.

"Oh, it could be Sarah's," answered Karin, hurriedly opening the envelope and pulling out its contents, "Yes it is!"

"Tell me all about it at break time," said Kenny and he disappeared downstairs to open up the shop.

Karin began to read Sarah's letter. "Dear Alyssia, Karin and Kenny, Some days ago I began to get flashes of intuition to go and visit a well. So I drove all the way to one by Sancreed and put my feet in it, and while I dried them I meditated there. Suddenly I was an old hermit, a woman who lived in a wood by a well in a very makeshift dwelling. People found out about me and would come to me for advice, healing, blessings and encouragement. Animals came too. I understood about herbs and the elemental kingdom. Spirits, fairies, gnomes and angels would talk to me and tell me of the natural order of things. Many animals approached, trusting that I could help them. I felt that many years passed like this in a peaceful and happy way.

One day a man came asking for help. He sat beside me and I offered some advice and gave him some herbs, he said they were for his father who was very ill, I said that I couldn't promise anything for I couldn't transcend the natural laws if that was meant to happen, but I would offer the herbs with my blessings in the hope that they would heal him, or at least ease any pain he was in. The man looked a little resigned and went away unsmiling. Later I thought of him often, hoping all was well. A couple of days later I think, that was roughly the time period I perceived, I was approached by a large man with an impassive face and asked me to follow him. I said that I didn't need to go anywhere and was happy to stay where I lived, but why did he want me to go and where? 'You'll soon see' was the curt response.

A gradual feeling of gravity came to me, especially as the man became less gentle as we proceeded and dragged me somewhat on occasions. Eventually we reached the town, which I had long ago left and found strangely disorientating. I soon found myself the centre of attention in the marketplace. There was a gathering there and I was the focus. I found myself on trial. The man who had brought me there pushed me over in front of someone who began the proceedings. He accused me of attempting to heal people with herbs that were long ago dismissed as useless by our society and then he called the witness. Well, it was the man who had come to me to ask for help with his father. He fiercely announced that I had given him herbs that would have killed rather than cured. I loudly said that I followed skills that had been handed down for generations, with recipes that were tried and tested, and never in my life would I ever wish to harm anyone or anything.

I could see that the whole trial was rigged and the man who had come to me, I sensed that his father wasn't ill at all, and was just a pretext to come to me. His father and himself, it turned out, were 'doctors' of a different variety. He prescribed herbs too, but not in my time-honoured way, preferring a new 'modern' approach, and I was in fact, an inconvenient rival who was too popular. Despite remonstrations from the crowds, I was convicted wrongly, and many people came to me with tears in their eyes. I smiled to them and said to 'be strong' and such encouraging statements, before I was silenced with a blow, which made me unconscious. I was taken away and my death was caused by being forced to ingest some noxious substance."
Well, that was my past life experience girls! Do tell me about anything past lives that has happened to you and I look forward to the next instalment. Love and blessings, Sarah."

Karin sat back, pondering on all three of their incarnation experiences. The three of them had all been women in past lives, she thought, and had experienced difficulties of one sort or another. Things that tested their faith, devotion and their whole lives had been turned upside down, and others around them too. She wondered what it meant in the context of the crystals and the image of the three Atlantean women who they had been. Perhaps more would come later that would shed light on that, maybe more regarding each of their lives that they had experienced, or even more lives still.

Kenny came up later and Karin told him of her thoughts, and he read Sarah's letter.

"It's fascinating Karin, I'd really like to meet Sarah even though it seems that only the three of you are involved."

"Well Kenny, perhaps someone who isn't directly involved is good to have around. I mean, to keep a dispassionate eye on things, you know what I mean," explained Karin.

"Yes, I think so. If more past lives and all sorts are going to come through, it may get rather intense and you'll need cheering up!" said Kenny, putting a dab of tomato sauce on the end of his nose and clowning around. Karin shook her head and then laughed.

"I don't know how we'd manage without you looking like that!"

Kenny grinned and wiped off the tomato sauce and said, "I know! It's a serious matter really however."

He tried to look serious, and despite his earnest attempt, he still managed to look comical, and Karin hugged him. It would be wonderful to have you there if it's right for you to come down to see Sarah."

Kenny murmured appreciation and smiled, and they had a cup of tea. Kenny returned to look after the shop, while Karin busied herself ordering more stock from suppliers, and researching new possibilities on the Internet.

Meanwhile, up north, Alyssia was travelling south with Vince, the van driver.

"What do you mean, I'm hooked on chocolate therapy!" retorted Vince, "I only have one chocolate bar a day," he pretended to look indignant.

"Oh really, what about the rest?" laughed Alyssia.

"Oh that! Well, I get them for the wife and kids you know!" he replied.

Vince looked at her slyly with a grin and gave a thumbs up.

"Shall I stop at Chester?" joked Vince with a glance at Alyssia, "it's alright, I can be on cake power for the rest of the way! It's not really much further to Oswestry."

Vince gave a backward glance towards the chocolate cake Alyssia had given him, that was stored in the back of the van.

Karin wrote a letter to Sarah, giving her full details of both Alyssia's and her own past life experiences, and added her thoughts about further stages that may develop that would link the three of them to Atlantis.

She told Sarah of Alyssia's move to stay with them. Once completed, she wrote a few other letters and went to post them all at the post box nearby. Before she went out the shop door Kenny stopped her.

"Karin dear, a parcel came just before; they've sent the wrong things. We'll have to return it. Sorry love," he said apologetically, knowing she'd have to go to the main post office.
"Ok, I'll just phone them about it and seal the parcel again upstairs, and then go to the post office. Hang onto these meanwhile dear," she said, leaving her post with Kenny.
Kenny looked at the far end of the shop extension and thought a mural would be great down there. Karin reappeared with the parcel and Kenny told her of his idea.
"Great Kenny! What should we have there?" she asked.
"I don't know exactly, perhaps you and Alyssia can think of something," Kenny paused a moment, thinking, "perhaps Merlin and some unicorns," he suggested.
"Sounds good to me!" answered Karin breezily and she departed for the post office with all the mail.
It was near closing time when Alyssia and Vince arrived with a beep at the shop entrance. Kenny dashed outside.
"Hi there!" he said to them both, "come on in. Do you need a drink?"
They said that they would just get Alyssia's gear out, and Vince said he had to return promptly, but was grateful for the offer.
"Technically I'm not really supposed to have gone further than Chester, so I'd best not linger," he replied with a stage whisper.
There was a flurry of customers just before closing time. Someone bought a large amethyst geode candleholder, another a collection of candles and incense and another got a couple of books and a rainbow coloured skirt. A bunch of schoolgirls came in wanting a bracelet each, and Kenny humoured them cheerfully, whispering to them to tell their friends to come along too.

Kenny closed the shop and went upstairs and helped Alyssia to get the luggage along from the kitchen to its final destination. They sat together at the kitchen table over a cup of tea.
"Have you told Alyssia about the mural?" he asked.
"Yes dear, Merlin and unicorns," replied Karin, "she loves the idea."
"I'd love to make a start on it tomorrow Kenny!" agreed Alyssia enthusiastically.

"Ok then, just buy the paint you need, and I'll reimburse you," said Kenny.

"Do you have any white?" she asked.

"Well, as a matter of fact, I do," he replied, leaning his head on his hand and looking quizzically at Alyssia.

"You know, I think that's all I need. You see, I can outline the figure of Merlin so that the background colour becomes part of his cloak," explained Alyssia, "and the unicorns are white, so I may not need anything else."

"That sounds impressive. Well, there's nothing to stop you then! You know, I really think that doing the mural will draw more people in, and also those who would want murals themselves," said Kenny emphatically, "especially when you re-do the shop sign outside. Something in me just knows that it will bring in more trade, and other things, though I don't exactly know what yet. It's like a voice whispering to me somehow, that all this is significant."

The others looked at him intently, half amazed at his response.

"Kenny, that sounds amazing coming from you!" exclaimed Karin.

"Yes, I'm beginning to sound like you two now. There's magic in the air!" he said with the usual twinkle in his eyes.

"You could be right there," said Alyssia, "and I was meant to stay with you guys too!"

"How could you have stayed away? It's the hub of life here!" said Kenny, "besides, we're going to get a resident healer of sorts to use that little spare room in the corner."

"Yes Alyssia," said Karin, "we don't know who it will be yet, but we have faith that the right person will come through the door."

"Sounds intriguing!" said Alyssia.

Karin had put a casserole in the oven and the smell of it was pervading the room. They set the table and Karin dished up.

Later, Alyssia made preparatory sketches of the proposed mural and also ideas for the sign outside, and the three of them discussed the ideas together.

Eventually, Alyssia started yawning. "It's been a long day so I'll just turn in now, and then I can be ready to make a start on the mural tomorrow."

They said goodnight to her and she went off to her room.   Karin and Kenny decided that a little flier or booklet by the counter advertising Alyssia's work would be a good idea.

"We could at least get some of her paintings up tomorrow too," said Kenny.

The next morning came, and it was sunny and warm. Kenny was already up and outside, walking in the park. He saw someone feeding some birds and he waved happily to the person, as he always waved to everyone.
The figure fed the last of the bag of crumbs she had and then approached Kenny. The figure was female and had a strangely interesting air, thought Kenny.
"Hello," he said, "you popped out for a breather like me?" he grinned.
The woman smiled serenely, "you could say so, I've just moved here. Nice to escape from unpacking."
"Well, why not pop into our shop, you'd be welcome. It's called Plas Myrddin," he replied.
At this the woman grew alert, "I will come, definitely."
"Sorry, got to dash back to the shop, but look forward to seeing you, it's easy to find, ask anyone!" said Kenny briskly and he dashed off.

Karin and Alyssia were in the kitchen preparing breakfast when Kenny entered.
"Did you enjoy your sprint around the park, Kenny?" asked Alyssia.
"For a moment or two, then I met this woman." Karin raised an eyebrow, "No honestly! You see, I think she'll have a connection to the shop somehow, you two!" he said excitedly, and he described her to them.

For the next couple of weeks Alyssia painted the mural at the far end of the extension, and Karin's new stock orders were coming in, so the room was gradually filling up with goods. Alyssia's paintings were up on the two side walls, with a few to spare. The new sign outside, which hung at a perpendicular angle to the shop front, was painted in the same theme as the mural, and there was an image of Merlin holding a crystal ball, with a faint reflection of a unicorn in it. Kenny was really pleased with it, and went around with a beaming smile on his face as much as possible! Karin and Alyssia worked on a flier to promote her mural and sign writing work, as well as business cards to place on the counter.

"I can get the info onto our website and the Oswestry T.I.C. and Board of Trade websites too," said Karin.

"I can feel an air of excitement about all of this Karin, it's just as Kenny said, there's definitely a strong sense of purpose which is our catalyst at work around here," said Alyssia animatedly.
"We just need Sarah up here now!" mused Karin.
"Don't say that! Her house will probably collapse or something like that in a storm, and she'll be forced to move up here," Alyssia responded.
"I'm sure it will be better than that!" corrected Karin, "she may get an offer she can't refuse, and with that in mind, get a sudden calling to come to Shropshire as a result, don't you agree?"
"I can't fault that! Everything is going so well, I'm sure everything else to come will just fall into place without a murmur!" said Alyssia.

"I think it's break time, Kenny hasn't been up yet, that means he's busy, so I'll take him a drink, Alyssia," she said, putting the kettle on, while Alyssia returned to finalising her promotional information and printing it out.
Karin popped downstairs with the tea and saw Kenny discussing something with a man who was dressed in a spring green velvet jacket with darker green trousers.
"There, you have it now! My job is done, good day to you sir," he said, "and to your girlfriend!" he added, looking at Karin intently and he smiled, then he exited the shop swiftly.
Karin looked at Kenny with a mystified look.
"And who was that Kenny?" she asked, "How did he know I was your girlfriend?"
"Could have been just a lucky guess," shrugged Kenny, "but somehow, from what he said, I don't think so."

Just then two more people came into the shop, and Kenny had one of them over at the counter straight away.
"I'll tell you later," he said to Karin with an emphatic look and raised his eyebrows up and down swiftly, then resumed attention to his customer.
Karin went upstairs again.

"Alyssia, Kenny's had an intriguing customer in the shop. He was dressed in green velvet, seemed slightly old-fashioned and he called me Kenny's girlfriend without knowing anything about me. Kenny says he has a story to tell us later!" she said happily.
"Hmm, the plot thickens! I can't wait! How long is it until Bertha comes?" asked Alyssia.

Karin looked at the clock, "about and hour and a half. Well I should get something rustled up for lunch by then," she commented.
"I've got these business cards and fliers sorted out now Karin. How about getting the info onto your website?" asked Alyssia.
"Just send it to this email address for our website hostess, and she'll add it on," said Karin, reaching for a notebook and showed her the relevant page, "she'll also sort out the T.I.C. and Board of Trade sites too."
"Lovely!" responded Alyssia with a smile, and she began emailing. Karin began chopping vegetables and boiled up some potatoes.

<u>CHAPTER 4 - THE INCANTATION</u>

Sarah looked at her watch, 'I thought that delivery was going to come at ten minutes to three, where is he?"
She waited a bit uneasily, looking out across to the west, the light catching her eyes as she followed the line of cumulus clouds, which were not as white as they had started out at the beginning of the day. She tried to ring the delivery man and left a message on his answer phone.
"Hello Pete, are you on your way, you did say ten to three, just checking that all is well and that the delay is nothing to worry about. Please ring me back if it is necessary," said Sarah.

Just then, Sarah heard the sounds of a vehicle approaching, and she span around as a smile lit up her face, relief flooding her expression, and she went to the door and opened it. A different man walked up the drive towards her.
"Hello, are you looking for somewhere?" asked Sarah.
"I'm looking for Mrs Sarah Blenheim," he said, his voice was deep and slightly gravelly, his face looked stolid.
"That's me! How can I help? I didn't ask for anyone," she said, a hint of the concern returning again.
"Your man Pete couldn't come today, so I've come instead to deliver your goods. I do odd jobs and fill-ins for people," the man explained, and he flashed an ID card.
Sarah still wasn't too happy, but thought she'd wait to see if he brought the items before considering slamming the door in his face.
He returned to the van and brought the necessary items to the door. Sarah said prudently that she would take them from there indoors. His prying eyes seemed to be looking around everywhere, and trying to peer behind Sarah to inside the house.
 "Would you like to pay me and I'll take it to Pete?" he asked, smiling graciously.
"If you don't mind, I'll just sort it out with Pete when I'm next in St Ives," she replied.
The man stopped smiling, gave her a subdued glare, turned on his heel and left. Sarah frowned and went indoors.

'Why do I get a very uneasy feeling about that man?' she thought.
Just then, a shaft of light came through the lounge window and alighted on the crystal casket, and Sarah was able to see it from where she stood.

Intuitively she linked the two together in a split second and she shuddered a little.

'Are there people out there who sense that this crystal tool is here and they want it for themselves? Oh my! I had never thought it possible, but should have considered it. How can these people know when it is tucked away? Perhaps intuition works for the wrong reasons as well as the right ones. I'll have to take it elsewhere. I'm in a vulnerable position here by myself. I'll ring Karin. No, I'll ring Geraldine first and see what she suggests,' she thought quickly, 'wished I'd never got this delivery of food etc., I seem to have lost my appetite!'

Sarah rang Geraldine, "Hi Geraldine, how are you fixed right now? Oh good, I've got a stiff back, just started this morning, I'd love a massage and healing session, just come over. Good! I'll get the kettle on."

Sarah's expression was a little brighter. She went to the casket in the cabinet and removed it. She took it to her bedroom and instinctively packed it in a large suitcase, and also filled it up with essential belongings. 'In case I have to make a dash for it. I could drive up to Oswestry. I think I'll settle my affairs here just in case,' she thought, 'I'll also take my manuscripts, especially the latest, and my writing gear with me for safe keeping.'

While she was busy sorting her belongings out, a car pulled up. Sarah thought of the van again momentarily and was relieved to see Geraldine's mauve car there, and her figure carrying her treatment bag up the drive.
Sarah opened the door and cheerily welcomed her with a hug and beckoned her inside.
"Well my dear, let's get you ready and I'll give you your treatment," said Geraldine. Her large blue-green eyes looked at Sarah gaily, and her blond head of hair was tied back in a bun.
Sarah beckoned her to the lounge and indicated for her to sit.
"Geraldine, something has happened," she explained, looking more serious, "I'm sorry to get you here under false pretences, but I feel that a delivery man who came today was trying to pry on my property. I'll explain fully Geraldine."

Sarah paused, ran a hand through her hair and looked at Geraldine, who by now was looking a little surprised and concerned.

"You see, I was expecting a delivery of the heavy stuff I usually get periodically, a sack of potatoes and that sort of thing, and it should have come by ten to three. Pete was going to bring it, he said he would. The time went by and no Pete. I rang his number but there was no one there. Just then, a van appeared and I thought it was Pete and this strange man came to the door. I wasn't keen on the look of him, the van had no name on it and he asked for me by name and showed his ID card too quickly for me to grasp it all, but he delivered the goods. He wanted to take them inside, but when I said that I would take them myself and pay Pete for the goods, his charm disappeared swiftly. His eyes were darting about, not obviously, but I sensed he wanted to see something inside. I wondered afterwards what he was looking for, and then a shaft of light landed on the crystal casket I've told you about, and I felt that this was what he was looking for, Geraldine," explained Sarah.

"Are you sure you aren't getting too paranoid about this Sarah, I mean, how should anyone know of this casket?" asked Geraldine.
"I know, I know! It's probably crazy, a woman on her own, miles from anywhere, getting neurotic about strangers!" and Sarah shrugged her shoulders, "but some kind of gut reaction made me feel as if there is some need for care and caution, or perhaps quick action to be taken if necessary."
"Why don't you try ringing Pete again and see what he says, it might allay your fears dear," suggested Geraldine.
"Good idea," said Sarah, rising from her chair and going to the phone.

"Hello Pete, how are you. What happened to you today my friend?" asked Sarah.
"Sorry Sarah, I got held up out in the sticks. My car broke down. I'll deliver the goods tomorrow, is that alright?" said Pete.
"What! But Pete, a man with a white van came to my door not long after I rang you at three-ish to see where you were, and he said that he'd come instead, showed me his ID, some firm called 'Do 4 U' and he delivered the very things you had planned to give me. I don't like the sound of this, Pete. If you don't know who it is, I'd better contact the police," exclaimed Sarah.
"Too darned right, I can't have odd characters popping out of the blue and nicking my customers. I'll ring them for you, did you see a reg number?" he asked.

"Yes, partly." Sarah gave what she had seen, "okay Pete, I'll expect the police around anytime soon."

Sarah wandered back to the lounge and sat back in her chair and gave a small sigh. Geraldine looked concerned.
"So Pete didn't know of this guy at all?" asked Geraldine, and Sarah shook her head.
"Nope, he never set eyes on the bloke. I thought it was worth worrying about," said Sarah.
"Yes indeed. I could stay here tonight if you like Sarah, but I must return tomorrow as I have some appointments. I'll just go home to collect my night things," she explained.
"Would you like to go now, before it gets dark?" suggested Sarah.
"Yes, it would be prudent to go immediately," agreed Geraldine, and she rose from her chair to depart.

While Geraldine was away, Sarah wrote out cheques for various items due, and settled her affairs. She rang an estate agent in St Ives that dealt with lettings to make inquiries, in case she decided to leave. The man was very helpful and encouraging and said that plenty of people were looking for quiet cottages these days around this area. Sarah asked him to come over and view the property first thing tomorrow.

Geraldine arrived back with her small suitcase just ahead of the police, who took all the necessary details. They checked the goods the man had delivered, and took note of Sarah's description of the man. Then she remembered that the man had gloves on, and they were beige coloured so she hadn't noticed unduly. The police checked all the items for potential fingerprints just in case. Finally they left the two women in peace.

"I don't think they'd catch that man on the strength of my drawing Geraldine," commented Sarah, almost breaking into a laugh, "I feel like a cup of tea now, do you?"
"Let me Sarah, you've had quite a day," insisted Geraldine.
"Well, let's do it together," Sarah answered with a hint of good cheer, and they both went into the kitchen.
"Why don't you ring your friends and arrange something?" asked Geraldine.
"I will tonight, and see what I should do next," said Sarah thoughtfully.

The doorbell went. Sarah panicked momentarily, but then got up, went to the door and opened it.
"Oh hello Jimmy. What's this?" she asked.
"Hello Sarah. I found this on my doormat this morning, don't know how it got there, but it looked worth delivering to you as soon as I could manage it," said Jimmy good naturedly.
"Thanks Jimmy, sorry you've had a journey to make," said Sarah kindly,
"No matter love, but a cutting from your garden wouldn't go amiss!" he added, laughing.
"Go on then!" cajoled Sarah with a smile, "just help yourself, there'll probably be some pots by the wall."
Jimmy thanked Sarah, and gave a parting wave as he headed towards the herb patch, hobbling slowly.

"It's a letter from Karin," said Sarah, eagerly opening the contents.
She sat in the lounge to read the letter, while Geraldine brought in the tea tray and began pouring out after a few moments.
"Alyssia was due to start a pottery job but it fell through, so she's staying with Karin and Kenny, and is painting a mural and a sign for the shop, and she also describes the past lives she and Karin have been experiencing," commented Sarah, "things are beginning to fall into place Geraldine."
"There's really something significant involving you three. I think you ought to be with the others, not here alone," Geraldine advised.

I've spoken to someone at Chandlers about possibly letting the house while I'm away," said Sarah, "and he said people are looking for properties like this, and he's coming tomorrow morning."
"I'd do it for you, but as you know I have to get back. Why not leave a key with the agent if you go in a rush. We can sort out what you need to take, and I could store the rest for safe keeping, eh Sarah?" asked Geraldine.
"Yes, thanks Geraldine. I'll ring Karin and see what they say up there. Best get planning immediately," said Sarah bringing the phone into the lounge and she dialled their number.
"Hello Karin! It's Sarah, just got your letter. Something bit urgent happening down here. Some kind of threat towards our casket," and she explained in detail.
Karin listened with concern. "Sarah! You must get yourself up here as soon as you can, can you come up tomorrow? If there's any further

trouble follow these instructions to the letter. Don't ask us where we got them now, just trust us!" she spoke emphatically.

Sarah listened and wrote down the instructions carefully, making numerous notes, going over the details with care and attention.
"Alright, I'll have my mobile, you've got the number haven't you?" asked Sarah, "good. Bye for now."
"Geraldine!" shouted Sarah, "They gave me these complicated instructions. It's to be used if the casket is in danger, and they gave it to me as an anagram for safety over the phone, can you help me?"

They sat together, poring over the information for a while and eventually they came to a conclusion.
"The word is amaranth," stated Sarah, "and the numerology for the word is 1,3,1,3,1,4,5,3, and the corresponding notes in an octave are c,e,c,e,c,f,g,e. Is it middle c or top c?"
"Sarah! Do you think we could get up there?" laughed Geraldine.
"Maybe not! Just joking really! Do we have to use our voices, or perhaps an instrument and tape it?" suggested Sarah.
"Let's try those notes at different scales, tempos, and also in reverse and see what we get," advised Geraldine.
"Okay, but I'll get my crystal, the one I should always carry around with me, but don't while at home, and see what we come up with too," answered Sarah.

With the crystal, things went smoother and more swiftly, and they came up with the answer.
"The intuition from the crystal made me choose, not the scale of C but E, from the numerology of the total sum of the word amaranth's letters being 21=3," explained Sarah, making notes to remember."

"Sarah, what's that on the side of your crystal? I could just see the light catching it. Just turn it over a little, just there by your thumb now!" asked Geraldine eagerly.
Sarah peered at the crystal and grabbed a magnifying glass. She looked astonished, "Geraldine! There's a symbol and it takes the same shape as the formation of the notes we've chosen," Sarah's mouth hung open a little as she looked at Geraldine.
"Well! Let's try it!" said Geraldine.

Sarah looked at the crystal again, "Oh, but it's in reverse! So that must be the way to use it. We'll practice it but not while I hold the crystal, being the catalyst. I have a strong intuition that I can only make this work for real when the designated time occurs. Oh dear, no chance for dress rehearsals then!" Sarah looked anxiously towards Geraldine; "anyway, we can at least get the notes right before then. I must get them into my mind so that it's automatic, Geraldine."
"What if the others need to know Sarah?" asked Geraldine.
Sarah looked at Geraldine and though a moment.
"Yes, that's a very important point, they should know every detail. It must be kept secret, so dare I use the phone? I wonder why the crystal hasn't glowed before now in any case. I'll phone them anyway later after our practice. We can recite it too while I'm packing up," ruminated Sarah.

They practiced so it was very clearly in Sarah's mind.
Then they heard the sound of a car outside and they both got up, looking at each other. Sarah went to the door and peered through the little window beside it. She saw the flash of a white van, and it sped off again.
"Geraldine, it's that ghastly man! But he's driven off again," said Sarah, composing herself.
"When is that letting agent man coming tomorrow Sarah?" asked Geraldine.
"Nine fifteen, so that's not too bad. I can have everything essential packed into the car by then," replied Sarah.
"I think it's important that the prowling man doesn't think you've gone," said Geraldine thoughtfully.
"But how can I do that? He'll see by the car not being there," responded Sarah.
"I do know someone who has a car like yours and a very similar registration," answered Geraldine.
"Yes, that's very kind," interjected Sarah, "but it would put that person at risk too."
Geraldine smiled, "don't worry Sarah. You see, we could both come here when you've gone. Martha's her name, and she could leave her car here having borrowed your spare key and we could potter around for a while until you are safely up to Oswestry. I would return here after my appointments."
"Yes, very good thank you, but I just hope he doesn't come by earlier and suss out what's going on," answered Sarah.

"Well how about plan B, in that we stack all your belongings in my car, with you lying on the back seat under some rugs. Make for Martha's house in St Ives and I leave you there with your belongings, and then I return to St Just. I get Martha to drive back here to your house; she likes wearing green like you.   Martha will deal with the letting agents, and then she will go to St Ives afterwards in your car, then she will collect her car and drive back to your house and stay there until I return, and we will both stay there as long as we can to give that man a red herring or two!"

"My goodness! You should have been a detective or film director!" said Sarah and they both laughed, "but it's giving me a headache trying to consider it." Sarah thought a moment. "Why don't I just go very early in the morning and leave you to see the letting agents?"
"Well, alright Sarah, but I'll ring Martha just in case we need a diversion, eh!" responded Geraldine with a slight smile.

Sarah got up and continued to sort out her belongings and went through all the points with Geraldine in preparation for the lettings agents. She ensured that all belongings not to be used by the lettings agents' tenants were placed in a lockable cupboard, and all things of value, either she would take with her or Geraldine would look after.

All essentials for taking up north were stacked neatly along the corridors, not wanting a prying eye to look through any windows and spot a suitcase. Geraldine came around to where Sarah was standing, which was in the end room.
"I forgot about my materials cupboard Geraldine," said Sarah.
"Don't worry, I'll take it back with me, along with everything else. Have you got some boxes?" she asked.
They both got them down from the attic and filled them up. Sarah also filled up a couple of boxes with her clothes that she couldn't squeeze into her cases, and also her best china.
"Just sell these, as most of it has just sat around for too long, as they do. Take some for yourself if you wish," said Sarah, and Geraldine smiled, and indicated that she'd do her best to sell anything. Sarah had a quick phone call to Karin to let them know she was coming as soon as she could in the morning.

They had an early night. A slight storm began to brew far out at sea, and slight rumbles of thunder could be heard intermittently, as well as the sound of gales blowing, which woke them briefly on occasions, then all went quiet and they both fell into a sound sleep.

Next morning soon came; Sarah was restless and awoke very early. She opened her eyes and reached over to the curtains and peered through. The dawn light was beginning to spread over the undersides of clouds and bring a pale tint along the horizon. Sarah looked at her travel alarm clock, it was quarter to five. She stretched and then sprang out of bed, as she was an early riser. She got dressed and washed swiftly and was into the kitchen making up some muesli for the two of them, with fruit juice, a pot of tea and lashings of toast. Geraldine came stumbling through having just dressed herself. She was yawning vigorously for the clock still only said twenty to six.

"Oh my! That's a big breakfast, wow!" said Geraldine.
"I reckon we're going to need it! Well I certainly am!" replied Sarah.
They sat and ate it in the lounge and then finalised the packing.
"I phoned Martha after you went to bed and she's able to come over once we go to her place!" said Geraldine with the remains of a mouthful of some left over toast she had decided to eat.
"Good, shall we get started then? I'll just get my crystal and handbag," asked Sarah with an earnest look.
"Oh Geraldine!" came a cry from the bedroom, and Sarah rushed back, "it's the crystal, it's glowing. I think I'm going to have to make a dash for it!"
She looked tense and paused a moment with her eyes shut as if divining what the best thing was to do.
She opened her eyes again after a moment.
"I know now isn't really the time for meditating, but somehow I feel I've just got to make a dash for it rather than hanging around anywhere in particular," said Sarah urgently.
"Well, if you feel that strongly, then you must do what is best. Don't worry about the letting agent, Martha and I will sort things out, you just get going Sarah," encouraged Geraldine. "I'll remember to tell Mr Chandler that you've had to go and visit a friend who is seriously ill etc., now off you go!"
Sarah got her coat and backed the car right by the door, and they speedily packed the boot and filled the car with belongings.
"Just negotiate a figure, you know the price range that is suitable," explained Sarah.

"Yes dear, it's alright, I've remembered what you said!" said Geraldine.
"Sorry, I get like this when I'm a bit on edge!" said Sarah apologetically, and gave Geraldine a hug, then got into her car.
"Goodbye Sarah, let me know when you get there safely, and just say 'oky doky' once you get past Okehampton, that will be enough!" said Geraldine knowingly.
Sarah nodded and smiled and then sped out of her driveway. Geraldine got out her mobile as she walked back indoors, and phoned Martha and told her of the change of plan and to be there before 9.15am.

Sarah felt a little more relieved as she speedily drove northwards to St Ives. She looked at her crystal that lay on her lap. The morning sun shone a little over her shoulders and caught the right edge of the crystal. She was well on her way to St Ives.
'Ah, this is Rosewall Hill,' she thought, glancing to the slightly craggy, steep sided hill which was approaching on her right, 'I've only just under two miles to go 'til St Ives.'

Just as she was coming past it the crystal glowed fiercely. There was a flash of a white van. It swerved in front of her and applied the brakes, making her do the same, she managed to grasp the crystal in time, which was still glowing brightly, and she could feel it pulsating with energy. Sarah drew breath and as the man leapt out of the van door towards her she sang out the notes while clutching the crystal tightly.
There was a strange tremor in the air. The man stopped in his tracks, looked at her defiantly. Then he was drawn backwards into his van, and the vehicle was pushed to one side as if by an invisible force.

Sarah looked in amazement, shook herself into action and turned her ignition key and raced onwards, checking in her mirror at the white van. She couldn't see the man's face; he must have slumped down on the seat. She soon lost view of the van and began to feel slightly more relieved by the time she reached St Ives. Passing through the town she continued along the A30, going as fast as she could manage, she couldn't say for how long. Instinctively, she periodically looked out of the window and rear mirror, anticipating the return of that white van, but he wasn't to be seen. Sarah stopped by the side of the road just past Okehampton and dialled Geraldine's mobile number. She could hear Geraldine calling out 'hello', but Sarah couldn't make herself be heard. She tried again, but it still didn't work. She sent a text, but it wouldn't go through.

'Strange,' thought Sarah.
She revved up her car and continued going north, and then saw a sign to a little village and decided to turn off.
'I'll try a phone box, maybe my mobile isn't working now,' she thought.
She pulled up by a phone box and got out, quickly looking around her as she went over to it. She dialled the number again and got the same response.
'I'll ask someone at their house, maybe they could help me,' she thought again.
She went over to one of the nearest houses in the village and knocked on the door. There was no response. She could hear voices from the inside and she knocked harder. The door opened and a man walked out and didn't notice Sarah at all.
Sarah spoke loudly, asking if she could use the phone, but it was as if she were invisible. At first she grew a little panicky, but suddenly she realised.
'It's the notes I sang. I must have to repeat them in reverse order to bring everything back into focus,' she thought.
She returned to the car and waited until the man had left and that no one else was around, looking around the area thoroughly.
'Just as well it's a nice quiet village!'
Sarah sang the notes in reverse order, holding the crystal. There was a tremor-like energy in the air again and she knew that she could ring Geraldine now, which she did.
She then swiftly joined the A30 again and soon linked up with the M5 at Exeter and continued northwards.

Just past the M50 junction to Wales, Sarah stopped at the service station on the northern side.
"Karin, Alyssia! I'm ok so far. Had a bit of trouble in Cornwall," she emphasised, "I'm fine now, and just north of Gloucester, not far from Great Malvern. Start making me something lovely for tea, I'll need it!" she said, trying to stifle a yawn. "I'm just going to have a snack and then push off again pretty swiftly," added Sarah.

She swallowed a bun she'd prepared that morning, then had a drink, and was on the road again within quarter of an hour.
As she was driving, she had a strange feeling of being watched, and instinctively looked around her, and through all the mirrors. She saw a fleeting image of the man with the white van and accelerated.

Her crystal wasn't flashing so nothing was imminent, but she tensed up anyway, and kept looking around every so often. She turned off the M5 and headed for Kidderminster, with a view to reaching the road that went via Shrewsbury. As she was approaching the Shrewsbury bypass, there was the fleeting image of the man with the van again, his eyes piercing and a smile on his face.

It was a rather haggard figure who arrived at Plas Myrddin during the afternoon, for she had driven as fast as she could, not relaxing for a moment until the town of Oswestry was within her sight.

Sarah realised how tired she was, and the others rallied around and got her car parked around the back and her belongings upstairs. She was so exhausted by her flight that Karin rang Geraldine while Sarah was asleep on her bed. She told Geraldine about Sarah's encounter near St Ives, and that they would regularly keep in touch, and that Sarah would ring her back when she was awake again.

Kenny looked at Karin and Alyssia.

"We'll tell Sarah about the gent who visited us when she wakes up, eh?"

"Ok, that reminds me!" exclaimed Karin, with a look of realisation, "I've been reading more about Atlantis since we got back from Sarah's, have you Alyssia?"

"A little bit, just before going to sleep mainly!" answered Alyssia.

Kenny scratched his head, gave a shrug and said, "Wish I'd had the energy to keep up with you lot, those workmen kept me on my toes. Anyway, better get back to duty. See ya later, mates!"

He darted downstairs just as the door chime went.

Around 4pm Alyssia took a cup of best Oswestry herbal tea through to Sarah, who stirred as Alyssia entered.

"Oh, a cuppa herbie," murmured Sarah sleepily and gave a slight smile. She indicated that she'd come through soon.

"Who was this guy with the green velvet jacket then?" asked Sarah with a slightly puzzled look, now seated in the living room area.

"We don't know, he never said where he came from. He just came, handed over some papers and said they were very important spiritual information required for certain mystical individuals, and then left," said Karin, "though Kenny thinks it was definitely meant for us as it had the information about the incantation for the casket within it."

"That information certainly came in handy," added Alyssia, "but there's more, and we haven't had time to read it yet."

"Perhaps we should do it now, after all," at this point Sarah lowered her voice instinctively, "just in case that man has inklings of where the casket and I went and is getting ready to pounce again."

"Point taken. Come on and gather round!" announced Karin as she reached for the relevant information, which was tucked safely underneath a pile of stuff. "I've made more copies, so we all have one each, though Kenny and I'll share."
Karin handed them out, and the three of them sat and read the pages.
"It's talking about planning a trip and what to take," said Karin.
"But to where?" asked Alyssia, "it only says to pack all kinds of survival type stuff as if we were going trekking in the Andes."
"Chance would be a fine thing!" beamed Kenny, who poked his head round the door, "any chance of a cuppa?"
"You could have called me, dear," said Karin.
"I wanted a biscuit right now!" stated Kenny and lunged for the last biscuit on a plate nearby, then cantered downstairs again.
Karin got up to put the kettle on.
"You don't think that it could involve the crystals?" questioned Sarah, and the others looked at her attentively, "I mean, like my experience today, crossing dimensional pathways."
"You could be right Sarah," answered Karin, "perhaps the answers to all of this lie elsewhere."
"In Atlantean time," interjected Alyssia, "can you imagine going there?"
"It all sounds exciting, but we don't know how we'd get there, and more importantly, how we'd get back again, that's if we could!" stated Sarah.
"We're going to have to think about this carefully," said Karin, reading a bit more and then looking up, "it mentions about making a kind of formation with crystals here, as a starting point for the journey."
"Do you suppose we'd be creating a time portal? Perhaps we should hold a meditation with our crystals," said Alyssia, "and see what we must do to safeguard the casket."
"Okay, let's do it tonight," concluded Sarah, and the others agreed.
Karin took the cup of tea down to Kenny along with a handful of biscuits.

Later they could hear the sound of Kenny locking up the shop. Karin and Alyssia were beginning to prepare the evening meal while Sarah unpacked a few belongings and got her room shipshape and Oswestry fashion, as she would say.
There was the sound of footsteps coming up the stairs before Kenny's head peered around the door.
"Great! Tea on the horizon I see. Full steam ahead!" and he briskly entered and half collapsed into the nearest seat.

"It's creamed vegetables, previously marinated in exotic herbs and spices, pecan and cashew nut roast, topped with coriander gravy and accompanied by creamed sweet and savoury potatoes," announced Alyssia. Kenny was about to respond when Alyssia held up her hand to stop him, "followed by ……" she emphasised, "superberry syllabub, Monsieur Kenton!"

"Wow! I'm speechless with admiration. What's the reason for this deluxe presentation girls?" asked Kenny.

"Just flexing our culinary muscles dear," laughed Karin, "we thought a little extra flourish would lift Sarah's spirits."

"Good idea too! It's working on me anyway," commented Kenny.

Soon enough the meal was served and they all sat at the table together.

"This is lovely, girls!" exclaimed Sarah, "well worth coming from Cornwall for every day!"

"You know that woman I met in the park?" commented Kenny, "well, she said she'd like to use our healing room and give intuitive readings to people. I said that we were interested, dear," he said, looking at Karin, who was beginning to look a little outraged, "don't worry dear," he said, putting his hand on Karin's knee, "sorry I didn't consult you first, but I just got an intuitive feeling that it was right to invite her here. She said that she'd come around after closing time to give us all a reading each, by way of a practical c.v, tomorrow. Her name is Maraya and she lived in Somerset for a year or two."

Karin's face had relaxed by now and began to look a little interested.

"Ok, let's see what her readings are like, she sounds quite interesting so far, do you know anything else about her?" asked Karin.

"She said that she'd lived abroad for quite a number of years, near Greece on Santorini, the western side of Morocco, as well as Cadiz, a brief time in Brittany, then over to the Scilly Isles before her stay in Somerset," answered Kenny.

"What an amazing selection of places to have chosen," remarked Alyssia.

"The Atlanteans were connected with western Morocco and Cadiz," mentioned Sarah.

"And the other places!" added Karin and Alyssia together.

"What! That sounds very deliberate to me, I think she's got to be connected with all this!"

They all agreed. Sarah told Kenny of their plan to meditate with the crystals to see what they should do next, and also how to safeguard themselves and the crystals.

"I'll just be the doorkeeper," said Kenny, "and make sure all is well round here while you're meditating," and he looked at them all seriously.

"Why don't we meditate in our bedroom, then Kenny can watch the flat door, the windows and down at the front of the shop," added Karin.

"I'd feel happier about that. Once the crystals become activated, then it could draw attention," remarked Sarah.

"Do you think we should use some other crystals meanwhile? So we don't attract attention with the casket ones," suggested Alyssia.

"Well, maybe we could try," said Karin thoughtfully.

"If it doesn't work, then we'll have to use the crystals from the casket," added Sarah.

"Right then! Let's get going!" announced Karin, ushering the others. Alyssia went into the bedroom and brought two chairs around to the place they would be meditating. Sarah got the casket while Karin brought a kitchen chair in, and Kenny stood on guard until they were all in the bedroom, then he looked out the window before seating himself facing the bedroom door.

The three of them held a crystal each from Karin and Kenny's collection, with a cluster between them all on the floor. Their chairs were in a circular formation, each facing the centre. They said a prayer and asked for the powers that be to help them to perceive how to safeguard the casket crystals.

Later they emerged to see Kenny with an expectant expression on his face.

"Well? Did you get anywhere? All quiet here, no mysterious characters looming about," said Kenny, and he sprang up to put the kettle on, put a pile of biscuits on a plate, and laid it on the table.

"I think, from what we deduced, that answers will come to us as we progress, but for now we must be very careful with the casket and not activate or use it until we know how to safeguard ourselves properly," said Sarah, and the others agreed.

"Also," said Karin, "I got the impression that you have an important role, Kenny, and that a doorkeeper acts as an anchor or homing place to focus on when returning from deep meditations. You see, I saw an image of a stone circle and its energy circuit, with an outlier regulating that energy as necessary."

"Amazing!" responded Kenny, "like holding the reins in a way."

"Don't get any ideas of power control dear!" said Karin with a laugh.

"Never entered my head, honest!" Kenny said with a look of mock innocence, raising his hands briefly to his head, he proceeded to dust an imaginary halo. Kenny glanced at the casket momentarily, and then a thoughtful expression suffused his eyes.
"By the way, what are the contents other than the crystals you've already used, is that everything?" asked Kenny, looking around at everyone.
Alyssia and Karin exchanged glances and looked at Sarah.
"We never looked further than those four crystals we've used, is there more?" asked Alyssia.
"Yes there is another layer underneath. I had to use that chanting method to open it up, like with the top. Below the lid I found another large crystal, fatter than the other, so it nearly fills the space. There was also a strange dust surrounding the crystal, of a pale sea green colour and in amongst it were some amazing seeds. I photographed them just in case they might perish, now that the casket's open," explained Sarah.
"Why don't we try to grow them," exclaimed Alyssia.
"Don't you think they'd be well extinct by now," remarked Karin.
"Maybe, but having been sealed up. It's like a time capsule!" insisted Alyssia.
"Ok! How about it then, we have nothing to lose!" said Karin excitedly; "There's some compost under the sink Kenny...dear!"
"I get the hint!" smiled Kenny, striding to the sink and grabbed some compost and pots.
Sarah had gone to fetch the seeds and soon returned, and everyone examined them closely.
"When did you take the seeds from the casket?" asked Karin.
"Don't worry everyone! I had taken them out the last time I opened it down in Zennor and had intended to plant them in some pots down there," said Sarah.
"We could attach a copy of my photos to each of the relevant pots, then we'd identify them better," said Sarah.
"Good thinking, you can just link your memory card into the computer Sarah, when you're ready," Karin replied brightly.

They duly potted up the seeds and labelled them.
"There are six of the spiky ones, three of the delicate lacy ones, five of the huge ones, and ten of the microscopic ones," stated Karin, noting details in a notepad, "I think we must monitor the growing cycle of these seeds."
"Do you think they're going to be relevant to finding Atlantis and are some kind of medical plants suited to those times?" ventured Alyssia.

"Maybe, a good thought," remarked Sarah.
"The Eden Project's got nothing on us!" laughed Kenny and they all laughed too.
They began on the planting. Kenny filled the pots with compost, while Karin, Alyssia and Sarah placed the seeds in them. Kenny decided on larger than expected pots since they didn't know anything about their growth cycles.
Once finished, Sarah yawned and said she needed to get to sleep and departed swiftly. The others talked together while deciding on places for the pots to go.

The next morning saw Kenny and Karin preparing for another day at the shop, bustling around busily while Alyssia and Sarah still slept.
"I'm looking forward to seeing one of those plants sprouting up!" exclaimed Kenny with a smile.
"I certainly hope they'll grow, even though I know it's a long shot," answered Karin.
Just then Alyssia made an entrance, yawned and sat down at the table.
"Any tea left?" she asked, but Karin indicated that there was none left, so Alyssia rose slowly to put the kettle on, still yawning.
"Bye girls, see you later!" said Kenny brightly.
"See you!" they chorused.

As Alyssia was finishing her toast and pot of tea, Sarah came through. She looked livelier than Alyssia.
"My! I've slept in very late today," she said.
"I think you deserve it after yesterday," said Karin and Alyssia smiled.
"Was it only yesterday when I arrived? Somehow it feels as if I've been here longer," said Sarah.
She sat down and put some toast in the toaster, which lived on the table, and managed to find enough tea in the pot to fill a cup.
"I have to tell you something girls," said Sarah, leaning forwards a little, and the others listened attentively, "I think that green powder I mentioned has to be put on the seeds to help them grow, as I kept on getting the words 'green powder' when I was going to bed and also when I awoke. It's not a fertiliser in the usual sense, somehow more sacred, is the impression I got."
"Ok then! Let's try a sprinkle on them once you've finished breakfast Sarah," said Alyssia.

They duly sprinkled the green powder in small quantities around the plants on the surface of the soil. Many of the plants were left on south-facing windowsills in Karin and Kenny's room, and others carefully placed in Sarah and Alyssia's rooms.

Karin went downstairs to get the mail from Kenny and told him about Sarah's impressions about the green powder, when they both heard screams from upstairs. They looked at each other in astonishment, and then Karin rushed upstairs.

She opened the door to the flat to see that the plants had grown upwards rapidly and were almost up to the ceiling. Karin stood with an open mouth, and then rushed back down to Kenny.

"Kenny! Kenny! It's those plants, they've grown about five feet already!" exclaimed Karin, almost breathless with shock, and with running up and down the stairs so quickly.

Kenny looked at her with amazement.

"Five feet high! How much more will they grow! I hope they don't fill up the whole flat. Let me know if they grow much more, we may have to do something about them," he said, frowning a little, "I wished I hadn't said that about the Eden Project, we may need their advice!"

"I could search for possibilities on the Internet," responded Karin, with a doubtful expression.

"Well, let's just see what happens, and follow our intuition," said Kenny thoughtfully, "you know, those plants are like nothing else! Think of the headlines if anyone got to know, and of course that would attract the element we wouldn't want!"

"You're right. We'll just have to sort it out ourselves," answered Karin, looking somewhat resigned, however.

"Cheer up, it's an adventure!" said Kenny, and he smiled, putting his arm around Karin.

Just then a group of people came into the shop, and Karin moved off. A couple of them came towards the extension and started viewing Alyssia's paintings.

"Oh these are nice," said one lady, dressed in orange and turquoise.

"I think I'll get this one, it reminds me of so many meaningful things in my life," said another dressed in shades of mauve.

Kenny rang upstairs after that to announce the sales of Alyssia's paintings.

The day went quickly and Kenny closed the shop door, turning the closed sign to face outwards. The late afternoon sun reflected off the edges of the door and windows, and for a fleeting moment Kenny wished he had been outside all day just leisurely wandering around somewhere rural and enjoying the sun, with no crystal casket and strange plants etc., to cause surprises they didn't want. He pottered around, tidying the shelves and counter and removed the notes from the till, and then went upstairs.

His face peered hesitantly round the door and exclaimed,
"Well, the hollyhocks haven't spread to the door yet!" and Karin and Alyssia laughed.
"No, they stopped growing not long after I came downstairs again to tell you about it Kenny. Sarah thinks if we'd put more powder on they would have grown either much quicker or bigger," said Karin.
"I'm glad you didn't, what would people make of a convex shaped building. But what are we going to do with them all, that's what I'd like to know?" asked Kenny looking at them both.
Sarah just came into the room then.
"I think we ought to enter a flower competition with the Oswestry W.I.!" she said, "You know, I'd love to find out what the green powder's ingredients are."
"Yes, don't suppose you've had any scientists in the shop Kenny?" asked Alyssia with a smile.
"Oh yes, old eccentric Emrys the alchemist," he said with a glint in his eye, "last of his kind you know, secretly stirring elixirs up the Cwm Rheiddol valley. He just came in a week ago."
"Well, you'd better ring him up then," laughed Karin.
"And ask for the formula," added Alyssia.
"When you've finished ad-libbing, when is the lady coming?" asked Sarah.
"Oh yes, Maraya. Hey, we'd better get shipshape as she's coming over at 5.45pm," he said.
"I suppose she may want some tea as well?" asked Karin.
"I think somehow she might be spending quite some time here," said Sarah, "don't forget that I'd brought a load of food with me, it's still in the car."
"Bring it in!" insisted Karin.
"I'll come and help bring it upstairs," Alyssia called out. Kenny and she went downstairs with Sarah's keys and out the back door, while Karin started chopping up some vegetables.

They discussed what Maraya might be like, and especially the readings, while the casserole was simmering in the oven. The shop bell rang and

Kenny poked his head out the living room window and indicated to Maraya that he'd come down to unlock the shop door to let her in.

"Maraya, this is everyone," announced Kenny as she entered, and introduced her to the others each by turn, "do sit down and make yourself comfortable."

She sat near the door and loosened a light, brightly coloured shawl. They could see her dark features more clearly and she had high cheekbones, but kept her eyes looking down quite a bit initially.

"Are you settling in all right Maraya?" asked Karin, "Kenny told us."

"Oh yes thank you. It's not as warm as further south, as I'm so used to Mediterranean weather, but we'll see!" and she laughed gently.

"Kenny told us about all those exotic places you've lived in. Santorini and Morocco, wow! What's it like there?" asked Alyssia eagerly.

"Very beautiful, especially on Santorini, so peaceful and calm, with a slow pace of life, and you can be almost self-sufficient without too much effort. It helps if you travel light and live simply anyway," and Maraya smiled sunnily.

"We have some food in the oven Maraya, and thought you'd like to join us for tea. Would you like to start on a reading now or after the meal?" asked Kenny.

"I don't mind making a start now, and continuing after," responded Maraya, glancing briefly at everyone.

"Right, should we go out of the room while you make a start on, say, Sarah?" questioned Kenny.

Maraya got out her crystals, "no, no. To be honest, I wish to give you all a reading together, it just seems right on this occasion," she said as she reached for her bag and everyone looked surprised.

"Are you sitting comfortably?" asked Maraya, and they agreed. Maraya said a prayer and closed her eyes while holding her crystals, which began to glow a pale mauve colour, with speckles of deep azure and gold flickering around in them. She opened her eyes and proceeded with the session.

"You have all come together for a purpose, and I know that it involves a box of crystals!"

At this everyone looked a little concerned, especially Sarah, but tried to hide it as best as she could.

"Do not worry my friends," reassured Maraya, "I only wish to help you, and know that there are forces that want to possess that box, and you are wise to not open it at present until you understand how to protect and shield yourselves from danger. There is much that can be done with it. I will show you how to protect it from identification by outsiders, who can link into any unusual activity with a kind of radar contraption if they need it."

Sarah went to get the casket and soon returned.

"You don't need to open it, just place it on the table," advised Maraya. Her crystal grew brighter still, and Alyssia couldn't take her eyes off it.

"Just picture yourselves connected to the large crystal inside and that the light is projected from it around you all and fills the flat," she instructed.

They did that and a white light began to fill the flat and wrap around everyone and the casket.

Just then, there was a loud pop and a kind of whistling noise like a firework display, and everyone looked startled.

"What was that sound?" asked Maraya.

"Oh, probably kids outside doing something they shouldn't," said Kenny.

"I think it came from inside," said Maraya.

Kenny went to look in their bedroom and the others saw him bending down to pick something up.

"What was it Kenny?" asked Karin.

"Something just fell off a shelf. Got too much stuff piled about, so something invariably drops off from time to time!" he answered with a grin.

Maraya looked intently at Kenny.

"You don't need to hide anything from me. I know you have some unusual plants here," and everyone looked a little awkward again, "the crystals are telling me that the seeds were in the casket and you planted them only yesterday, and now they are beginning to germinate and drop seed pods. Correct me if I'm wrong," stated Maraya, and she looked around at everyone reassuringly.

"No, you are right," said Sarah, and she leaned forwards, "do tell us exactly why the casket is so important to hostile forces?"

"I'd better take you one step at a time, but due to the urgency, I'll have to be swift. Let me see all the plant varieties you have please, as it's necessary information," asked Maraya. Sarah led her round and she examined them all in detail.

Once back in the living room she sat down and looked at everyone.

"You have some very useful plants indeed, I'm impressed that they've grown so well after all this time, very impressed," she commented, "the spiky shaped seeds are Amaranth."

At this everyone looked surprised.

"But Amaranth are smaller and completely different," remarked Sarah, "I've worked with plants for years."

"I know," answered Maraya, "but these plants are from another time, Atlantis! Plants then were much larger and originally people worked intuitively with the land and the nature spirits, and so much more was achieved. The original people who began the Atlantean civilization came from…." said Maraya, looking around.

"The Pleiades!" came the chorus from around the table, and Maraya smiled.

"Yes, the Pleiades. So they brought a lot of Pleiadean resources with them, including seeds like these and they probably had some fully grown plants on board. According to some sources, they could cross the time barrier and travel to places in a very short space of time," explained Maraya, and she looked over to the Amaranth plants in Karin and Kenny's room, their emerald green leaves glowing, "this species of Amaranth can be used to heal all manner of ailments, and is a food source too. If you take off some of the leaves, flowers, fruits or seeds, they will not perish for quite some time, especially the seeds, as you know!"

"What is that green powder Maraya?" asked Sarah.

"Could you show me it again Sarah," Maraya asked, and Sarah picked up the bag of the powder from inside a carrier bag, which she'd brought through from her room along with the casket.

Maraya looked at it and put a small bit on her fingertip.

"You know, you can ingest this. It is regenerative, as you can imagine, but because Atlanteans were so much bigger, it would be a disadvantage for you to be too small. I'll demonstrate!"

Everyone looked attentively as Maraya took a pinch of the green powder and put her fingertip in her mouth, and then sat back with a smile. After a moment or two she began to look a little bigger, maybe only an inch or two, and then she stopped.

"Are you going to grow any more?" asked Kenny.

"Doesn't it hurt growing so quickly?" asked Karin.

"Don't worry!" smiled Maraya, "there's a momentary gestation period involved, so that the compounds within the powder seep into the system allowing this growth to take place without harming the body in any way, nor causing any pain or undue discomfort," explained Maraya.

They all watched with fascination as Maraya now proceeded to expand and grow. She had to stand up to avoid breaking the chair with her weight and then had to bend forwards to avoid hitting her head on the ceiling, and continued until she was bent double.

"I am roughly about eleven or twelve feet high now. Do you have any seeds from the ten small seeded plants yet?" she asked with a quizzical look on her face.

"Not yet Maraya," replied Kenny, looking slightly concerned, "would any leaves do?"

"I'll try a couple, they'd help to stop me getting a crick in my neck!" she replied.

Kenny picked off a couple of leaves, and then took another for good measure, and handed them up to Maraya. She chewed on them swiftly and then she began to shrink a little, by a couple of feet. Suddenly there was a slight stirring sound in the bedroom and Kenny went to look.

"Hey! That plant I took the leaves from has just produced a seed pod. Everything works fast round here!" exclaimed Kenny.

He returned and gave Maraya one of the seeds and she swallowed it, and soon enough, she shrank back to her original size and then sat a moment with her eyes closed, and on opening them, she looked at everyone with a smile.

"I expect you are wondering how I know so much about these plants?" she asked.

"You could say so!" responded Kenny, "I still can't believe that you've just done that!"

"By the way, which plant is the green powder from?" asked Sarah.

"Sorry Sarah, you asked about the powder before. I guess there's so much each plant can encompass! The powder is from the huge seeds you planted. They are very bushy and if you prune them a little, like the others, they'll produce huge pods full of large seeds, about ten seeds per pod. The names of the plants, well I could never remember the formal names but the huge pods are known as the 'elixir' plant, the tiny seeds are called the 'withering' plant, not being negative, but was often used to stem infections and diseases, and it is also used for disappearing in a hurry, but as I said, a reduction in size is a disadvantage there, and there are other ways to disappear, which brings us to the fourth seed type," explained Maraya.

"Yes, those delicate lacy type of seeds," commented Alyssia, "that's what I call them."

"Indeed, have they grown yet folks?" asked Maraya.

"Yes they are beginning to and they are in my room," answered Alyssia, "there are a few leaves on each plant."
"Bring one through Alyssia!" asked Maraya, "better still, best bring them all."
Sarah and Alyssia went through and returned with the pots, and placed them on the table. Maraya looked at them, and she sang a strange archaic chant, "Ah-lay-mah, keh zel-i-an-os kur-i-ah" several times over. The delicate leaves of the little plants stirred slightly, and then they gradually moved nearer Maraya. She indicated for them to rise upwards and they gently and gradually rose higher until the plants were about three feet high, and had only been three inches before.
"You'd better learn this chant for the next lot of seeds, they love being sung to, even the adult plants," informed Maraya, and she proceeded to teach them the chant. "Of course the plants are growing a bit more with our chanting, and look, they're producing seeds too!"
Sure enough, little fronds lengthened, thickened up and became rectangular shaped pods with lacy fronds at each corner.
"These are called 'blue mist' plants and you'll see in a minute!" explained Maraya, and took off a small pod.
It was a little like the black egg cases that got washed up on beaches, Alyssia thought. Maraya opened the pod and extracted a seed.
"This little seed can be made into a tincture if you want a supply to last a while for several occasions, but if you want to be invisible for up to a week or two, just crunch a seed per week." Everyone looked rather concerned at that. "I'll show you how to make the tincture, as I want to demonstrate how you use it."
Karin showed Maraya where the kitchen equipment was and she started preparing the tincture.
"First you have to split the seeds a little," and she squashed several seeds by putting the seeds in a mortar and pestle and she pressed on them, "and then put them in a glass jar. Pour a pint of cider vinegar over the tops of the seeds and close the lid," which she did. "Shake the jar well twice daily, while keeping it in a warm place for two days. Decant the liquid after that, and then put the residue into a muslin bag and squeeze out any remaining tincture, remove the pulp and bag, and then store the tincture in a dark glass jar." She then finished the demonstration after shaking the jar and handed it to Karin to put in their airing cupboard. When Karin returned Maraya continued.
"I have a finished jar here with me!" and she held it up with a mischievous smile.

"Maraya, all the while that you've been telling us about these plants, and you have your own tincture. You've obviously got your own seed supply, either through another casket of your own, or you've somehow been time travelling to Atlantis the way most people go to Tesco's!" he uttered, and everyone laughed.
"I have to agree on some of those points," Maraya smiled, and then became serious, "I don't have a casket, but knew someone who did in Morocco, and I obtained some seeds from there and so got to know their properties, and yes, I have been to Atlantis a few times, I went with the group of people I knew in Morocco."
Maraya looked round at everyone's intrigued and amazed faces.
"It may seen outlandish and impossible, but can be done if conditions are right and you are well prepared, and know how to keep those unwanted forces at bay. I will help you," explained Maraya.
"But why did you visit Atlantis, was it anything specific or just for an adventure of a lifetime," asked Sarah.
"There are deeper reasons than an adventure, and I can only tell you the full story in time, for it is a safeguard to you if you don't know the full story, for the hostile forces will not be able to detect the knowledge. I will show you the disappearing act, and though you'll become invisible, you are still in the three-dimensional world, so, bumping into things or people who don't see you is still as unpleasant!" explained Maraya.

She opened her tincture jar and asked for some hot water, and Karin heated the kettle, and then poured some water into a cup with a teaspoon of the tincture in it. Maraya stirred it and drank the liquid. A strange blue haze appeared around her and then evaporated to conceal an invisible Maraya!
"Are you still there Maraya?" asked Kenny, instinctively looking round.
"Yes, I'm still seated. The liquid will wear off after a short time, roughly half an hour. Anyway, it means I can go home without being seen again!" laughed Maraya.
"What do you mean, again?" asked Kenny, "you mean you arrived here with a dose and only appeared once you approached the shop?"
"Yes that's right! Now I must go, as I have things to do at home, besides, it's late now. I want us to meet up over the weekend, are you closed on Sunday?" asked Maraya.
"Yes we are," Karin replied.
"I'll tell you what we will do when I come, meanwhile if you could make a good lot of tincture supplies from all the seeds and the green powder too,

though I shall supply you for this occasion as yours won't be ready in time," and she left instruction sheets on the table, "can I come reasonably early, say about 9.30-10am, then I'll tell you what we will do then!"
"Certainly!" answered Kenny, "we're all used to getting up early, aren't we girls!" They all smiled at Maraya.
"I look forward to seeing you again," said Maraya.
"Yes, but if we all have to be invisible, we'll all be saying that!" remarked Kenny with a chuckle and everyone laughed. He escorted Maraya downstairs to the back door.

<u>CHAPTER 6 - THE FLIGHT TO CHALIDOCEA</u>

Alyssia was the first to rise on Sunday, as she got the morning sun streaming into her room. She could just manage to see over some of the fairly dark rooftops, set against the bright luminous duck egg blue sky, with wisps of white cirrus striated diagonally. Something in those lanky stretched shapes that made Alyssia think of their attempt to link from one time period to another.

As she was dressing she thought to herself, 'I hope we followed Maraya's instructions on the green powder correctly. I'll go and see, then tell the others that it's worked, hopefully!'

She padded through quietly, thinking of what they had done last night. Kenny joking as usual, had reached for the largest casserole in the cupboard, as the huge seeds had to be baked inside a container with a lid, on a low heat for several hours. The seeds, Maraya had said in the instructions, tend to break open in heating, spilling their contents about when dried.

Alyssia went over to the cooker. The casserole, which was a smaller one than Kenny's choice, stood on top of the hot plates. She opened the lid very slightly and gradually, like opening a newly fired kiln, just in case there was an unexploded seed lying in wait, she thought. Alyssia could begin to see that all had turned to powder, and she lifted the lid off in glee.

There was a stirring in Karin and Kenny's room, and a sleepy looking Kenny appeared through the door.

"Hi Alyssia, is the potion successful?" he asked, gravitating towards the kettle.

"Yes, it looks good. We'll have to put it in a container I suppose," said Alyssia.

"I've got some very small plastic bottles, I'll swill some of them now, and dry them in the airing cupboard, we might need some today," said Kenny, hunting for the bottles, as well as crockery and cutlery for breakfast. "Ah! Here's the bottles, and they're clean too, I was more organised than I thought!" and he produced a sealed bag of them, which he plonked by the cooker.

"Are you worried at the thought of time travel Kenny?" asked Alyssia, "I mean, letting us all go, and you'll have to wait here."

"Tell you the truth, I've tried not to think about it too deeply, just been keeping it at the entertainment end of the spectrum," he said with a serious look, but I am able to deal with things like this as I just tend to switch off and think about something else. I learnt about that a bit when I was a night security guard in metropolitania. There was a lot of hanging about, but a lot of tension, anticipating inevitable break-ins."

"I see Kenny, it sounds as though this experience we are embarking on could get difficult," responded Alyssia.

Karin came in and greeted them cheerfully, and they prepared breakfast. The smell of toast lured Sarah into the kitchen, and they all sat down to mushrooms and tomatoes on toast.

"You don't know when you'll get the next meal in Atlantis!" Kenny said.

"You could be right there!" responded Sarah, "let's tuck in!"

Later, they were all congregated in the living room with a rucksack each, packed with food, first aid gear, a selection of ready made diluted solutions taken from the mother tinctures, some green powder and a little spare clothing.

Maraya arrived about 9.30am and they could hear a knock on the back door. Kenny went down to open it just as Maraya was becoming visible.

"Good morning Maraya, nice to see you again! Come in," Kenny whispered as she entered in case any of the neighbours were listening.

"Good morning Kenny, are you all ready?" she asked.

"All present and correct," he replied, and they went upstairs.

"Hi everyone," said Maraya, and they all responded, "there are a few more points to go over before we get going, so do sit down."

They put their rucksacks in a pile by the flat door and sat down.

"We still haven't gone over the essentials of how to make the casket invisible to anyone. Do you have it to hand Sarah?" she asked, and Sarah brought it out from a bag round her waist.

"You still have your Atlantean crystal out of the casket don't you Sarah?" asked Maraya.

"Yes, it's here in the bag too," and she drew it out and proceeded to take the crystal out of its little green velvet bag.

"Have you two got your crystals as well?" asked Maraya.

Alyssia pulled their crystals out too and placed them on the table.

"Well, that's an advantage, so you don't need to bring the casket with us. Do you all know the chant that Sarah used on her journey here?" and the others said that they did, "good, it will be of use, but in order to veil our thoughts and the opening and closing of the casket, we have to create some constant white noise for those occasions. If you could get your crystals ready and follow what I do and say. Hold your crystal so that the thumb is on the base, turn your radio on so it is out of tune and project that thought to the crystal to create that noise on the ether as well as physically."

The three of them concentrated hard until all three crystals were making a deafening sound. Kenny put his hands over his ears.
Maraya found it hard to make herself heard with all the white noise, so she showed with her crystal that by running a finger or thumb of the other hand downwards over the crystal, that this would regulate the volume of the white noise. She showed them how she could manage to do it with one hand in case the other hand was occupied.
"This stops spies in their tracks!" she said.
She paused while everyone tried the volume control, and Kenny could take his hands off his ears with a sigh of relief.

"Now I want to ask you something," said Maraya, "how many times have you actually used the large information crystal in the casket? What did you see on those occasions, and were you all present at those times?"
"Well," said Sarah, pondering a moment, "as I've been the keeper of the casket after the girls found it, I'll make a start. The three of us were together when we saw our first scene of the past. It was a terrible view of the last moments, with a military commander called Azorca who was the spokesman. He described the downfall and the need to send off the crystal casket urgently, once they had done the final touches of placing information from the spiritual library into that large crystal."
"Any other occasions?" asked Maraya, "I'll comment afterwards, once I get the picture."
"Yes, there was another time with the three of us, not long after," said Sarah. "It was a time, probably also in the last days. We saw a young woman witnessing many beleaguered people being moved around, like in a Nazi invasion. We were seeing it from her point of view. She befriended a young girl and took her home, and explained how crystals had been tampered with, so people couldn't express their opinions. Anyway, the girl and she escaped the city one night as she'd de-activated the crystals in her house. They met up with other independent thinkers and all managed to escape from Atlantis."
"Is that everything?" asked Maraya.

"More or less, but I did get a feeling of concentration camp type terror around that time which pervaded, as if emanating from the crystal, and it invaded my dreams. Maybe because I had left the crystal out in the sun quite a bit, indoors and out, and so it had become over-energised," said Sarah, "oh yes, it was because of that, that I asked Alyssia and Karin to come and stay with me, but that feeling evaporated once they arrived."
"Did you two see anything beyond those occasions?" asked Maraya, looking intently at them both.
"No, we didn't," they replied.

Maraya composed herself, gathering her thoughts before answering. "Right, we have here the last days of Atlantis, as you said Sarah," said Maraya, "the first sighting was obviously the last moments. Several caskets were sent off like that by those in charge, either priests, warriors, or in your case, a band of priest-warriors.
In the second sighting, this was in the latter times also, but a few decades earlier. People had been impregnated with tiny crystals under the skin, programmed to interfere with bodily mechanisms over time and confuse thinking processes. Many crystals all over Atlantis were controlled by large crystals, which were programmed to influence all the small ones. All this was created by the priesthood to subdue people, but they of course, had means to protect themselves from the crystals that were contaminated, having programmed the main crystal to avoid influencing the priests and warriors of the establishment."

"It's hard to believe it possibly happened," murmured Kenny.
"It does seem like a very bad dream," said Maraya.
"Maraya," asked Kenny, "is it possible to re-run that information on the crystal for me, or others to see?"
"Yes it is, and will show you all in time, for you will need to control it, to access what is necessary when you want to," answered Maraya, "good point Kenny," and she smiled at him and turned to the others also.
"Now to Sarah's visions of the concentration camp like atmosphere and images. It did happen, for quite a percentage of people couldn't cope with the effect of their confused state and it strained them mentally. The priests re-considered this subjugation and toned it down a little, though the damage had been done to quite a number of the populace. With some coercion, the healing temples, which had been closed due to all manner of corrupt activities, were re-opened, and many of those affected, were healed to a fair degree and felt more peaceful, but it was only temporary

and the priests or greycloaks as they were called by the populace found excuses to have them closed again," and Maraya paused a moment.

Maraya then leant forwards a little with a questioning look on her face and said to them all, "You know, you have been shown the worst aspects of Atlantis first. Do you know why?"
No one ventured a reply so Maraya continued.
"It was a safeguard instilled into the crystals of the casket, in order to deter the curious from seeing the more valuable information contained in it."
"Which we've yet to see!" responded Sarah.
"Yes, and that's what the hostile forces want to stop you from seeing!" added Maraya.
"Why exactly were the healing temples closed Maraya?" asked Karin.
"Because that is where the problems with the crystals started, for that is where all the impregnation of crystals into peoples' bodies happened, and once that was achieved, then they made excuses for the closure of the temples gradually as more people felt the effects of the crystals and were not mindful of the usual need to stay healthy, and the crystals were programmed also with reluctant suggestions for people to avoid the temples. They also said they were 'too costly to run', and so there was little resistance to making gradual cutbacks until they all closed," replied Maraya.
Everyone looked pensive. Kenny frowned a little; Alyssia looked serious and let her eyes wander around the edge of the doorframe, and Sarah fingered a knot in the pinewood table.

"Now I'm going to safeguard the casket!" announced Maraya, and everyone came out of their reveries. "Sarah, could I ask you to place the casket on the table near the wall by the toaster, but not too close to it. I want to make it disappear for safety's sake while we are gone. Karin, if you could get out the mother tincture of the 'blue mist' plant please, a little bowl and also some hand cream or almond oil."
Sarah put the casket on the table near the back, by the toaster. Karin went to get the tincture from the fridge, and a bowl from a shelf nearby. Kenny obliged by getting the oil from their bedroom.

"I'll just put a little bit of the tincture in the bowl," said Maraya, "roughly half a teaspoonful, add a tablespoon of oil, and then rub this all over the casket and then you'll see, or won't see!" laughed Maraya.

She finished applying the oily tincture mix, and the characteristic blue haze appeared around the casket and it vanished.

"Hey! Is there any left?" asked Karin, "I could put some on our biscuit packets, that would stop Kenny for a while!"

Everyone laughed and Kenny put on an aloof expression and folded his arms.

"Right we can go now folks!" exclaimed Maraya, "but I think I'll do my disappearing act before we get there, in case we are being watched."

She took a very small mouthful of the diluted tincture and soon vanished in the blue haze.

They decided to travel in Alyssia's pale mauve car rather than Sarah's as it may have been recognised, or Karin and Kenny's deep purple van with 'Plas Myrddin' on both sides!

"Which places would you recommend as being energy sites?" asked Maraya.

"Pistyll Rhaeadr for one, and also Old Oswestry hill fort," answered Alyssia, "and I've been to both."

"Are those places regularly visited, because we need somewhere really quiet," replied Maraya.

"I'll get my map," said Karin, opening it out quickly, "if you take the B4579 towards Selattyn, Alyssia. I can see a castle mound in a wood tucked away from any footpaths, Maraya. Just turn left when you get to a kind of crossroads, the roads are tiny and the right one goes to a farm, and the left one goes to a hamlet called Brogyntyn."

They turned off towards Brogyntyn and travelled slowly down the narrow lane until they came to a junction and decided to just park around there and walk from there on.

"The mound is at the end of this wood above two little lakes," explained Karin, as they got out of the car.

"Sounds magical," said Alyssia.

"Can I ask you what we might expect to a degree on our journey, and is it possible to direct ourselves accurately to a destination and time period?" asked Sarah, looking around for Maraya.

"I'm here!" she said, "and should re-appear shortly. It is possible, and I shall explain all by the time we reach the top of the woods. When we hold our crystals, we merely have to think of a time period and ask for a date. The problem with that is, of course, that none of you know a thing about the dating system then, or which period would be safe enough to go back to."

They had walked along the road for a hundred yards while talking, and had just entered the wood. At that moment Maraya reappeared and looked around at everyone with a smile.
"The original dating system in the early days was as follows. For each year they used the names of the sons of Poseidon, and other divine beings on the earth then and also those in the heavens, that Poseidon had told the earth people who ruled the Pleiades and the galaxy. Later each year was named after the current arch high priest of Atlantis, and if he were in office for more than one year then the number of years in office would be applied, for example, 'the Year of Kriyothos 3'. They saw no reason for recording time chronologically to the degree we see it necessary today. They knew astrology in great depth and so paid more attention to that, and the various age periods like Pisces, Aquarius etc.," said Maraya, "let's settle for a nice period of time eh! Let's say 12,000 years ago BC."
"That was the golden age, we'll go for that," cried Alyssia, and the others agreed too.
"Let's get to the place of take-off then," said Maraya.
They had been walking up through the long thin wood and soon reached the mound. They put down their rucksacks and awaited instructions.
Maraya pulled garments from out of her rucksack, "I should have told you before about your Atlantean garments, girls, but we've covered a lot of ground and I forgot until this morning, and here's a little bag each to carry your potions etc.," she said, handing them around, and she got hers out too. Kenny turned away while they changed, and told him he could look and was impressed by the refinement of the garments.
"Put your clothes in this bag girls!" said Maraya. They did so and left it by Kenny.

"As you're not familiar with timing, just link your crystals to mine and we'll all get there safely together. If at any time anyone needs to return, just think of this time period, the exact date and time," said Maraya.
"Just give me time to have a flask of tea and some biscuits!" said Kenny.
"Ok twenty minutes then! That makes it 29th August at 11.30am for our return," announced Maraya. "Now we must all drink a small portion of the elixir juice, and once we've grown to the right height, then we take the blue mist juice. I find it better to be invisible in case we land in the middle of a crowd or someone's house etc!"

"How do we make the crystals work?" asked Alyssia, "I've tried concentrating on them before, but certainly couldn't imagine time travelling would happen."
"The secret is that it does work when you are 12 feet tall! It's the combination of the larger size and the effects of the elixir, as it gives you an expanded energy and capabilities, just wait and see!" said Maraya.
They took a measured portion of the elixir and grew to the required height, and had to bend down so as not to collide with the overhanging branches. Kenny nearly got bumped by Karin's rucksack, which, like the other's rucksacks, had expanded with them as they were holding them. Then they took the blue haze, waving to Kenny as they disappeared.
Then they all concentrated hard on their crystals, which were pointed at Maraya's. Strangely, they could all see each other since they had all disappeared simultaneously. They were amazed by being able to see their energy streaming from their heads with concentration, and directed to their crystals, which in turn made Maraya's crystal glow brilliantly, and then their surroundings faded.

Kenny saw nothing of what happened, but eventually after five minutes he got up and wandered around feeling tentatively to see if they were there. On realising they had really gone completely, he felt a strange feeling of amazed happiness that it was successful, followed speedily by a sense of loss and sadness that he wasn't with them, and also concerned about what hazards time travellers could encounter, but told himself to 'shut up' and that 'they'll be back in twenty minutes' and tried not to think about anything else on that subject. He proceeded to have a cup of tea and biscuits as he sat on the brow of the mound, looking through the leafy glades and down to the silvery rippling surface of one of the little lakes.

The four women found themselves on the mound again, and three of them wondered if anything different had happened, though Kenny wasn't visible. It felt warmer and they noticed that the sun had a brilliance that was more like tropical climes.
"It's warmer because the sun is nearer to the earth," whispered Maraya initially; then noticed that there was no one but themselves, so stopped whispering. "That's why it's brighter too! By the way, try not to look so amazed at everything once we reach more populated areas, people might wonder what's going on."

The others gave a thumbs up and then they moved away from the mound and down to where the little road was, except the wood they were in was larger now and there was open meadowland instead of roads.
"Let's go down here," suggested Maraya, and they turned right, heading for Oswestry direction.
"Look at that over there!" exclaimed Alyssia, peering through the trees, and looking to the horizon.
"It looks like some kind of airport!" said Sarah with wonder in her voice.
"Let's check it out!" said Maraya, and they needed no encouragement.
"Pity the car got left behind!" said Karin.
"We'd never fit in it," said Alyssia.
"We could put some elixir in it in future!" said Karin, and Alyssia laughed.
"We can walk quicker being bigger and more vital, like superman or women," said Maraya, laughing.

They indeed began to find that their larger bodies and the effects of the elixir was giving them increased vitality, and especially when they stopped to sip some of the amaranth juice. It only seemed about five minutes until they got to the airport, as they ran for a fair stretch of the way.

Once there, Maraya approached one of the officials there to ask for day return tickets for all four of them.
The others looked around, observing their surroundings carefully. Everyone was dressed in brightly coloured clothing, but no one seemed to be talking to each other, they thought, they would look at each other, laugh, smile and the usual gestures. Then they saw Maraya doing the same, so she, like the others, was asking telepathically for the four tickets, and wondered how they could do the same when the occasion was thrust upon them.

The aircraft was a curious thing, and was oval in shape like a zeppelin, with three sets of fins on either side, in the position where legs would be on an insect. There were numerous jet engines on the fins, the base of the craft and along the tail fin. It was a bright silver colour. The craft was sitting on some kind of docking structure that supported the body of the craft, but you could see around the supporting struts to view the base of the craft.

Maraya ushered them onto the aircraft that awaited departure. They seated themselves and got strapped in. Maraya beckoned the three of them to come closer and she whispered in a very low voice.

"This aircraft will go very fast, so watch out, but it will be safe. Don't worry, you'll pick up telepathy soon!" whispered Maraya, and smiled reassuringly.

Alyssia indicated to Karin and Sarah to look at the crafts exterior for here and there were touches of oricalchum, its familiar reddish-gold tints dazzling in the sunlight.

Suddenly the motors started and revved strongly. The craft took off vertically to about 80 feet above ground and hovered a while. Alyssia began to see a bright light around the craft and indicated that to the others, as well as that they were on Old Oswestry hill fort! The craft changed gear and suddenly the craft lurched forwards by 50 feet, and Alyssia, Karin and Sarah eyed each other covertly with concerned expressions. The engines revved higher, head rests lifted up behind each person. Securing straps and large cushioning structures wrapped themselves swiftly around each person, so that they couldn't move and then the craft shot off at tremendous speed.

Alyssia, Karin and Sarah shut their eyes and tried hard not to cry out. There was a flash of brilliant light and suddenly everything was calm and still as if in slow motion. The three of them opened their eyes to see the craft approaching a continent across an ocean. Tall pinnacle shaped mountains hugged part of the coastline and in amidst them lay a flat plain, multicoloured with lush vegetation, and small villages and hamlets could be seen with their houses arranged in circular formations.

The craft sped overhead until they could see a city, but not like the ones in their time period. This one had gleaming towers of golden hue, and not as outrageously huge as ours, Alyssia thought.

Alyssia, Karin and Sarah saw something white on the far side of the city and realised it was a unicorn running along, and then they saw two more. Needless to say, their expressions were of amazement.

The craft came to the Atlantean airport, which mirrored the one they'd seen on the Old Oswestry hill fort. They hovered overhead before landing vertically, and once the engines stopped, all the straps, cushioning and headrests retracted again.

As they descended off the craft via some steps, Alyssia could smell the perfume in the air, and she looked at the others, Karin looked

appreciatively and Sarah sniffed at it enthusiastically. Maraya came up to them and Sarah looked at her and pointed to her watch and glanced at the craft. Maraya understood that she was asking for the return journey time. Maraya indicated the choice of 3pm or 5pm. "Have more amaranth," she whispered, as if to indicate that it would help their telepathic powers develop quicker.
The three of them took a gulp each, once they were outside the airport, and then started looking around the city.

Alyssia instinctively expected to see cars, and then they saw little hovering buggies trundling people about. One stopped for them and the driver indicated for them to hop in. Maraya swiftly got in, and so the others, not wanting to be left behind jumped in too. The buggy flew swiftly along the street, which followed a wider circular route than in the villages, being on the outskirts of the city.
The buildings were all beautiful and of different styles. Some were decked in jewels, some in wonderful coloured wood and ornately carved, and others looked as if they had been modelled in clay, for they were of flowing shapes, and looked as if they had pigmentation with something like oxides, thought Alyssia, and also burnished. They reminded her of Gaudi's architecture. Where the buildings were of stone, the colours were predominantly red and black. There were shops, dwellings, craft workshops and it dawned on the three of them that everything was made to share with the community. There were people sitting around resting, communicating with others or looking at all the craftwork. Their clothes, like what the four women were wearing, were all graceful and elegant, with a slight sheen to them, and the priests and priestesses were recognisable by the headband and their different coloured robes.
The buggy then took a left turn, and Alyssia and Karin looked at each other when they saw the large impressive building at the end of the only straight street there, for it only went to the building. It was situated in a square until Alyssia realised that the building was hexagonal and so was the square. The hover buggy stopped and they all alighted. Maraya thanked the man telepathically and they went up to the steps of the building. As no one was present Maraya whispered to them again.
"This is the main healing temple, if I take you in here for a healing, your telepathic abilities will come. I'll tell them that your abilities have waned due to some incident in the provinces, something that occurs occasionally. I will explain further when we return, but such traumas usually affect telepathic abilities, so they'll give you a routine healing for that ailment,"

she said with an encouraging look, and the three of them smiled broadly as they entered the building.

It seemed a little like a hospital, Alyssia and Karin thought, as they would compare notes later. There were countless healing rooms as to be expected, with offices and staff looking after the services. Except that the atmosphere in the building was one of such deep peace and contrasted so deeply with the usual hospitals hustle and bustling atmosphere that they soon forgot the hospitals back home. In the main foyer area there was a large indoor fountain, with a mass of pink and mauve flowers growing around it, set into a sunken bed, and the whole area was constructed in white marble. The leaves of the plants were bright emerald.
There was a seating area around the plants and a variety of Atlanteans sat, many with eyes closed in meditation. Alyssia, Karin and Sarah saw a group of fairies tending to the flowers, and an elf walked past. They then noticed some huge crystals by the walls with one or two gnomes standing beside them, and they would touch the crystals now and again, and then a little pulsating light entered each crystal with that action.
Maraya indicated to them, removed the phial of amaranth tincture solution and pointed to it, and the others realised that these flowers were another kind of amaranth too. They went over to the flowers and touched the leaves, and knew they were there for their healing qualities.

They then walked away from the foyer area, and followed Maraya to the end of a corridor and up a flight of stairs. At the top they saw a circular notice with a head on it, and knew they were in the part of the hospital that dealt with problems of the head area. Maraya took them inside and told the staff about their supposed plight and the three were allotted a healer each. The healers indicated where each of them had to go to get partially undressed and put on gowns, and then they would lie on healing beds lined with crystals.

Alyssia, as the others did, lay on top of her crystal bed, expecting it to be uncomfortable, as they were unpolished amethyst quartz. But as soon as she lay on it the healer activated something on the side of the bed and Alyssia felt herself become almost weightless, and merely rested gently against the crystal bed without any pressure bearing on it. The healer concentrated on her head, sending brilliant flashes of energy in multicoloured hues throughout all parts of it, and then occasionally down her spine. Alyssia then became aware that the amethyst bed was having a scouring action on her system, which left her feeling brilliant and more vital than she'd ever felt in her life. A deep peace instilled into her of such magnitude that she felt very moved. She was aware of beings around her. When she opened her eyes she realised that they were healing angels and healing priests she could see in spirit.

She began to hear voices, knowing that they were other people's thoughts and at first she couldn't tell which thoughts belonged to whom, until she thought of one person, namely the healer beside her, and then she was able to hear the healer's thoughts the clearest and the other peoples' thoughts became peripheral.
Alyssia smiled and thanked the healer telepathically. The healer sent a kind thought back to her and then gave Alyssia a hug.

Alyssia got dressed and met the others, sharing their experiences together telepathically, about how amazing it was and how energetic they felt. They could see radiant energy around each other as a result of the healing, and also around everyone else they saw.
They left the building and Sarah asked Maraya telepathically what time it was and she said it was quarter to three.
The others looked apprehensive, but Maraya just smiled and called for a hover buggy. One came immediately and they returned in time to board the aircraft.
The return flight didn't seem so bad for Alyssia, Karin and Sarah, and thought afterwards that it was the healing that had opened up their telepathic powers and strengthened and refined their bodies, which helped them to withstand the high speeds.
On landing at the Old Oswestry hill fort, they could see a bright line of light along the route they had just taken. They strode up the wooded hill to the place where they had entered Atlantis and concentrated upon 29th August, where they had been at 11.30am.

There was Kenny just finishing off his cup of tea and replacing it onto the flask. He turned to see them again and a wave of relief flashed over his face. Everyone took some of the withering plant juice and returned to normal size again.
"I'm so pleased you're all back, it's seemed the longest twenty minutes ever!" said Kenny, coming over to them and held Karin.
"Not as long as ours!" said Karin, talking out loud again and she smiled at him.

"You all look different somehow," said Kenny with a curious look, "sort of younger in one sense, but older in another, and your eyes are more alert."
"We all had a healing," said Karin, making a sweeping gesture, which included the others, "we'll tell you on the way back, it was in Atlantis and we flew there."
"What! In twenty minutes!" uttered Kenny.
"What is time?" said Maraya.
"Yes, I know in theory that it's like an elastic band," admitted Kenny, "ok, so you've had a two week holiday on the Atlantean Costa Brava!" and they laughed.

As they approached the car Maraya did her disappearing act again and they soon returned back to Plas Myrddin.
"You know Kenny, the airport was on Old Oswestry hill fort!" said Alyssia.
"Really!" exclaimed Kenny, "do you think the aircraft followed ley lines, or at least made use of energy sites to give the craft a boost?"
"That's interesting Kenny," remarked Sarah, "I've just read recently that all the ley lines were originally created by Atlanteans, and follows what we saw and felt. Perhaps they created them, not only to keep the planet and its inhabitants well and healthy, but also to empower their transport."
"The ship did hover for a good ten minutes over the fort didn't it Karin?" asked Alyssia.
"It certainly did, the craft was charging itself up," replied Karin.
"I wish I could go to Atlantis too," said a resigned Kenny.
"Don't worry," said an invisible Maraya, who sat between Kenny and Sarah, "there will be things for you to do, besides, both Jadeir and I will show you what your crystal can do. You'll need to know how to use it and be a link to both worlds!"
"Oh, it could get exciting then!" said Kenny, looking more cheerful.
"I think you can bet on it," replied Maraya.
"By the way, what was the name of that city we visited Maraya?" asked Sarah.

CHAPTER 7   KENNY'S EXPLORATIONS

"Kenny, these leaves are for you!" said Karin, proffering five emerald green leaves at him, "they're from the healing temple. Maraya said you should eat them."

Kenny took them, "all the way from the main healing temple in Atlantis, amazing," and he looked up from the leaves with a look of wonder, and then it changed to a cautious look, "what effect will it have on me?"

"Maraya said it would help you to become telepathic too. These leaves are more powerful than the ones we have, even though the plants there were a bit smaller," Karin replied.

He chewed on them, expecting them to taste awful, but was pleasantly surprised.

"You should begin to feel some kind of effects fairly soon," said Karin, and Kenny gave a thumbs up.

"Hey, you two are quiet!" he said to Alyssia and Sarah.

"Sorry Kenny, we find we can read each others minds so were talking to each other telepathically. Sorry, it's a bit rude, and we'll just speak out loud around you, we're just exercising our skills and is so much easier than speaking," said Sarah.

"I suppose you can hear them too Karin?" asked Kenny.

"Yes I can, but hope you'll be able to join in soon. Watch out, I'll know when you want to raid the biscuits!" laughed Karin, and Kenny put an arm around her to restrain her.

"I'll just have to keep silent," he replied.

"Oh look! There's the casket again!" said Sarah, as it re-appeared while they were all resting.

"What do you feel like doing this afternoon?" asked Karin to everyone.

"You know, I just feel like having a lovely meal and watching a good film," said Kenny with a rather stolid expression.

"What! It's a lovely day, why don't we go out somewhere!" said Karin, laughing; "teaser!" and she prodded Kenny.

"How about Pistyll Rhaeadr?" asked Alyssia.

"Just the place!" answered Kenny, "you get the sandwiches and I'll get the biscuits dear!"

They prepared what they needed to take and set off in Karin and Kenny's van. Of course they had to make the casket disappear again.

As it was Monday the next day, Kenny was back in the shop. Alyssia was inspired to do some more painting and Karin did some admin work, sorting out bills and paid some attention to literature from the tax office.

"Worth going to Atlantis to escape from!" said Karin to Alyssia. They all communicated telepathically while Kenny was out of the flat. Sarah came into the living room as she'd been sorting out things in her room.

"I've just phoned Geraldine and asked her to send all my materials, thought I could run off a load of small bags for crystals for starters, and then make some handbags. How would that do for the shop Karin? I've got to earn my keep while I'm here too!" she said.

"Oh great Sarah, they'll be good to have in the shop as it's ideal to have local goods," replied Karin, "do you have all the supplies you need? I mean, we could search the Internet if need be."

"I'm fine for now, but is there a fabric shop in town where I could get beads, thread and all that paraphernalia?" asked Sarah.

"Yes, I'll show you on the street map, you may as well get just as acquainted with Oswestry as with Atlantis!" laughed Karin, and the others laughed too.

"I'll just sort out something in my room for a moment girls," said Sarah, and went off again.

She felt as if she needed to meditate on something. She lay on her bed a moment and the impressions returned. She could sense a spiralling energy, and a female impressed herself on Sarah's mind.

"You are the keeper of the casket, I know. I am a mentor and am here to help you. You do not know it yet, but there is danger lying ahead, but you have help to guide you. Watch out! Make sure you have all the equipment that you need," said the visionary being.

"Who are you?" asked Sarah, "and what is the danger?"

"I am Rhianah, and the danger is not imminent, but look inside the casket for something is missing and needs to be found. I can help you in your mission, just call my name!"

"I shall try to ask Maraya what she knows about this when she comes," replied Sarah.

Rhianah gave affirmation, and Sarah sensed she was smiling and then her presence faded away.

"She didn't give much away. I wish we knew what's really going on here, and if it's something we want to get involved in," thought Sarah ruefully.

She got up and tidied things around to ensure there would be enough room for her belongings due to come from Cornwall, then she went through to the living room.
The phone rang and Karin answered.
"Hi Kenny. Ok, a cuppa it is! Oh, you're coming up, ok," answered Karin. She put the kettle on and looked over at Alyssia's painting, "that image looks good Alyssia."
"It's beginning to take shape now I'm giving it some detail," explained Alyssia cheerfully.
"Love those mauves and emerald tones on that figure," said Sarah, and went to sit down.

Kenny popped his head round the door.
"I've just come up quickly to drop off this note for you all to read; it's from Maraya. Good, a cuppa! Better dash as usual, the customers are downstairs," he said and smiled when Karin handed him his plate of biscuits.
"I'll read it to you if you like," said Karin, "telepathically eh!"
The others looked at the letter in Karin's hand and Alyssia stopped painting and sat at the table.
" 'Dear all, I've come into the shop to test the healing room to see if it would be a good route to Atlantis. Because of the various architectural changes etc., over time, we don't know what objects will be where at any time. I'm taking a chance from inside a building, and because it would be so convenient, I'm taking that chance! While you are reading this letter, I shall be away trying out a few time periods to see how it fares. I shall be back in time to start my first readings officially, and then come and talk to you afterwards. Kenny will put up a sign for me that I have made, once I have returned and re-adjusted again. Then, after closing time I shall come up and explain to Kenny about his crystal. With blessings and love, Maraya.' And she's put a playful sketch of a little swimming dolphin next to her name," said Karin.

Indeed, by the time they'd finished reading the note and pondered on it, there was a phone call and Karin answered it.
"Hi Karin! Maraya's just returned safely, just thought I'd let you all know, and I'm about to put a little sign on her door too, as well as the larger one which I've just fixed up by the main door, next to Alyssia's," said Kenny.
"Oh great, I'm so relieved that she's back safely," replied Karin. She turned and gave the thumbs up as she replaced the receiver.

At lunchtime Kenny and Maraya came upstairs.

"Well, I've had two short readings already!" said Maraya cheerfully.

"Bertha's here to take over for the afternoon," said Kenny, "what's for lunch?" and he rubbed his hands expectantly.

"Lots of salad, a bowl of rice with veggies etc in," answered Karin, putting the bowls of food on the table with Sarah's help.

"I've brought something too," said Maraya, and produced some homemade scones, and Kenny's eyes lit up.

"How was your trip Maraya?" asked Sarah, and everyone immediately looked at Maraya with interest.

"It is fortunate that most places are favourable from downstairs, except for 10,000 years ago at the final destruction for obvious reasons. I did make the mistake of going there once out of curiosity, as one of the Morocco group told me of a scene like your description that he'd viewed via a scryer from previous times. In my enthusiasm, having watched too many TV dramas at one time, I went back to that time, though I didn't hold onto that date for more than a second as I saw tidal waves approaching the coast and blackened skies, and just managed to change the date in time. It was terrifying seeing a black wall of water approaching extremely fast," she paused a moment, "but another time was much earlier, about 50,000 years BC, which I did downstairs. As soon as I linked to that time, I found myself on open grasslands amongst a herd of huge rhinoceros type of creature, and they began to gallop towards me, so I left very quickly then too!"

"Boy, I don't blame you!" exclaimed Kenny, "hope you'll be taking me to beautiful places with sunken gardens and tropical fruits!"

"I can try, and there are places like that, but not immediately here at this latitude," smiled Maraya, "even though it was a bit warmer in Atlantean days."

They all finished their meal and Alyssia talked to Maraya about her painting she was doing, for she was painting an image of figures in an Atlantean setting.

"Now I think I'll describe what Kenny and I will be doing later," said Maraya.

"Will I need a camouflage jacket and stout boots?" asked Kenny.

"If that would make you happier!" joked Maraya, "but it's better to wear the clothing of the time you have to visit if possible, or something that won't attract attention."

"Have you got some costumes yourself?" asked Karin.

"I do have quite a collection, though in some time periods it is not so important, as some areas of the country haven't a clue what people are wearing elsewhere, so it doesn't matter too much. Most people in Morocco wore the Middle Eastern type attire similar to that which can be seen today. I'll show you what I've got Kenny."
"I don't fancy wearing a woolly rhinoceros hide tunic!" responded Kenny.
"Don't worry, I don't have one!" laughed Maraya, "now I'd better get on with telling you in case someone wants a reading downstairs. The idea is to take you back to certain time periods when the Atlantean cultures were at their heights, and at the best times, as well as the not so good. Some, we'll spend some time there, others for just a glimpse. The danger is minimal with just glimpses."
"Are we looking for a general view of Atlantis as a whole, or is there something specific that we are looking for?" asked Kenny.
"Well, yes we are looking for something, and there are others who are involved, I mean who are looking as well. Those people in Morocco are the ones involved, and we as a group got the impression that there is another casket at large, but we don't know where it is based. Can you get the casket Sarah?"
"I certainly can," and Sarah left for her room, and returned with it, carefully placing it on the table in front of her.
"We want to do the white noise sequence," explained Maraya, "because we need to open the casket and remove the large crystal for Kenny."
"Oh yes, of course!" responded Sarah.

The five of them created the white noise, and then they proceeded in the ceremony to open the crystal using the note E above middle C by chanting. They focused on the crystals on top of the box going round clockwise and holding a compassionate energy, and they went round the crystal group three times.
The box made its strange noise like a vibratory hum, echoing the chant, then the familiar sound of the voices singing. A beautiful pearly light surrounded the box, and also a reddish hue, which turned to the deepest purple. Then the box lid flew open, making Kenny jump this time.
"There's the seal," said Sarah, then she looked at Maraya, "we never got round to finding out what it's for."
"It's the identity key for that casket and batch of crystals, and it has a code of some kind encrypted into it," replied Maraya.
Sarah picked it up and examined it closely.
"I can't see anything!" she exclaimed.

"You won't because it's done through the vibration that the group of crystals will resonate to, and can only be heard clairsentiently. The seal also holds a group of key words we will need at some point," explained Maraya.
They all looked curiously at Maraya.
"And the key words, what will they be needed for?" asked Alyssia.
"In order to find a missing object from the casket," said Maraya.
"I'll just get Kenny's crystal out," said Sarah, carefully lifting up the divider between the layers. The scryer crystal lay on the top layer, and Kenny's crystal lay beneath.
"Oh Sarah!" said Maraya, "let Kenny take out his crystal, so that it links to him directly."
Sarah put the top layer of the box onto the table and pushed the box over to Kenny and he took out the crystal.
Immediately there was a glowing energy pulsating through the crystal, of rainbow colours, and Kenny almost was on the point of dropping it in surprise, when Maraya put her hand on his arm.
"Just hold it for a few minutes until it stops flashing. It's just awakening and linking to your energies," explained Maraya, "I think it may like you, they always do when a golden glow comes at the end!"
Sure enough, the crystal suffused itself in gold, beaming brightly, and Kenny gave a little chuckle, which made everyone smile.
"Did this happen to your crystals? I don't recall you mentioning anything," asked Kenny.
"No, we weren't as fortunate Kenny," said Karin, "you must be privileged."
Kenny gave a fleeting look of glee and then said, "that probably means I've got something difficult to do!"
"Do you think we should take this scrying crystal out and then the problem of opening and closing the box will cease?" asked Sarah.
"I know it would be handy, but inside the box, the crystal is more secure because the orichalcum creates an interference to various methods of detection," replied Maraya, "have you looked under the lid?"
Sarah, Alyssia and Karin looked surprised.
"Is that where the missing object is? I don't think there's anything there, is there?" asked Alyssia, looking at Sarah and Karin.
"Well, I'll have another look," said Sarah, and she tried to find an opening, then gave up, "I can't get in! Maraya, how do you do it?" and Sarah looked at Maraya.

Maraya took the box and got out her crystal. She pointed it towards the lid, the inner casing detached itself and the covering slid off. She turned the box around so everyone could see that it was empty.
"Feel the lid area and you'll see the shape of the object that should be in there," she explained.
Alyssia, Karin and Sarah all drew up their chairs together and examined the lid.
"It's so shallow, there's no room for a crystal," said Karin.
"It feels round," said Alyssia with a puzzled look.
"Perhaps it's a disk, a very thin disk of some kind," mused Sarah.
Kenny picked up a CD from the shelf across the room.
"Would this fit in?" he asked.
"I don't think Atlantean priests would have listened to folk music!" laughed Karin.
"I'm sure they didn't dear," smiled Kenny, "go on! Just try it in to see if it's the right size and thickness, so we know what we might be looking for."
"Ok!" said Alyssia, who reached for the CD, as Kenny slid it over the table, and she placed it in the casket lid.
"Just a little too big, by 2 or 3 centimetres, but it's roughly right," said Sarah, "though the thing we are looking for might be slightly thicker. The only problem if we do find it, is how to detect ours if there are a whole mass of them."
"Good detection work, folks!" replied Maraya, "it is one of many, but there is an encoding that is given both in your crystals, in Kenny's and the seal. Once you have the disk, you can see all the other contents on the scrying crystal in the casket."

"Right, we'd better get the information from the seal then!" said Sarah.
"I'll do it," said Maraya, "please just be quiet a moment while I concentrate. Anyone got a piece of paper?"
Kenny reached for a sheet of rough paper off the shelf plus a biro, and then everyone became very still.
Maraya closed her eyes and then concentrated hard. After a minute she opened her eyes and wrote on the paper.
"The word is there on the paper, have a look! Do close the box now Sarah to keep the seal safe."
Maraya placed the seal back in its position in the box, and then Sarah closed it up. Then they all looked at the word.

The word was 'vilapo' and they all looked up with a puzzled expression. Maraya took the paper back and added 'I see', and then passed it back with a slight smile.

"It's old Atlantean, though not all Atlanteans spoke this way," said Maraya, turning to Kenny, "it's your turn to get the next word. Just focus on the crystal and mentally ask for the word for the password, the crystal will help you."

"I hope it's feeling in the mood!" he said, looking a little concerned.

He shut his eyes and focused on his crystal, which began to glow faintly with a shade of pale yellow. Then he looked up and opened his mouth to speak. Maraya indicated for him to write it down and not to speak out loud.

Kenny took the paper and pen and wrote the word. He showed it to Maraya so she could add the English.

Sarah, Karin and Alyssia did the same to obtain their words.

The sentence read out in Atlantean was 'vilapo – tria – piloz - ighonias – galanos' and in English it was 'I see – three – tall – corners – blue'.

They all still looked puzzled, understandably.

"What on earth does that mean?" exclaimed Kenny, shaking his head.

"Could it be a building?" asked Sarah.

"Possibly," answered Maraya, "but the crystals know, so there's an advantage. I can't tell you which time period it will be in, but we could meditate together once I've got Kenny familiarized with his crystal."

"But don't we need a crash course in Greek to catch this information and know how to communicate in Atlantis?" he asked.

"Don't worry! These crystals, when taken into Atlantis transcend language barriers," replied Maraya, "you managed all right girls when you went, didn't you?"

"Yes," said Sarah, "somehow, with all those plant potions, the effects of growing larger and the crystals, we didn't have any problems," and the others agreed.

Maraya got up and motioned for Kenny to come downstairs to the therapy room. He got up and said "see you later, or will it be earlier?" and the others smiled.

"We'll get some tea ready while you're busy!" said Karin "won't we girls!"

"But don't come back too early!" added Sarah, giving him a wave.

"Okay, we'll give you half an hour," said Maraya laughing, and they departed downstairs.

"You've made this a really nice space Maraya!" said Kenny.

Maraya smiled and then reached down to a chest, which had padded seating over the top. She removed the seating and opened the lid and pulled out some clothes.

"Here! These are for you!" she said.

Kenny took them, looked at them a moment. There was a long deep blue cloak and silver undergarments consisting of trousers and a long tunic top. He went behind a screen and changed.

He came out and saw Maraya had put on her garments too, which were an iridescent green-blue long dress with a high collar and also a deep blue cloak that had iridescent green thread work all over it.

"What magnificent garments. Whereabouts did they come from in Atlantis?" asked Kenny, as Maraya handed him some deep blue and silver boots, and she put on some shorter green and blue boots also with an iridescent sheen to them.

"These garments automatically belong to the people who receive the casket and I have put Sarah, Alyssia and Karin's clothes in here too," she said.

"How did you know about all this clothing?" asked Kenny with a curious look, "I mean, surely they weren't hanging on pegs with our names on!"

Maraya gave him a mischievous look.

"With being in the Moroccan group, we were able to explore around," said Maraya, "we visited various temples and talked to them about the caskets and they said that we should take the clothing as necessary. I took the liberty of obtaining your clothing as the priests could see that I would meet you."

"Weren't they surprised that someone from the future was just popping by to talk about one of their valuable objects which was now in the future?" asked Kenny, "and shouldn't it belong to them and be taken back?"

"Yes," said Maraya, "I'm sorry about all the secrecy, but it is part of the law of the casket holders that the recipients have to ask all the questions and find out what is going on. That's what makes the casket holders able to develop their own skills of deeper understanding. I can tell you so much and often have to stop myself from telling you all everything." And she looked at Kenny apologetically. "To answer your question directly, the priests in the high temple in the mountains know about the timeless value of the caskets and knew that they would be opened in future times, so they allowed the clothing we wear, to be made available for when we visit. We were shown that there was clothing for three caskets, and the clothing for the third casket is still there presently, and as far as they are aware, no one had found the casket yet."

"Did you find the disk from your casket?" asked Kenny.
"Yes we did, but unfortunately it got chipped, which rendered the disk virtually useless," she said with a serious look.
"Where did you find your disk?" asked Kenny.
"In a different place to yours because the code phrase was totally different," explained Maraya, "and your time period may be a different one."
"Was it a peaceful period?" asked Kenny.
"It wasn't too bad, but there were some difficulties to encounter, like security," said Maraya.
"Don't they hold back-up files or duplicate copies you could have gone back for?" asked Kenny.
"Yes, I'm sure they would have. We did look, but it was in a different place, and of course the code phrase would be irrelevant," answered Maraya, "unfortunately the security gets more difficult, the more decadent the society gets."
"Would the crystals not help in any way?" asked Kenny.
"To a degree, they can only give a hint of an indication, and once you've found the right place by a flash of light," said Maraya.
"They obviously have an extremely organised filing system, something you'd need to know from the inside. Time for super sleuth Kenton!" exclaimed Kenny, "except I don't feel like one yet Maraya," he said with a worried look.
"Don't worry yet Kenny, we're going somewhere nice right now. I'll explain the travel plan," said Maraya.

"Remember what we did at the hill fort, we take a mouthful of the elixir juice and then we'll grow to twelve feet high, okay," said Maraya.
She reached for her bottle and Kenny got his out and they took a sip and began to expand. They had to bend down increasingly as their bodies enlarged.
"Now take a sip of the blue mist juice," said Maraya, and the familiar blue haze surrounded them, "concentrate on my crystal and point yours towards me, okay."
Kenny and Maraya sipped the juice and disappeared, yet they could see each other. Kenny focused on Maraya and her crystal, as she in turn concentrated on hers, and in a flash they were back in time.

As things began to redefine themselves Maraya whispered to Kenny.
"Try not to speak too much, for people here commune with their minds.
I'll take you to the temple where the others went in order to help your
clairsentient skills. Just follow me, there'll be no problem and I'll secure a
place on the aeroplane, ok," explained Maraya.
"Ok," said Kenny, "lead on."
Maraya looked at the ground for there were half-protruding boulders
scattered around, and she indicated for Kenny to observe them as a
landmark. He noticed five boulders around themselves. There were no
buildings immediately around them, but he saw water springing from the
ground over to the west and realised that it was St Oswald's Well, and
there were a group of rounded dwellings beside it.
"Let's go Kenny!" whispered Maraya.
Kenny stopped gazing about and quickly followed her to the airport to the
north. They found an aeroplane awaiting departure and boarded.

On approaching Atlantis, Kenny could feel his crystal glowing a bright
silvery-gold colour, and he showed it to Maraya and she looked
approvingly.
Kenny looked amazed at the coastline of Atlantis as they approached. The
plane skirted round the tall coastal mountains and touched down vertically
at the airport.
Maraya hailed a hover buggy like the last time and they arrived at the
healing temple.
Kenny was given some healing on the crystal bed by a male healer, and
then he was left on the bed for several minutes. Kenny fancied that his
crystal was glowing just like he was, and was pleasantly surprised to see
that it was, once he was getting dressed again. He realised that he was
now telepathic like Sarah, Alyssia and Karin.

He insisted to Maraya that he wanted to sit by the water feature. He
noticed the fairies tending the amaranth plants, and the gnomes sending
energy to the crystals, and a few people sitting in meditation on the seats
nearby.
Maraya gave him an amaranth leaf to eat, which he did. They could now
both commune together telepathically.
"I've got this feeling of expectation here Maraya," said Kenny.
"Then we'll stay!" encouraged Maraya, smiling.
Next thing Kenny just about jumped out of his seat, as a green smiling
face peered round at him from behind. He said something and stood in

front of them. He bowed profusely to Kenny and kissed Maraya's hand. Kenny bowed from the waist in response.

"I'm saying to myself, I haven't seen you before," the green person said, looking intently at Kenny.

"Oh well, I live in a different part of the world. What is your name my friend?" asked Kenny.

"Jadeir's my name and what's yours?" he asked.

"I'm known as Kenny in most places!" said Kenny with a broad smile.

"I'm glad to meet you Kenny," he said grinning, and shook his hand, then quietly said, "I know you've come here to awaken your telepathic skills for a purpose."

At this, Kenny looked at Maraya and she ushered them to leave the temple so as not to disturb the other people sitting there, and they walked outside and down the steps.

"Kenny, Jadeir knows me well, and is familiar with the caskets, and what we are trying to do, and he could be helpful."

Jadeir and Kenny smiled at each other, and Kenny indicated that he understood.

"Jadeir wonders if you'd mind if he comes back with us," asked Maraya.

"No problem I'm sure," said Kenny, thinking he only meant on the hover buggy or to the plane.

"Thank you, I'd like to see where you live," answered Jadeir.

"Oh I see!" said Kenny, realising, and turned to Maraya, "is that all right, will it be safe?"

"There'll be no problem at all, and he'll have his own crystal too!" she replied quietly, not wanting their thoughts to be overheard by passers by.

"But where will he get his...?" asked Kenny, but was interrupted by Maraya.

"You'll find out later!" she said, "let's walk onwards and catch a buggy and find somewhere in the countryside, eh Jadeir."

"Yes Maraya, we'll visit my people," said Jadeir.

Kenny looked intrigued and smiled at the other two.

"Well, I've got to see where you live if you insist on seeing mine!" he replied.

"Well come on!" exclaimed Jadeir, pulling Kenny along suddenly, to a green hover buggy, "this one takes us to the far outskirts of the city and also to my village."

Jadeir waved his hand at the hover buggy driver to make him stop. Kenny noticed another passing by with two gnomes and an elf in it. They all got into the buggy and set off.

The buggy moved along through many streets, linked like spokes in a wheel to the concentric route layout of the city, which finally led up to the perimeter of the city of Chalidocea and stopped at a gate. Kenny observed it closely, and told the others later that it was wider at the base that at the top, and there appeared to be a lookout at the very top, with some living quarters below. He realised that gateways were quite relaxed and informal places, and served as places to exchange information.
"It's like an information centre here!" commented Kenny, looking at the others.
"Oh yes," piped up Jadeir, "excellent. Traders come for miles, asking if certain items are needed in the city in exchange for what they might need. Sometimes people ask if a friend they've lost contact with is living there, or ask directions, or where to learn certain skills. It's our information centre all right!"
"We have places like that at home but they are called libraries for general information, or for tourism, tourist information centres," replied Kenny.
"What is tourism?" asked Jadeir, "is it a spiritual following of some kind?" and he looked at Kenny with such a keen sincere expression that Kenny had to keep a straight face.
"I wish it was!" Kenny replied, "it is only for people who want to travel from one part of the world to another, to visit places, friends or for work purposes, but sometimes people do go to see sacred places."

Kenny turned to look out of the hover buggy again and saw that they were approaching some woodlands, and were about two miles away from the edge of the city gateway.
"This is as far as I go, just call me when you want me to return!" said the hover buggy man.
They thanked him and started walking to the woods.
Kenny looked in wonder as a flying horse glided over to the tops of the trees nearby. As they walked into the woods, Kenny was amazed to see scores of fairies tending flowers, gnomes bringing energy up from below ground, and elves working with both gnomes and the trees. Kenny looked at the trees more closely and could see the spirits of each of the trees. They looked like illumined green shapes within each tree, with facial features protruding slightly from certain gnarled spots on the tree trunk. Some of their faces looked severe to Kenny, but he realised that it was just on appearance, and that they were very kind really.

"I'll introduce you to my community!" announced Jadeir, he said telepathically as usual, for all conversations throughout Atlantis at that time period were telepathic, and he looked at Kenny.
"Oh thank you, I'd love to meet them all," Kenny said with a broad smile, looking around in wonder as he kept on noticing something new. He looked at Maraya expectantly.
"Oh, it's alright, I know the community already, as I came here when we first found the Moroccan casket," she said, "but I'm very happy to come round with you and meet them all again."

"Come and meet the fairies first. Hey stop working so hard folks! We have a new friend!" shouted Jadeir.
The hovering fairies flitted over speedily and crowded around Kenny's face, which had an amazed expression.
"Hello," he said, "I can't believe I'm talking to fairies!"
"Enchanted," they said in unison, "we are very happy to meet all manner of people, but do you not meet us all the time in your daily activities?" they asked.
"Unfortunately, no, because most people where I come from do not see you and some don't believe you all exist," said Kenny.
The fairies looked puzzled, "but which part of the world can that be, we've never heard of such a thing."
"It is not in your time, but 14,000 years in the future," said Kenny, and the fairies looked astonished, "I'm afraid things don't always get better as time progresses, but I think more people are turning to better ways of living and your kind will be accepted again."
"We hope so, that is a very sad world you come from indeed, but we are glad some people care and accept us there."

The fairies talked amongst themselves a moment and two of them flew off a moment and quickly returned, holding something between them.
"Here Kenny! There's something for you to take back to your world, and they held it out to his outstretched hand and they dropped the item onto it.
"How lovely! It's a little jewel!" exclaimed Kenny, and he held it nearer his eyes to get a good look, and it began to glow, and he saw something stirring in it, and he looked up curiously.
"If you wish to contact us, we can talk to you through the stone wherever you are, just think of us strongly," they said, and smiled at him, "the

movement in the stone is the crystal's energy awakening, ready for action of some kind."
A strange ethereal sparkling light surrounded them and swirled round the stone, some of it entering it and then surrounded Kenny, and he felt as if he was truly connected to the place. He was lost for words and was almost overcome by emotion.
The fairies looked at him kindly and sprinkled a purply pink mist over him and he felt calmed, and he smiled back through the haze.

The fairies then flew off back to tend to more flowers. He watched them working as they gently gave energy to the flowers, casting that sparkling energy around newly formed buds.

Jadeir gently ushered Kenny over to see the elves next. He could see the resemblance between Jadeir and the others, for Jadeir was around six feet high, wiry framed, with pointed ears and green skin. Their eyes, like his, were a dark green, and very piercing without being intrusive, simply very observant, and their thoughts could be louder than anyone else at times, and they were also very chatty.
"This is Pireus, and this fellow is Galen, and he is Calani, and that one there is Derien, and they all don't work as hard as I do!" said Jadeir laughing, and they all leapt towards him, looking him closely in the eye with folded arms.
"I don't mean it, honest!" said Jadeir, edging back, and they all laughed and hugged each other.
Kenny and Maraya smiled at them and looked at each other.
"They're a jolly lively lot!" chuckled Kenny.

"Let's show you what we can do!" said Jadeir, and he took Kenny over to a tree bole. "Look down at the ground while we are working."
Jadeir and the others bent over, looking at the ground, and were talking to someone.
"Yes, a bit more energy needed for this tree please, and for the roots of the plants to the left," they said.

Kenny peered closely and could just see a gnome's face peering up through the ground, and then the gnome activated some energy, and Kenny watched with a fascinated expression as a shaft of light came out of the ground to the tree and the plants nearby. The energy was then taken up into the plants themselves once the elves gathered round them. They drew it up into the stems, and then up the trunk of the tree, so that the tree and plants glowed happily, and a slow smile spread over the face of the old tree, and the tree winked!

"Time now to go to the next place! You have to meet someone else Kenny!" said Jadeir, ushering him over to the pathway which brought them into the wood. They took a branch off the path a little further into the wood itself. They wandered down to the left, turned a corner around a group of old trees. Jadeir greeted them and they smiled back. Kenny and Maraya greeted them too. Then the land dipped down to the river that flowed so gently, that Kenny hadn't heard it before now. They stopped by the waters edge and Jadeir called someone's name.
"Saliera! Saliera!" he called loudly, and waited in anticipation.
Soon a pale blue face appeared out of the water; she had large dreamy eyes and long pale hair. She also had scales here and there on her arms and body, of a lustrous sheen, which were also pale blue. She also wore what appeared to be a gown that was actually part of her body, Kenny realised after a while.
"Ah, hello Jadeir. I was just tending to the plants on the river bed, and cheering up the fish in the hollow," said Saliera.
"Oh!" replied Jadeir, "what's wrong with the fish today?"
"Some of their babies are missing, so I told them not to worry and I'd go and find them, so I'd better dash!" she replied.
Saliera looked up and saw Kenny and Maraya, gave a sweet smile before vanishing underwater.

"She's so attentive to the needs of all in the river," remarked Jadeir, "you know, the river runs for hundred's of miles, and she covers half of that, and links all waters of the world, ensuring that it stays healthy. There are many tiny beings who help her in the river, and they mainly tend to all the living creatures in it. Sometimes Saliera gets more closely involved and helps them out directly. She cares as they all do, for every tiny living thing that inhabits that realm."
"Well, I find that quite touching really," said Kenny, "many people would think you were crazy if you so much as pondered on such an idea. I know all life is sacred, but so many don't think like that at all, and I find it very sad."
"Yes, but can your people hear each other like you can here?" asked Jadeir, "Because without knowing at least some of the deeper things of life, the understanding becomes confused."

"No people in our time can't hear, but some can to a degree. Though I can't speak for anyone of course, as it's a subject people keep to themselves about" answered Kenny, "and yes, it is very difficult to feel truly calm and at peace without deeper insights, and being in touch with life as I feel here in Atlantis, it's truly wonderful."
 "I think we'd better make our way back now, Jadeir, and thank you very much for showing us around," said Maraya.
"We'd better go then!" responded Jadeir.

They retraced their steps to the elderly trees, when they heard a cheerful call from the river.
"Jadeir! I found the baby fishes and am taking them back to their parents now, they got lost!" said Saliera loudly.
"Glad to hear it!" replied Jadeir, and he smiled, and the elderly trees chuckled happily.

They returned to the gathering of elves, fairies and gnomes, though the latter were only partially visible, and said goodbye to them.
"I'm going with them everyone, it should be an adventure!" said Jadeir, and he walked over to the tree bole.
"My friend Ganus, do you have a spare crystal around down there?" he shouted.
"Here you are my friend Jadeir," replied Ganus.
Ganus the gnome stretched up his hand with a crystal in it, which appeared just within some soil at the base of the tree, and Jadeir dug down a couple of inches and retrieved it.
"Thank you, this is a beauty!" he exclaimed, as the crystal glowed a beautiful peach colour. He looked at it for a moment and then placed it carefully inside a small bag he had round his waist.

Jadeir, Kenny and Maraya waved goodbye to all the woodland beings as well as three deer that had come by at that moment, and the deer looked at Kenny gently.
"Go and quickly greet our deer friends Kenny," whispered Jadeir, and Kenny stepped forward.
He quietly advanced until he was within two feet of the middle one. They looked at each other, and a sense of unity came between the deer and Kenny. There was a gentle peace, and he could see the earth, the trees, the sun and the moon, and all those images seemed to be within the

deer's eyes. Then he saw a large being with deep brown eyes, set in a powerful tan coloured face, who radiated kindness.
A strange feeling of timeless wisdom flowed through Kenny and he somehow felt as if he had been standing there looking at the deer's eyes for centuries, yet it was only seconds.
Kenny smiled to the deer, and the deer moved forwards and touched Kenny's cheek with its nose. Kenny waved to all three of them before turning to leave with the others, and they walked out of the woods towards Chalidocea.

CHAPTER 8 - JADEIR VISITS PLAS MYRDDIN

"Just in time for tea!" exclaimed Kenny, "but how are we going to explain about Jadeir?"

Kenny and Maraya took their portion of the withering potion and shrank back down to size.

"Don't worry," said Maraya, "I'll go upstairs and tell them, and when I return we'll show Jadeir the external route to the stairs."

"Ok, I'll just explain to Jadeir about the shop," answered Kenny, and Maraya went through the healing room door, and upstairs.

"Jadeir, there are four of us who live here, and we live in our flat upstairs, it's a type of dwelling without a garden, and is above our shop, which is a place where we either make objects ourselves, or buy them in from other people who make them, and we sell them in our shop," explained Kenny, and Jadeir looked curiously, "we could show you the shop later when everyone's gone."

"Ok, but what is selling? Don't you share things?" Jadeir asked.

"We would if we could, but our society always exchanges items by using a medium for bartering, which is called money, and it consists of coins, which are round pieces of metal, and also paper, and both have their value put on them. Unfortunately, people need to work hard to obtain enough money to pay for all our needs," said Kenny.

"Oh dear, it sounds a difficult existence here, not relaxed enough to see the beauty and wonder in life," replied Jadeir.

"No, it isn't, and in many places, life is very stressful for people, or people are poor, or no work due to machines taking over their jobs, or that there are wars on their doorsteps," said Kenny.

"I'm not sure I like the sound of this world and think I'd prefer to go back, after seeing your flat Kenny," said Jadeir, looking a little sad.

"I'm sorry to sound so cheerless, but if it helps, there are quite a lot of people who would love to see the world a happy and harmonious place, and do their bit to make it better," said Kenny.

Jadeir's face began to look a little happier again.

"You know, some people create lovely gardens, others make and sell good wholesome food, others make lovely crafts and paintings, and there are those who care about the planet and they spread the message how they can," said Kenny encouragingly.

"It makes me think of the olden times amongst humans on the first lands of Atlantis, when there were the people who cared and wanted peace and harmony, and the others who only wanted power for themselves," said Jadeir, "and the latter people just keep on re-appearing to cause problems all the time."

"Yes, unfortunately," agreed Kenny, "but I guess if we try our best to stick up for what is right, then it is not only doing good, but we benefit by growing stronger and more determined."

"I see, for humans the world is like a place of lessons, and for us, the elves, fairies, gnomes and undines, it is a realm that we must look after and preserve, for we are all very peaceful and calm as you know, and don't need lessons," replied Jadeir.

"I wish I was one of your kind sometimes!" said Kenny with a chuckle, and Jadeir looked at him and smiled.

With that, Maraya returned.

"I've had a good talk with them upstairs, and they are all happy to see you Jadeir, and know where you fit into our journey with the crystals," she said.

"I can tell you all about that, I'm sure!" said Jadeir, "and if I don't know anything, I just ask the great creator of course."

"How amazing," said Kenny, "you'll have to teach me how to do that."

"You mean you can't!" said Jadeir, looking amazed.

"I'm afraid not many people can do this, but maybe in time," answered Kenny, "hey! Let's go!"

The three of them went out the back door and Kenny showed Jadeir the way back inside through to the stairwell. Maraya then returned upstairs via the healing room, while Kenny and Jadeir tiptoed up the stairs to the flat, so Bertha and any last customers wouldn't hear them. As they were tiptoeing by, Kenny could hear Bertha clearing up, so she would be locking up very shortly.

"Hi everyone!" exclaimed Kenny, "this is Jadeir folks!" and then he went to hug Karin.

"You have that look of inner peace as we did when we returned from Chalidocea, Kenny," commented Karin, "doesn't he, girls!" and they all agreed, and Kenny smiled broadly.

Jadeir smiled cheerfully, looking at everyone's faces observantly as they all introduced themselves.

"I do hope you like our type of food," ventured Karin.

"I do eat vegetables sometimes," responded Jadeir, "is that what you eat here, as in Atlantis the humans there have vegetables, either raw or cooked, depending on the time of year, or their preference."

"We have both here, and we have a baked vegetable stew with our usual salad, and some rice, oh and there's a pudding to follow," said Karin.

"Please tell me what a pudding is," asked Jadeir, looking around to see if he could identify it.

"It is a sweet tasting dish, often soft," explained Alyssia, "and we made a cheesecake today."

Jadeir looked interested, "I'm looking forward to trying human food from 14,000 years ahead!" His eyes lit up and he laughed, and as he did so, a strangely effervescent radiance emanated from around him.

"Wow, that's amazing!" cried Alyssia.

"Have you never seen it before?" said Jadeir, looking surprised again, "ah, all of us folk can do that. It's called radiating, that's the nearest word I can think of that will make sense to you, we do have our own word in our own language though, and means something like 'seeds of our being in light'."

He collected the small amount of energy in his hands and tossed it over everyone's heads in the direction of the plants and it looked as if he used telekinesis, for the radiant energy landed amidst their foliage and the plants seemed to radiate with a silvery light for a moment or two. Everyone looked with astonishment.

"You must give that all the time to the plants," remarked Sarah.

"Yes we do. We also give more concentrated versions of it as given from the angels," replied Jadeir, as everyone listened very attentively.

Karin turned around to get the food out of the oven, and they all gathered around, choosing places to sit. Sarah handed out cutlery to each person from the table dispenser, and Karin dished up.

"I like this food in the distant future!" said Jadeir with his mouth full, and tried to smile at the same time, which made everyone try not to laugh with their mouthfuls also! Jadeir enthused about the cheesecake too and said he'd like the recipe to take back home. They then had a large pot of herbal tea and Jadeir liked that very much as well.

It is important that I meet the elves and others somewhere, as I need to talk to them," said Jadeir.

"We can go this evening if you like, Bertha closed up the shop herself today, so we are able to go earlier," said Kenny.

"Could I see the shop before we go?" asked Jadeir, looking inquisitively.
"Ok, I'll take you down shortly, after our tea," said Kenny taking quick sips.

"This is a nice place you have. It feels good here, because it's welcoming and feels sincere. I don't get quite the same feeling from some areas around here, not that they have a bad atmosphere, for the town is generally welcoming. I just mean that your shop has, by far, that extra something," explained Jadeir.
"That's very kind Jadeir, though I think most places you wouldn't prefer are more likely to interest humans," said Kenny, and Jadeir nodded and grinned good-naturedly.

Jadeir wandered around, examining all the items for sale, and studied Alyssia's paintings too.
"I can tell she's been to Atlantis!" smiled Jadeir.
"Most of those were actually painted before she went!" remarked Kenny.
"This time! She has had some connections to Atlantis already," replied Jadeir.
"You're right there, because Sarah, Karin and Alyssia all thought that they'd had lives as priestesses in Atlantis," said Kenny.
"I agree with that. It is more than possible, and probably why the casket came to them, and your involvement?" said Jadeir, turning to look at Kenny intently.
"Well I don't know," said Kenny, scratching his head, "I haven't had any insights so far, but I guess I was involved at some time, perhaps a slave!"
Jadeir laughed, and peered at Kenny's face closely, "a high priest!"
Kenny looked half amazed, bemused and amused all at once!

They returned upstairs again. Kenny said Pistyll Rhaeadr would be the best place to go. Everyone was eager to go, until they realised that they wouldn't all fit into one car, so Maraya, Alyssia and Sarah decided to stay put and let Karin and Kenny have some time together.

"How can we travel along the roads with an elf sitting in the van, we'll cause a crash!" stated Karin.
"Oh don't worry," replied Jadeir, as he made his legs disappear, and Karin looked amazed.
"Can you make your top half disappear too, as that will be on show the most!" asked Karin.

"I think I can disappear entirely," answered Jadeir thoughtfully, "I wasn't sure I could do it here as well as I can in Atlantis," and he faded slightly, "I've needed time to adjust to being here."
"Let's get to the van!" shouted Kenny, and they hurried off downstairs, having said goodbye to the others.

The leafy greenery at the top end of the Pistyll Rhaeadr valley, which usually looked especially green, was beginning to show yellow foliage in many places now.
"Not far now Jadeir, we're almost there!" said Karin.
"I've managed to spot one or two elf colonies up this valley already," said Jadeir.
"I've never seen any beings up here at all!" stated Karin, "how do you manage to see them?"
"Since I have elf eyes, it's easier. I can see what humans can't!" he explained.
"It's such a shame we can't see the fairy folk easily," said Kenny, "but we are very glad there's a lot about."

They came to the car park and got out, breathing in the pure air and listened to the sound of the waterfall for a moment.
"Where would you like to go Jadeir?" asked Karin, "you could sit by the waterfall, walk past it and climb up the track beside it or wander back down the road to somewhere near the woods."
Jadeir paused a moment looking around.
"Let's go to the waterfall, as I can see a couple of elves approaching it right now, and they're telling me they're bringing some friends," he said.

By the time they had reached the waterfall, Jadeir said that there were masses of beings around them. Karin and Kenny watched Jadeir communicating as he had appeared to a degree by then. They could hear what he was saying, but tried not to listen too closely since it may have been private, and they looked at the waterfall together.

"Can you see something glowing up there Kenny? Just above the lowest part of the falls?" asked Karin.
Kenny peered for a moment, "yes, I wonder what it is. It seems to be expanding, how strange!"
"There's more of them!" exclaimed Karin, "what on earth are they Kenny?" and she turned to look at him.

"I can now see that they have faces and long blue green clothing, and they are half in the water," replied Kenny, "look!"
Karin observed for a while, "oh yes! Are they undines?" she asked, "like the one you saw in Atlantis."
"Yes," said Kenny, focussing on them, "I do believe that is what they are!"

"Karin, Kenny!" cried Jadeir, who became more visible to them when no one else was around, "I think the last of the visitors have gone for a while, so the other elves say. I wanted to tell you that life with the elves is much the same as Atlantean times with them all, except that there are fewer trees now. They have to work harder, along with the fairies, gnomes and undines, to counteract the effects of pollution instead."

"We've just seen some undines up there, Jadeir!" said Kenny, pointing upwards towards the top of the falls.
"Ah, yes, they've been listening in to our conversation," explained Jadeir.
"Can you tell me what other things undines do when they're not helping minnow babies?" asked Kenny.
Jadeir laughed and said, "most of the time they are energising the water, in the way that I did earlier in the flat, keeping it vital and pure and swim back and forth so that their energy permeates everywhere."

Just then there was a flurry of energy in the atmosphere, and Karin and Kenny saw wispy shapes swirling around them.
"Hey! It's making me dizzy!" said Kenny, as the swirling intensified.
A group of fairies appeared to both Kenny and Karin, waving to them as they span around.
"Look at them, it's marvellous to see them! Hey Karin, can you see them, eh?" exclaimed Kenny in delight.
"It's wonderful, and I can!" answered Karin, laughing happily.
"You can see us!" they chorused, "you will see more of us from now on! Jadeir told us you have a fairy gem, which can link to us too, so use it if you need us."
"I will, and thank you," replied Kenny.
"We can return to your home now Kenny, and leave these folk in peace," said Jadeir, "bye, my friends!" and he hugged as many elves as he could and waved to the other nature spirits.
They walked back to the car and drove away. Jadeir, meanwhile, slowly faded away as they progressed.

Plans were afoot for the next evening, as Maraya and the others had been discussing a return to Atlantis for Karin and themselves, but without Maraya.

"We'll have no problem following your instructions, Maraya," said Sarah, "I'm sure they'll be perfectly straightforward."

"You get a hover buggy to the eastern gateway, for Kenny went to the western one. You have to take a route that winds away up into the mountains. You must take the one with the waterfall beside it, for only that one takes you to your destination, and is the third turn off along the way. You will obtain transport when you get to the waterfall," said Maraya.

"I wonder what the transport might be, surely not a taxi!" said Alyssia, smiling at Maraya.

"Not at all!" laughed Maraya, "you'll see. It's a surprise! As once you are on that route, transport always comes!"

"It must be a magic carpet service, sent by the high priests, having spotted us via their electric eyes in the side of the mountain," chuckled Sarah, which set the others laughing too.

Karin and Kenny returned from their trip with Jadeir, and they told everyone about seeing the fairies, and the importance of the fairy gem, which Kenny then took out of his pocket. It was diamond shaped, pearly coloured stone.

"When this stone is concentrated on, it will emanate a bright emerald green light, once the crystal has awoken and finished with stirring its energies around," explained Jadeir.

The first of the autumnal mists were making themselves apparent that morning, and Karin had to awaken Kenny.

"I feel extra tired today, do you think it has anything to do with my trip yesterday Karin?" he asked.

"Yes Kenny," said Karin, "it probably has. I felt a little disorientated myself when I returned, but it soon wore off. Just take it easy for a bit longer, and I'll call you when breakfast is nearly ready."

"I'll do the same for you tomorrow morning after your trip tonight dear," murmured Kenny, and he turned over and fell asleep again instantly.

"Did you sleep alright Jadeir? I wish we had another bedroom for you to stay in, and hope you found the camp bed comfortable," asked Karin, as she made a start on preparing breakfast.

"Oh I was fine, though I got up in the night as I saw a bright light outside," replied Jadeir, "when I looked out of the window I noticed that it

was in the sky, is it a planet? We never had that in Atlantis," and Jadeir looked very puzzled.
"It's called the moon. Most people assume that it has always been there, yet Kenny and I have read that it came at the end of Atlantean days," replied Karin.
"Really! How did it come?" asked Jadeir.
"It either appeared to be roaming in space, or was a moon of another planet somewhere, and got pulled into our solar system and gravitated towards earth," said Karin.
"I shall have to meditate on this and see what comes," said Jadeir.
Jadeir looked out of the window again, and the incoming light reflected brightly in his eyes. Karin fancied that it was the moon's reflection being echoed by his contemplating upon it.

He turned and started looking around the living room at all the memorabilia Karin and Kenny had displayed. Images of themselves a number of years ago in various parts of the world, either travelling or where they've lived. Other images were of friends and relatives, and now there were a few with Alyssia and Sarah adorning the walls. Jadeir amused himself as Karin concentrated on getting lots of food onto the table. She made a huge pot of tea with plenty of spare hot water in another jug, lashings of toast, with several spreads, and a big container of homemade muesli. By the time she had nearly completed everything Alyssia came through.
"Oh lovely! I'm just in time!" exclaimed Alyssia, "my turn tomorrow!" and she greeted them both, "did you sleep well Jadeir?"
"Very well thank you, though I got up in the night to acquaint myself with the moon, as we don't have one in Atlantis."
"Oh really?" replied Alyssia, and she thought a moment, "oh yes, of course. I do recall now, it being mentioned in one of our books."
Sarah came slowly into the living room, yawning a little.
"Oh dear, I'm the last as usual. You know, I used to rise much earlier than this in Cornwall, must be the air here!" commented Sarah, looking a little tired.
"That could be a useful excuse for being absent minded around here!" retorted Karin, and everyone chuckled. "I'd better get Kenny up, he said he felt extra tired after his trip yesterday," she said, and went towards the bedroom, "just start eating everyone!"

Sarah and Alyssia eagerly offered toast and cereal to Jadeir, and he helped himself. Soon enough Kenny entered the living room about ten minutes after Karin returned, looking a little tousled, but lively as usual.
"Hi Jadeir, I hear you had a good night! Hey, don't take all the toast!" laughed Kenny, as Jadeir piled his plate with a happy grin.
"I need extra nourishment. The atmosphere on earth in these times differs greatly from our time!" said Jadeir inbetween mouthfuls while Kenny gave him a wry look; then Jadeir helped himself to another piece.
Kenny looked abjectly at the last piece of toast, which had a broken corner, which set Alyssia laughing.
"Don't worry Kenny, I'll do a few more pieces," said Karin, smiling at Kenny's expression.
"Here Kenny, have some tea," said Alyssia, pouring a cupful and slid it over the table to him.
"Thank you kind madam," he said, "I still feel quite tired you know, I need a little pampering today!"
"Can I try some more of your tea please?" grinned Jadeir.
"He's loving every minute of this!" commented Kenny with a chuckle.
"He needs pampering too!" responded Sarah with a twinkle in her eye, and she poured more tea for him and pushed the cereal towards them, "there, I think you both need that!" and Kenny filled a bowl for himself, before Jadeir could get to it!
Karin gave Kenny his toast and he buttered it quickly.
"Lovely, dear! Ah, it's a marmite day today!" and he spread some marmite onto the toast, "thought I'd better start getting my toast covered before someone thinks its another spare one!" Kenny put his arms around his food protectively, eyes darting around, looking at Jadeir who laughed inbetween munches.

As Karin was finished, she went to their amaranth potion bottles in one of the cupboards and brought them to the table.
"I think we all need a pick-me-up, especially as we are all travelling tonight too."
"Good thinking!" was the chorus.
Once they had all finished eating, Kenny, still seated, started to gather all the plates, when Jadeir looked at Kenny attentively.
"Allow me Kenny!" he said, and with a click of his fingers all the crockery piled up in front of Jadeir, and with another click, they all flew over to the sink and arranged themselves neatly on the bench. Kenny watched them go with a surprised look.

"Please! It's too early in the morning for such dynamic activity," said Kenny, and Jadeir laughed.

"What's your next trick Jadeir?" asked Sarah, who had gone out of the room to collect her sewing equipment, and just returned in time to see the flying crockery. She sat down to start sewing crystal bags.

"I expect it will be a disappearing act," laughed Jadeir.

"Let's see," mused Karin, "Kenny'll be in the shop all day, Alyssia needs to keep painting and Sarah is making a start on her bags. That leaves only me, Jadeir. Is there anything that you'd like to do today?"

"I need to look around this area, as I want to know what the town is like and other places nearby," replied Jadeir.

"If I give you a street map to study, would that help?" asked Karin, "and I'll tell you how to read it, or shall I come with you?"

"It's all right, I'll go out myself and give it a try!" and Jadeir smiled.

"Do you wish to go back today Jadeir?" asked Kenny.

"I may, if I've managed to find my way around well enough, though it depends on a lot of things," he answered.

"I'll have a word with Maraya when she comes in, and I'll let you know if there's any developments," said Kenny, "well, I'd better start the ball rolling downstairs!"

Kenny bounded from his chair quickly and dashed off downstairs.

Jadeir discussed the finer points of map reading with Karin, while the other two concentrated quietly for a while on their work. Meanwhile, downstairs, Maraya had arrived, and Kenny was receiving a crowd of customers, and so their day of working had begun with earnest.

"I can hear what people are thinking as they wander around the shop," thought Kenny, "most of the time it's fine, but I don't want to intrude. I'll have to ask Maraya how to switch off. Now I'm beginning to see the energy fields around people too. Wow! That person's got a lovely peaceful blue colour!"

Maraya came out after her first reading and Kenny asked her telepathically how to stop listening to everything that people are thinking.

She said, "Kenny, just focus on your own thoughts, or an object in front of you to break the focus of concentration, for it is just like you do when people are speaking out loud. Place your focus elsewhere, you just have to concentrate a bit harder, but it's easy once you've got the knack!"

"I guess we'd better speak out loud to each other, it will look a bit odd to others that we are just standing here silently!" said Kenny, "ok!" he spoke, "how was the reading?"

"Very satisfactory," she replied, "I do love giving readings, they can be very interesting, and encouraging for the clients."
A young lady approached the counter, and asked about having a reading done, and Maraya invited her through to her room. "See you later!" she said telepathically to Kenny.

After Kenny closed the shop at the end of the day, he came upstairs with Maraya to see food ready on the table.
"Did you manage to find what you were looking for Jadeir?" asked Kenny.
"I did. I told the others I was just looking around to see the geography of the place, and also to view the energy fields around the surrounding area. I was able to link with other elves and nature spirits to enhance the energy lines around here, because it is necessary," stated Jadeir emphatically.
"Why is that so, Jadeir?" asked Kenny, Sarah and Alyssia all together.
"Because of the work we are doing, and travelling back and forth through time, it does help," Jadeir replied.
"Does it act as a protective force, as well as allowing us to travel easier?" asked Sarah.
"Indeed it does. We shall all be much safer!" smiled Jadeir.
"I'll let you off for eating all that toast then!" smiled Kenny.
"Talking of which, it will get cold, everyone!" hinted Karin.
They all eagerly started eating, and murmurs of appreciation of the food were uttered.

Alyssia, Karin and Sarah prepared to get ready for their journey downstairs in the healing room, and changed into Atlantean clothing.
"You've remembered to massage the casket?" Karin asked Sarah.
"I certainly did!" Sarah replied.
"Well, Here goes! Let's get bigger!" said Karin, and they all drank some of the elixir tincture, and then drank the blue mist tincture, and disappeared gradually. They brought out their crystals and focused on 12,000 BC, and decided on the morning as previous, and around 9.30 am, and promptly vanished from this time period.

Upstairs, Jadeir sensed that they had departed.
"They've gone off now Kenny, Maraya! I can see that they've gone, and if I concentrate hard," at this he half closed his eyes and concentrated, "ah! They have definitely arrived and are making their way to the airport. I can see them, all is well!"

"Oh good. That's amazing that you can check up on things like that," replied Kenny.
"Quite a lot of us elves can, you know, we need to as we are always on call at home," replied Jadeir.
"Now we must plan our moves," said Maraya.
"Which time zone are we going to?" asked Kenny, "one that isn't so harmonious I expect."
"Yes, I'm afraid we must go and visit some of them. It will be a variety between 12,000 and 10,000."
At this Maraya paused in thought, "you see, the disks could be in any time, since the perpetrators could have hidden them anywhere," Maraya sighed, "I have to tell you that there are beings from that time who can travel in time too, like the person who followed Sarah. They are, of course, aware that we have a casket, but not aware yet that it is here in Oswestry. It is not necessarily people from our time who are hunting the casket, but ones from the darker Atlantean times."
At this Kenny's expression looked alert and thoughtful.
"I see, so we are going to have quite a job on our hands. Can those high priests help?" asked Kenny.
"They can certainly travel all right!" replied Maraya, and her eye caught the sheet of instructions from the man with the green jacket. "Do you know the person who brought those instructions?"
"No, he never gave his name, and I didn't think to ask, it was all so unexpected of course, and I had customers at the time. As he was about to leave, he noticed Karin and knew that she was my partner immediately. I wished afterwards that I'd asked his name," said Kenny.
"He is from Atlantis, Kenny. Just know that he is helping us. His name is Hudlath," replied Maraya.
"Ok. Hudlath, that's an interesting name! What does it mean?" asked Kenny.
"It means magic wand in Welsh," replied Maraya.
"What does an Atlantean want with a Welsh name? Even though it fits him to a T!" asked Kenny.
"He has several names, whatever suits the time span," replied Maraya.
"Ah! That's an interesting idea. I'd probably forget and start getting my names out of context, knowing me!" laughed Kenny, and the others smiled. "We should have told the others before they went," said Kenny with a concerned look, "about Hudlath."
Maraya gave an enigmatic smile, "don't worry, they'll find out soon enough. Anyway, we must plan our own itinerary soon enough."

"Could you tell me more about your trips with the Moroccan group?" asked Kenny.

"Yes Kenny, we had travelled several times, and on one occasion we went to see the high priest, Anchorin, who Sarah and the others are visiting, as our clue to discover the disk was to go to the temple," replied Maraya, "Anchorin showed us imagery as the casket portrays it.

"I could show you those images again Maraya," said Jadeir, "I'll just get my crystal out as we all need to focus on it."

He pulled the crystal out of a green pocket, which matched his green attire, and they all concentrated on it, by thinking of a man called Gareldo who was involved. Suddenly, there was an outpouring of energy from the tip that filled an area about a foot high above it, and then images began to appear, and they all watched closely.

They saw images of Gareldo from the Middle Ages. He was sitting at a table in an alehouse, with another man, and they were conversing. The vision showed them how this man was threatening Gareldo. His accomplice came over to talk to Gareldo while the first man slipped a drug into Gareldo's drink. The seated man also had a hand-held death ray gun, and held it on his lap, pointed at Gareldo. He coerced Gareldo to hand over a disk. Further scrying by Jadeir and Maraya showed Gareldo as a casket holder. He decided that he couldn't deal with it, so he rowed out to sea one night, unwatched, and deposited the casket. The physical appearances of the two people who harassed Gareldo are described as follows; one was tall with a long serious face, with moustache and beard, and the other was an irritable character, and quite a stocky build, with a glaring expression. Maraya recognised this latter person.

"That stocky man was the one who tried to attack us in Morocco," said Maraya, "I was horrified when I saw him at first."

"I'm not surprised. So these men just keep on re-appearing whenever in time the caskets are!" said Kenny, leaning back in his chair with a thoughtful expression, "but where is that casket now?" he asked, turning his head to look at Maraya.

"It's here, it was delivered to me recently," replied Maraya, and she picked it out of a deep blue velvet bag at her feet, and, don't worry, it's been made safe." Kenny looked at her curiously, wondering how it could get to her and why the others in the Moroccan group didn't have it any more, but Maraya continued speaking without a pause. "The wording for our clue, by the way, was 'to seek the sequestered dome', which was the temple in the mountains that we visited. If that man knew we were all here in Oswestry," and she gave a worried look, "but I think it is better that we all stick together."

"It is indeed," agreed Jadeir, "despite the risk of them seeing both caskets here, that is why I came and strengthened the energy fields and made links with the elves and fairies here, for you all."

"We're grateful Jadeir," Kenny responded, and Maraya smiled, "do you have any more clues as to where either of the disks could be?" he asked.

Jadeir looked intently from one to the other.

"Yes, Anchorin told us that these characters come from 11,659 BC, and we've tried going there, but they are very elusive," explained Maraya, "we need to find some people from that date who could help us, I can't see any other way of doing it."

"Yes, that sounds the best idea," Kenny replied, "Maraya," he asked, "you haven't mentioned the members of the Moroccan group much. I don't want to pry, but it is important, so that we can work together fully."

Maraya's eyes held a fleeting look of anguish, then she composed herself quickly, "the two others with crystals, like Sarah, Alyssia and Karin, are two men called Sagario and Danuel. I keep in touch with them, and they have been asking about the group here, and considering what to do next."

"Who was the doorkeeper?" asked Kenny gently.

"A man called Costillo. He went to various time periods in case those men had dealings elsewhere. He got to the stage where he could scry from the flat in Morocco to view activities in different time periods," explained Maraya, "although we knew those men came from 11,659 BC, they moved through time, and so we had to do the same."

"Where is Costillo now, Maraya?" asked Kenny, becoming concerned.

"I don't know," said Maraya in a strained voice.

She got up and walked away towards the window. Kenny attempted to go over to her, but Jadeir gently restrained him.

Maraya continued, "I returned from one of our searches with the others and he wasn't there. His crystal was still there; it was lying on the floor under a little table with a cloth over it in the corner of our living room. Sagario found tiny bits of crystal in the centre of the room as if Costillo had dropped the crystal just before he disappeared, and it had rolled across with the impact of falling. That man obviously would have taken the crystal if he had seen it. Other than that, I don't know anything more."

"Yet!" said Kenny encouragingly, "do you have the crystal with you, as it may have some kind of memory on it."

"Yes, I do, but there is nothing tangible enough, we all looked at it over and over, but to no avail."
"Let's pool our resources and see if we can get further on with it all," said Kenny, "we have Jadeir and the nature spirits."
Maraya turned around and gave a smile, and returned to the table.
"We must keep on trying, and keep our hopes up," she said.
"Definitely," responded Jadeir, smiling warmly at Maraya, "do you have that crystal, I could examine it over the next day or two and see if I can spot anything."
"Oh yes please Jadeir," she said, "I always carry it with me."
Maraya handed it over to Jadeir, and he put it in his pocket.
"I'll keep it safe while we do our peering practice," he said.
"Kenny," said Maraya, "you do know that being a doorkeeper is dangerous, for once that contact is made to all time spans in Atlantis via your crystal, then it is hard to stop yourself being detected."
"You have me with you all the time," said Jadeir, "none of you need worry as much now. I'm not saying that there's no danger any more, but that you will be as potent if not more so than those two characters."

"Hey, I've just remembered something that Sarah told me a while ago," said Kenny, "she said she had a vision of a being called Rhiannah, who told her of danger ahead, but Sarah only told me. Do either of you know her?"
"Yes," replied Jadeir, "I've heard the priests talk of a priestess of that name, and she has visited them from what they say." Jadeir had to concentrate hard for more information. "I'm scrying to ask about which time period she comes from. Ah! I'm getting that she comes from 11,659 BC."
"Well, what are we waiting for!" said Kenny, "let's get in touch with her."
"That's so encouraging!" said Maraya happily, "she could help us a lot Jadeir, Kenny."

"I'll put on my thinking cap and see what we can do next," replied
Jadeir.
In an instant he had a little green cap on his head, which was covered in small quartz crystals. Maraya and Kenny looked at each other in astonishment.
"Yes!" exclaimed Jadeir, "I have it! I saw an image of Rhiannah's world. It is not such a beautiful place anymore, for the city is not called Chalidocea, but Huanca, and has been for a while, but Rhiannah's temple

is to the north on some land that has gentle hills. She is a high priestess there.

In our day it was all green countryside around there, but now many buildings have been put up, and many more are being constructed too. Those in power are beginning to tighten up people's freedom a great deal. I see a humble building, which looks like a house on the outside, but it is cleverly adapted as a temple inside. The nearest landmark is a slight crag half a mile away to the west, and the house is on a main route, and has a green gate. Everything's very plain and nothing or no one looks happy there."

Jadeir looked sad a moment.

"Did you really need that cap Jadeir?" asked Kenny.

Jadeir looked a little coyly, "Well, no. That is, I can see into various time periods without it. It was a present of sorts from my friends; we give each other silly presents at times. I only wanted to lighten your spirits a little. I will show you how to look into windows of time safely, Kenny. Come on, let's go downstairs and try before the others get back."

Jadeir pulled at Kenny's arm, and the three of them went down to the healing room.

"Examine your crystal Kenny," explained Jadeir, "can you see the various indentations and shapes on it?"

Kenny studied his doorkeeper crystal very carefully for a few minutes, turning it around and examining every crack and mark on it.

"Is this anything?" he asked.

"Yes it is. What does it remind you of?" asked Jadeir.

Kenny thought a moment, "it's a bit like an Indian archway, perhaps it's a door?" he gestured.

"Yes, that's right, it's a door, and you need to press on that while you're concentrating, in order to see. Have some more amaranth Kenny!" advised Jadeir.

Maraya passed it to Kenny and he drank some of it. Meanwhile, Maraya got a notebook ready in case anything important would be viewed in the session.

"Let's concentrate!" announced Jadeir, and they all focused on linking with their crystals, for Maraya's crystal energy would be supportive to the other two. A halo of light formed around them all, emanating from the tips of the crystals.

"I'll concentrate on my crystal too, as it has the same symbol Kenny," said Jadeir, "though I can do this without a crystal as you know. Think of Rhianah, and the year 11,659 BC."

Kenny concentrated hard, and an image came up of the type of landscape Jadeir had described earlier.
"I can see it! That landscape you described," exclaimed Kenny. Maraya looked over their shoulders.
"Ask for Rhianah's temple to the north, near the crag," explained Jadeir, "it should bring us roughly to that area."
There was a movement over the landscape; swiftly flying due northwards, and the sea was visible in the distance. Then the image focused on a row of houses, with a crag just visible behind some trees.
"There's a green gate!" exclaimed Kenny, "let's focus on that house!"

The view of the house concerned came closer in and right up to the walls of the house, then there was a blurring of vision and they were inside. There appeared to be false inner walls without it being apparent. There was a basement and downstairs they saw the hub of this temple. A lady with the usual long attire and scarf over her head was focusing her attention upon a crystal on her altar. The altar and herself were suffused in light.
"Oh Danuih, Heliona, I ask for blessings on our world at this time. Bring those to me who need spiritual help, I pray, so that together we can bring a stronger oasis of hope to the world that belongs to us all."
The three of them could see a group of lit candles on the altar, casting a warm mellow light on the surroundings. The walls were completely round, in sharp contrast to the square dwellings they had seen.
"Do you think she had it constructed herself?" asked Kenny.
"Yes, there are still some architects who know how to make round buildings well, but they keep their knowledge secret," explained Jadeir.
"To deviate from what is expected in those times was a serious matter," said Maraya.
"How do we contact her?" asked Kenny.
"I was waiting for you to ask that!" responded Jadeir, smiling, "just link to her crystal and ask the goddess source that we become visible to her."

They concentrated hard and began to see her crystal change colour to a golden glow, with a few incandescent bursts of energy.
"Oh! Who are you people and where do you come from?" she asked.

"You contacted my friend Sarah, telling her she was in danger for she holds one of the caskets, and I am from her group," said Kenny, "and this is Maraya who holds another casket. We are from a time 13,659 years in the future, and our elf friend Jadeir is from the past, 1,659 years before your time."

"Really! It is good to hear from you!" answered Rhianah; "I was given the knowledge of the caskets from scrying into the past and know that they are somewhere in time, but are not intact. Can I ask you what you seek?"

"Yes, the two caskets are incomplete as you say, and a disk from each is missing," said Kenny. "We know of two men who come from your time who have them. One man is stocky and aggressive looking, and the other is tall with a long serious face, and has a moustache and beard."

"Can you give me an image of them both?" asked Rhianah.

"How do you do that Jadeir?" asked Kenny, looking intently at Jadeir.

Maraya pressed her crystal deftly and thought of Anchorin's visionary playback, until it focused on a still of both the men.

"Here! Kenny, Jadeir, I have it!" exclaimed Maraya.

"Oh good! That's right, just hold it up so Rhianah can see it better," said Jadeir.

Kenny revolved the crystal so that the images were projected outwards rather than viewed by themselves. Rhianah peered closely.

"Thank you, I've got their faces in my mind now. I shall begin to search for the whereabouts of these people," she replied, "and then I'll be in touch."

"I wish to say that they dart from one time period to another, so it is all pretty tricky," added Maraya.

"I understand and shall try to follow their routes," she answered and smiled, "farewell for now and may the deities be with you."

"Rhianah, there's a third person we need to find," said Kenny, "he is called Costillo and is from Maraya's group, but has been captured and he disappeared from our time. Probably taken by those two men," said Kenny.

"Ah, I see," answered Rhianah, looking concerned, "how long ago, and what does Costillo look like?"

"Several months ago, Rhianah. He has very dark straight hair, cut fairly short, brown eyes and sallow complexion, with a pencil moustache. He was very tall and fit looking and was wearing a white shirt, dark blue trousers and a slightly lighter blue jacket," answered Maraya.

"Is that every requirement now?" said Rhianah, and they affirmed that it was, "farewell for now and may the deities be with you."

"Thank you," they replied, "and with you."

"Do contact me when you find the information Rhianah, as I shall pick up a signal easiest," said Jadeir, and Rhianah affirmed that.

Kenny decided to ask Maraya about how she got the Moroccan casket.

"Maraya, how did you get the casket from Morocco?" asked Kenny.

"It was Hudlath, he brought it to me," replied Maraya, "and he told me that Sagario and Danuel wanted me to be the guardian of it, as they felt it would be more secure with me."

CHAPTER 9 – ANCHORIN'S MOUNTAIN TEMPLE

A shimmering effect was apparent in the healing room and Maraya ushered the others away towards the door into the shop.

"It's the others, they're returning!" she uttered.

Sure enough, three huge figures re-materialised and they sipped the necessary potions to normalise themselves.

"Oh hello!" said Alyssia gaily, "I hope we haven't interrupted you!" "Don't worry," replied Maraya, "we have just finished."

"Let's all go upstairs and compare notes," said Kenny, "I'll tell you what we did first as you lot look a little weary!"

"Just sit down and I'll make us all a pot of tea," said Kenny rushing about. He glanced at Karin and noticed she had a bright, animated look in her eyes even though she was tired, and he noticed that the others had the same expressions as well.

"I put some biscuits in the box earlier, Kenny!" said Karin, and there was a flash of movement in their direction!

"That sounds like a good step forward, that you were actually aware of Rhianah, and that there was a two way rapport," said Alyssia, trying to stop her eyes from closing.

"So I wasn't dreaming when I sensed her presence," added Sarah, looking very lethargic.

"You kept that quiet!" said Karin, smiling sweetly.

"I wasn't entirely sure about what or whom I was sensing," explained Sarah, and she avoided mentioning about the danger warning.

"You all look as if you had a good trip, but extremely tired. How long did you stay there?" asked Maraya.

"About four days I think," replied Karin, "we never stopped!"

"My goodness! You'd better get some rest now, and we can continue this conversation, and ask about your trip tomorrow. Off to bed girls!" answered Maraya, ushering them off in a humorous manner.

It was lunchtime the next day before the group could get together, and with Bertha assisting downstairs, Kenny could hear what happened in Atlantis. They all gathered as usual around the table and Kenny could see that their bright, animated look was still there.

"Your eyes all look so different," remarked Kenny, "since the three of you returned. You'll have to tell me how it happened."

"The story will explain itself," replied Sarah, "well, I'll start, since I replied!" and she chuckled.

"As soon as we left present time and took off in the plane to Atlantis as usual, we all commented on feeling an air of expectation and excitement. After we landed we took a hover buggy to the base of the mountain, and found the waterfall. It looked so beautiful that it made other waterfalls look insignificant," and she glanced round at everyone.

"Yes," said Alyssia, "those glinting lights we saw all around it, and when we went closer we realised that they were fairies, and they were talking to beings in the water and the rock, undines and gnomes. I couldn't believe it."

"And the powerful energy that radiated from that waterfall was phenomenal," added Karin, "energy just seemed to extend, like a waterfall of energy cascading over the countryside around, with an iridescent light that you can see in soap bubbles."

"We'll have to go there on our holidays!" said Kenny, which started everyone laughing.

"Then as we passed the waterfall, very reluctantly, we came to the turn off up to the mountain temple, and started climbing," continued Sarah.

"It was the strangest road," mused Alyssia, "because you'd set off briskly and the going seemed good, and then when we got a bit tired, the road appeared to get steeper and seats appeared out of the sides of the mountain path, facing towards the centre."

"After that happened a couple of times, a kind of mountain style buggy came down towards us. It gave a beep, announcing its arrival because we were scanning the extensive view over the plains of Atlantis, and we were naturally engrossed in looking at as much as we could see. We said things like 'Oh look! There's the healing temple in Chalidocea, and there's the wood that Kenny went to, etc.,' and we had pointed in the relevant directions.

Sarah continued, "The buggy took us up into the mists that seemed to often cover the summit and the temple during certain times of the year, though it wasn't cold. We arrived at the entrance and noticed that, despite the humbleness of the building, it had a dome of orichalcum.

We went inside and asked to see the high priest, Anchorin. He came forward out of a side door after a few minutes, and said he had been giving advice to several people. He was tall for an Atlantean and had deep violet eyes," explained Sarah, and she paused for thought, "although sometimes they appeared to have an electric energy and power within them, with a deeply penetrating expression, and at other times, calm, very compassionate with more than a glint of humour, and then again, a look a deep meditativeness as if you could just lose yourself if you looked at his eyes for too long," and the others agreed.

"He was dressed in white, with gold edging and had a sky blue belt around his waist, also with gold thread woven into it. He also had a gold and silver headband with crystals around it. Can either of you remember what gems they were?"

"Amethyst and plain quartz, I think," answered Karin.

"That sounds right," agreed Alyssia, "you've been there Maraya, would you agree?"

"Ten out of ten girls!" replied Maraya, "spot on so far!"

"We went through to a meditative room, though, of course, the whole temple was like that," continued Sarah, "it was so peaceful, as the atmosphere was of constant stillness, very powerfully uplifting. It was awesome! Now, would someone else like to continue?"

"Anchorin asked us why we had come," asked Alyssia, "and we told him about both our caskets and the missing disks and our connection to you Maraya. He looked at us closely and then said, 'follow me!' and we went along a corridor to an entrance, which had lettering over it that we couldn't understand. 'This is the temple room of inner searches' and we went in. The room, like most of the others, that we saw later, looked like a cave when it dawned on us that the whole temple itself had been chiselled out of the top of the mountain. As soon as the realisation came Anchorin looked at us and nodded, 'that is so! The mountain gave us permission to do this.' There were images painted on the walls directly of high priests and many deities who we didn't recognise carved into the rock itself. Anchorin watched with slight amusement as we gasped with wonder all over the place. He indicated for us to kneel by a pool, which had an equally strong resonance of stillness. There was a huge stone plaque at one end.

Anchorin started chanting and burned some sweet smelling incense mixed with a resinous ingredient, which produced a thick white smoke and it filled the room. We were told to look at the pool closely. The surface ceased to look like a pool of water to that of bright yellow flames and at least one of us blinked at such a sight. The flames became smaller and formed into a circle, and within that an image formed of Rhianah scrying. Her image was of the two men who had the casket disks. We could see they had the three disks. We wondered where the third casket was, as we could see Rhianah tracking down the whereabouts of the disks, and linking to Hudlath, to communicate this information, and for a fleeting moment we could see his face flash onto the scrying mirror that Rhianah had in her basement temple."

Alyssia looked at Karin, "how did it start with the priestess images, did they just appear or what?"
"The image of Hudlath and Rhianah vanished and then Anchorin looked at us expectantly and said 'you know you came for more than just seeking the whereabouts of the disks, don't you?' " replied Karin.
Alyssia continued, "and then he gave a wry smile, with humour in his eyes, when the three of us looked somewhat perplexed. 'You did see a vision when you were in Cornwall, of your connection to our world, or have you forgotten completely?' he said with a schoolmasterly look now. 'The priestess vision! Of course we had, then exclaimed as much, and he looked with some approval then. We apologised and said that so much had happened since then, but yes, we would be extremely interested to know more. He said to look again, and he increased the amount of incense and it filled up the room even more. We all felt strangely dreamy, and then adjusted to the smell. The smoke then parted so that we could see both the plaque and the pool of water. Suddenly the plaque became a mirror, flashing with bright light, which cast a strong shaft of light onto the water towards us. Strangely, each of us saw the images of our priestesses' past lives from our own individual perspective simultaneously.

We felt very familiar with these women right from the start as you could imagine. One was a scryer, seeing into the past, present or future and that was Alyssia," said Karin, "and another priestess was a healer and lived by a waterfall and that was Sarah."
"And I realised it was the waterfall that we passed at the bottom of the mountain, for I was the one who dragged my feet the most on leaving," Sarah commented.
"I was a spiritual instructor on healing," continued Karin, "and I also linked with those peoples from the other worlds, who came to visit and exchange wisdom, for there was a huge amount of interchange at that time."
"When was that time period?" asked Kenny.

"It was about 200 years before Anchorin's time," replied Karin.
"Yes, I remember you all! Commented Jadeir, as he had scryed for their images on his crystal, "though I was busy elsewhere, we all knew what was going on in the human world, as we do today!"
Sarah, Karin and Alyssia looked at Jadeir with interest.
"What else did you see?" asked Kenny.
Karin thought a moment, "it was like we fell into the images, and could see, feel and hear etc., everything about our lives then. I was working at the mountain temple, and so was Alyssia. We met those beings from other worlds, which was amazing. They would appear, and materialise in three dimensions, and land just in front of the temple in their spaceships, the usual disc shaped ones, and then enter the temple. They brought new information on how the network to other worlds was progressing, and to teach priests how to link to their worlds and develop their powers.
Anchorin had set up a powerful vortex energy within the earth, which was focused through a pyramidal structure. The energy was directed out around our planet to keep the energy of the earth stabilised, and also a strong beam across the skies towards the outer atmosphere of the earth at its strongest, and then a thin beam which linked outwards beyond there to link with other planets in our solar system, and then beyond to places like Arcturus, Andromeda, Sirius and the Pleiades. Anchorin described how they sent a resonance of a particular frequency to each star system or planet, so that it was like a route guider or motorway planner to get to destinations easily and safely."

"It was especially moving to experience our old lives, and have brought back something deeply moving and so close to our planet earth and earthly life that the experience was a timelessness, with a total linking to planet earth," explained Alyssia, "nothing like today, where we are always trying to get close to nature, and always get drawn away again back into human existence and all its scurrying activities. The Atlantean priesthood life was so simple, and it ran at a slow pace so that everything invited you to be close to nature. Everyone appeared to be in a permanently meditative state. I then moved away to experience the lifestyle of a sea temple, for I was to scry there and teach others to do so as well. Those sea temples were magnificent, and were like a swimming bath, but with carved temple walls, and an opening towards the sea. Dolphins came and we communed and held ceremonies there with them, it was marvellous."
"What if it got stormy?" asked Kenny.

"The sea was very calm in those times and rarely became more than a slight breeze," replied Alyssia, "it was a wonderful sight to see the high priest flanked by other priests and people all sitting around the edges of the pool, with only the high priest standing. Someone would ring a bell underwater and soon a group of five or six dolphins would enter and place themselves facing the priest and the ceremony would begin.
Everyone would end up swimming with the dolphins and a lot of interchange between the dolphins and swimming priests would take place," said Alyssia, "we always finished the ceremonies in a state of euphoria."

"Could I ask more about your life by the waterfall, Sarah?" asked Kenny, "what did you do there apart from enjoy the ambience!"
"Oh, I enjoyed that alright!" laughed Sarah; "I was a seer and herbalist person then. Though the temples were all working well, I chose to work alone and very close to nature, as some of us did and I linked with the nature spirits too, and they would tell me much, which I would then impart to those who came, and quite a lot did come during my lifetime. Is that to your liking, Mr Kenton?"
"Satisfactory, Madame Blenheim!" Kenny replied, with a comically haughty demeanour.

"We all feel so different after seeing those lives," remarked Alyssia, looking round at the others, "that somehow we feel as if we have changed something fundamental within," and the others agreed.
"Just being in Atlantis in their golden age on Poseidia is enough to encourage any spirit, and then see our lives as priestesses helping and instructing others in such clarity, and we all could relate to it, and memories came flooding back."
"Yes, it has strengthened us inwardly quite a lot," added Karin, "seeing ourselves in a life full of spiritual purpose without any doubts or sorrows, it's so encouraging!"
"It so ties in with who I am," said Sarah, "you know Kenny, I have been a herbalist and given spiritual advice in this life too, though gave up helping people in my practice due to ill health, and had to use it on myself. I have learnt so much more as a result, I could write a book."
"Go on! Then you can sell it in the shop!" said Kenny happily.
"Right! You're on!" replied Sarah, "once we've sorted out our assignment with the caskets. One thing we haven't mentioned was the inner temple where usually, only Anchorin and a few of his senior priests go. He asked

us to come and view it, since we qualified as fairly senior priestesses at one time. He showed us how energy was sent around Atlantis and across the world along those ley lines. We went in and saw a huge clear quartz crystal standing vertically like a standing stone, its pointed tip facing the roof. Within the roof's domed apex masses of clear quartz crystals were inset in the centre in a circular formation. Surrounding them were a concentric ring of lapis lazuli, and after that a concentric layer of amethyst. The energy of the huge crystal below seemed to resonate with the crystals above and an energy field was created, glowing brightly. It shone in bright shafts of light out the sides of the temple through windows, which were angled down to the temple in Chalidocea and other places. From there energy would be sent all round the world to all the other temples, and the airplanes took those energy line routes as you know."

"Is there anything else you want to know Kenny dear?" asked Karin, teasing him for asking lots of questions.

"Well, just one more!" he replied, "can I ask if you know whether those characters who have the disks can see any of their contents?"

"Anchorin said that they couldn't get at most of the information, only small bits of it, that is why they look for the caskets. Once the disks and caskets come together, the connections between all time zones start to rapidly close down. So it is vital to obtain those disks," answered Sarah.

"There's the third casket to find as well, if only we knew who had it," said Kenny.

The phone rang and Karin answered it, "yes, ok Bertha, I'll send her down," and she replaced the phone, "Maraya, someone wants a reading."

"Ok, thanks Karin. That's brought us down to earth!" she said and swiftly went downstairs.

"Jadeir, can you see where the third casket might be?" asked Kenny.

"I'll have a go, as this problem will only stop once we have the caskets all safe and complete," Jadeir answered, as he pulled his crystal from his pocket.

Everyone went silent and watched Jadeir intently while he scryed with the crystal.

"I'm asking for the third casket. There's an image coming up. The casket is sitting inside a dark space, perhaps a cupboard. I'll just try to expand the view to a wider scale, so I can see beyond close up range. Now I am getting an image of a chest of drawers and they are quite old fashioned.

There's no one in the house right now, so I'll just pan outwards to see what the house is like. It's a small, whitewashed house not far from the sea, and there are cacti growing around it and it's very sunny," commented Jadeir.

He kept on panning further out until he got to such a scale where he could see which country it was.
"It's Southern America, not far from Mexico I think. Where would that be Kenny?" asked Jadeir.
Kenny had a look, "that's the Yucatan, very exotic!"
"I'll have to get someone to call over there and see if they can investigate it," said Jadeir.
"Better get Hudlath," said Sarah, "he knows what he's doing. Can you contact him directly Jadeir?"
"No, but I can link to either Rhianah or my folk, and they'll pass on a message for us," replied Jadeir.
"I guess you'd better do so quickly, in case their casket has been spotted," answered Sarah.

Jadeir started to link in with Rhianah.
"Ah, she's in! She knows I'm contacting and is going to her temple now," said Jadeir. "Hello Rhianah, Jadeir here. I've found the whereabouts of the third casket. It's in the Yucatan, near a town or city called El Cuyo Odzah, on the north coast."
"That's good, Jadeir. Which time period is it in?" she asked.
"The present time period I'm in now, I just want you to keep an eye on it and see if anyone is using it," said Jadeir.
"I will keep you informed. I'll try Hudlath to scout around and report back, either directly or via myself, all right," said Rhianah.
"Thanks Rhianah," answered Jadeir, "goodbye."
"May the Goddess be with you," she replied, and everyone chorused back "and with you!"

"By the way," asked Kenny, "did any of you see those space beings?"
"Yes, of course!" responded Sarah, "we did, how could we have forgotten to tell you!"
"Bad memories!" chortled Kenny.
"We'll give you a bad memory!" responded Karin, lifting her mug as if to throw it at him and everyone laughed.

"I didn't mean it, honest!" Kenny replied, holding up his hands in a defensive pose and laughing, and Karin put her hand on his shoulder.

"They had very bright eyes, luminous and incandescent, very peaceful yet observant. We all felt instantly more peaceful than ever before," said Alyssia.

"There was a group from Sirius who were tall as well, with birdlike features, and feathers like a crest at the back of their heads," said Sarah.

"The Pleiadeans had large soulful eyes and were a bit more thickset, but not stocky. They both had attire on. The former were blue-green in various shades with silvery highlights, and the latter were a deep blue, royal to indigo. The most fascinating thing, apart from their appearance were their gadgets. The Pleiadeans had globe-like objects, which told them plans for their journeying and information about different planets, as well as a link up with their kind back home. The Sirians had crystals with them that they used to pick up information and link to home with and to teach healing methods to Atlanteans, for they had different types of crystals there on Sirius unknown on earth."

"Do you have any images of them?" asked Kenny, "on your crystals."

They showed him and he looked fascinated.

CHAPTER 10 – THE COUNCIL OF TWELVE

The Council of Twelve consisted of Sirius, the Pleiades, Betelgeuse, Arcturus, Andromeda, the Hyades, Castor, Pollux, Antares, Lyra, Ursa Major and Cassiopeia, and are the active forces in the heavens over the northern hemisphere of planet earth.

When a meeting was scheduled, which usually happened every two months by earth time, all members of the Council would meet in their space temple. It was constructed in a circular design, within which an octahedron area was housed, where they had their meetings. It was designed to allow them all to focus on their meeting more effectively, and communicate to those back on their respective planets.

The way they were able to do this was by looking into specially designed mirrors that were double sided, like inverted pyramids and about two feet square, which were situated at the threshold of the octahedron. Everyone would sit in a circle in silence, like in a Quaker meeting-house, and would then discuss matters in a meditative way, for the members would speak when useful information came to them. Once this meditative discussion was concluded, they would turn around, facing outwards towards the inverted pyramid mirrors, which were called stellarscopes. The messages were transmitted telepathically, and they could conjure up mental images of things too, as mentioned in their communications to portray to those on the respective planets.

"Now, let us finalise the talks today with a thought or two for planet Earth," said Zanadar, who came from Cassiopeia, "we know that our teaching and encouragement had produced a beautiful adherence to our wisdom, and we have been successful in the continent of Atlantis and a fair part of the rest of the world too, but …."

"But yes, Zanadar," interrupted Gelsior genially, who was from Pollux, and looked a little like a Buddha, "we all know that not every person on the planet is of the same mind and once the sources of power latched in at the next period after the golden age, then things began to deteriorate again. It always happens on that planet," he said with a sigh.

"We know Gelsior," gestured Aurion, who was from Sirius, and had silvery-blue colouring and bird-like feathers like a crest from the back of his head, and very kind but piercing eyes, "but it is part of Earth's evolutionary process and it will cease at some point in time."

"In the past we considered what to do about the caskets," said Zanadar, wanting to recap on details to see if it brought new thoughts to mind, "when the energies deteriorated, the caskets were at risk and so we ensured that they were kept safe somehow." Zanadar sat, pondering thoughtfully.

"Yes, Zanadar, everyone!" said Aurion, "and we ensured that the caskets were sent out to sea so that they were washed up and found by people who were kind and brave. In order to have reached that conclusion, we had to have a constant line of people who would be guardians of the caskets all through the various Atlantean time periods."

"Yes, and we all know that the present problem facing these people who picked up the caskets from the sea is that the disks went missing before the final collapse of the Atlantean continent," said Zanadar seriously, "we must break off from our usual work to pay Earth a visit to discuss the matters with Anchorin," said Zanadar, "how does that sound to everyone?"

He looked around at everyone and they all had a positive show of hands in favour of the idea, and Zanadar's orange-pink face broke into a warm smile.

Kelaré from Ursa Major then spoke, "I am unable to come immediately as I have a lot of commitments, and I had better keep my contact with the Light Year Command, for we have much to sort out with all the other younger planets across many galaxies. Though I shall be able to join you all within a few days!"

"Don't make it a light year Kelaré!" chuckled Gelsior.

"Might have known you'd say that!" responded Kelaré with a smile.

"Who would like to start things off?" asked Zanadar.

"I shall!" announced Siral, a tall streamlined figure from Andromeda.

"And so shall I!" responded Maeron, another streamlined figure with eyes like jewels, and came from the Hyades star cluster.

"We must now send our inspired thoughts to all concerned throughout the ages on planet Earth, to ensure order is restored and that the caskets become safe again," said Aurion.

"We will take that matter in hand together," said Golan from Arcturus, Gillan from Antares, and Talar from Betelgeuse, in unison, as well as Silaron from Castor, Melkior from Lyra and Salaron from the Pleiades.

The all focused hard on projecting light and peace out towards Earth, and a stream of golden white light went out from their temple towards Earth. If an earthly person could see all time periods on the planet simultaneously, then they would have seen that light go to each being and fill them with a brilliant sparkling light, strengthening and inspiring all inhabitants. All those who were clairsentient would sense this energy peacefully, and all those who were strongly against harmonious living would feel uneasy.

Siral and Maeron set off to descend to Atlantis from the space temple in a small circular craft. Siral was a graceful being and higher than most Atlanteans, whose skin was a translucent silvery sea-green colour. Maeron had a very long aquilinear face and very observant eyes, which could see through to the bare essentials of any soul, and who was slightly smaller than Siral and more slender still. He had a very bright sparkling deep blue cloak, which toned in nicely with his pale turquoise-blue skin. Zanadar, had quite a stocky build, with his orange-pink skin, and had a crest on the top of his head. He also had glowing brown eyes, very benign and the shortest of the three, and he accompanied Siral and Maeron.

Aurion, Melkior and Salaron followed on a little later as they discussed various concerns with beings in a neighbouring galaxy for a short while.

"Now that the little problem has been solved, we can catch up with the others and get down to see Anchorin," said Aurion.

They said farewell to the other six members who would keep up the connections with other regions of the universe and beyond.

"I would like to come down to earth, but I am going to be kept busier than I thought," said Kelaré.

"Don't worry," said Aurion, "there will be six of us down there, and that is enough really."

"Thanks Aurion," answered Kelaré, looking briefly to one of the stellarscopes and he looked at it with a searching gaze, and then looked back at Aurion. "It looks like I'm going to have to visit that planet again!"

"Don't tell me, Zenuit!" answered Melkior.

Kelaré gave a knowing look and a shrug.

"You've guessed right, but this time the shuttle craft is coming to collect me," replied Kelaré, "it may be a golden age on earth now, but there's certainly not much gold to be seen on that planet! Besides, as it's their kali age cycle in their universe, that's their excuse!" and he smiled wryly.

"We'll think of you and send out some good energy," said Salaron sympathetically and Kelaré smiled more positively.

Siral, Maeron and Zanadar alighted by the temple in the mountains, and they noticed the temple's orichalcum dome becoming visible through the habitual mountain mists. They went indoors and asked for Anchorin.
The tall figure of Anchorin, with his striking features, came down the corridor, and he beckoned for them to come.
"Come in, come in!" he announced in a welcoming voice, ushering them into a side room in the rock-cut temple, "aren't there more of you?" he asked.
"Yes," said Zanadar, "Aurion, Melkior and Salaron should be following us very soon."
Anchorin nodded and asked a priest to watch out for the three extra-terrestrial beings due to come, and bring them to the meeting room immediately.
"We can't really start until the others arrive, but make yourselves comfortable," said Anchorin and he gestured to the spring water jug on a central wooden table, "help yourself to the spring water if you wish, it's full of mineral salts and vital energy!"
They all got up and poured themselves out a cupful and took a mouthful, and each gave an impressed look.
"I've never tasted anything like it!" exclaimed Zanadar, "I can feel the energy rushing around me, it's very impressive."
"Just the thing for long journeys," added Siral, "where does it come from Anchorin?"
"This drink is available over most places in Atlantis, through some sources of it are slightly better than others, such as here!" Anchorin said, smiling broadly.
Maeron just smiled happily, looking a bit like a contented cat, and carried on sipping.

With that, the door opened and the other three entered.
"We got held up, Anchorin," said Aurion, giving Anchorin a low bow, and held his hands together, palms touching.
Once they were settled and also enjoying the vitalising spring water, Anchorin started to talk.
"Right everyone," he announced, "I must tell you what has happened so far with this casket business. Developments in that quarter have been so rapid that I thought I'd wait until a certain stage that seemed expedient

before contacting you for a meeting. You see, once that group of people in Britain found the casket, Hudlath went to ensure they had instructions on how to use it. Then, from the Moroccan group, came Maraya with her group's casket, she came and helped the British group to grow their casket seeds."
"Ah yes! The seeds, which are descendants from plants on the Pleiades," said Salaron.
"And Sirius too!" said Aurion, and Salaron nodded in agreement.
"All right, yes, but.." said Anchorin.
"Excuse me, but it is important," explained Aurion, "for the elixir plant and the Amaranth are both from Sirius, and the blue mist and withering plants originated from the Pleiades."
"And of course, the crystals are from Sirius and the Pleiades too," said Anchorin, "but what is the importance in this instance, for it won't help knowing that, in order that the people involved can be enabled to complete the caskets' contents."
Anchorin looked steadily at Aurion awaiting a valid reply.
"It may," replied Aurion, his eyes very piercing, "because those discs were made from substances from Sirius and the Pleiades, there may be ways to free those discs from being under the control of the renegades. I feel we must meet those casket people when we can, Salaron, the others, and I. We must meet everyone involved in order for any of our plans to work."
"Yes, a very good point," said Anchorin, but he still looked somewhat intrigued as to what Aurion's plans were, exactly, when they all met together, but he knew better than to ask too many questions, for, unless these beings were ready to reveal their reasons for plans or actions, no amount of questioning would make them say, and he would only get a strange feeling of invisible walls of energy surrounding them, or receive piercing looks.

"I must continue to tell you about the caskets!" continued Anchorin, "all of the guardians of the caskets have travelled at least once. The Welsh group, for though the group is actually based on the borders, their shop has a strong Welsh energy to it."
"What do they sell?" asked Maeron curiously, "anything that you have here?"
"Crystals, books, paintings, cards and the like," answered Anchorin, and the others looked pleased.
"As I was saying," said Anchorin quietly, "they were accompanied by an elf from Atlantis, who is residing with them in their abode in Oswestry,

and is proving to be a great asset. They have contacted Rhianah the priestess who is on the lookout for the beings who stole the discs. The third casket has been found in the Yucatan, in Meso-America."

Suddenly a light appeared on the wall in front of them, for they were seated in a semi circular manner. An image of the continents appeared, and the scale reduced in size, so that the land masses increased and the focus was on Meso-America, and the image homed in on the north east coast of the Yucatan.

"This is where the third casket is, and we are having a bit of trouble with it, for Hudlath investigated it recently and got confronted by the renegades. You will help us stop the renegades from entering the earth's atmosphere".

"What we can possibly do is alter the skin of the earth's atmosphere so that entities such as these cannot enter as easily," explained Aurion, "we'll see what we can do, though it is often temporary, for to do it on a permanent basis would alter the fabric within time itself, and then we wouldn't be able to get through to you as we are doing now. What we can do is create a distortion so that they get sidetracked."

"Yes," said Zanadar with a grin, "we can create an illusionary state so that they end up somewhere completely different in the universe, and with any luck they won't have a clue where they have been sent to, and it will take some time before they return, maybe a few hundred years if we're lucky, but it will certainly give us plenty of time to make progress, but it's a long shot, as you say."

"Sounds reasonable if it could work!" answered Anchorin with a twinkle in his eyes, "if we manage to get all the renegades who are either present or on their way through the vortex."

"Don't worry, it would be several groups at once, so, we'll get working on that set up as soon as possible," answered Zanadar.

"I'll help sort out the group meeting from our side," said Aurion, and Salaron agreed to help also.

"I shall inform Rhianah about everything and she will contact Kenny, Jadeir and the group," said Anchorin, who by now had a grave look on his face, "I also have to tell you that one of the Moroccan group went missing some months ago, and despite every effort, he has not been found; do you think he might have been taken by the renegades somewhere?"

Maeron and Sirol also looked concerned, "we shall look into that and link with all their outposts," Sirol answered, "what is his name and what does he look like?"

Anchorin brought up the faces of the Moroccan group in his wallscreen device, the dark features of Maraya, and Costillo, who was quite stocky, with keen, dark eyes and jet black hair, which came over his ears. Sagario was thin faced and quite serious looking, and his colouring was a bit fairer than the others, and finally, Danuel, whose face was rounded and gentle looking, with sympathetic eyes.
The scene then changed to that of Oswestry, with images of the group there. There was Kenny's shock of hair, Sarah with short grey hair and keen eyes, Alyssia's cheerful look and her plaited hair, and Karin's bubbly expression and her short, dark hair; and finally Jadeir's green face with bright eyes, which seemed to penetrate straight out of the image.

"Where are the other two of the Moroccan group?" asked Zanadar.
"We don't know, for Maraya said that they stayed behind in Morocco in case Costillo re-appeared there, and there has been only minimal contact involved between them and Maraya, but should we be more organised and encourage them over to Oswestry, as they ought to remain involved, I feel concerned about their isolation, as they'll be vulnerable" said Anchorin, "also, an important point is that Maraya has Costillo's crystal, so he is unable to return on his own."
"I can get the vortex energy increased between our planets of the 'Council of Twelve', and we can ask Atlantis to help us in this work to succeed," said Zanadar looking appealingly at Anchorin.
"No!" said Aurion shaking his head vigorously, "you can't do that because it will help renegade energies to come through from those future times, enhancing time travel when we need to find a way to curb it."
"Well, I don't know if curbing it is a good idea either," said Siral, "after all, we want all doors open so we can see what is going on and investigate; and any limitations may stop us from finding them, even though the freedom of movement will be to their favour too."
"Is there nothing we could do to try and limit selectively?" asked Salaron.
"I think a large supply of the blue mist plant is going to be the best substance to be used!" suggested Anchorin with a wry look, "and forget about all your marvellous ideas at present!"
"You're probably right," answered Salaron, with a jovial look.
Zanadar looked thoughtfully over everyone's heads and then spoke, "Anchorin there is one thing we could do," and his expression was serious, and he looked at Anchorin in the eye.
"Oh Zanadar," replied Anchorin with a look of anxiety, "I couldn't do that! It would be jeopardy, surely."

"The garden has been tended well, over time, but must be entered in times of crisis, and it has always been said that this was its reason, to be there for humanity in times of great need," emphasised Zanadar.

"But its energies would begin to deteriorate once someone has entered," exclaimed Anchorin with a sigh, "the dear Garden of Eden has always been a wonder to behold, which we can look upon, and know its healing powers stabilise our continent, its…well," and Anchorin sighed a little heavily, "if it has to be done, then I must go inside the garden," and he looked down into his lap, head in hand, with his expression concerned and subdued.

"They all know that this would happen a long time ago," said Zanadar gently to Anchorin.

Anchorin looked up at Zanadar and nodded in acceptance.

A shimmer of movement brought Hudlath to his destination, unseen, he wandered slowly in the scorching, bright sunlight. It was a striking contrast to the lovely warm atmosphere on Atlantis, which lacked these blistering extremes he had to contend with. He could easily see the whitewashed walls of the little red roofed cottage he knew would be harbouring the third casket. Behind him, about half a mile away, he could hear the lulling sound of waves lapping the shore; also an unfamiliar experience and he looked up and saw the moon, the reason behind the tidal pull.

As he didn't find anyone's whereabouts around, he went over to enter the cottage. Hudlath could walk through walls by using his crystal to go into a neutral gear, so that he was slightly out of every time slot. He wandered cautiously around the house, still invisible, until he came to the bedroom with the chest of drawers. The piece of furniture was ornately carved with relief imagery of foliage around it and the drawer handles were picked out to look like part of the foliage. He could see a flickering energy around the chest of drawers and decided to work on it to see what was causing it. Energy emanated from his crystal towards the chest of drawers, illuminating its exterior and surrounding it with a bright white energy. Immediately an energy shield disintegrated like the cracking of an egg, and Hudlath was able to approach the chest of drawers. He swiftly opened each drawer, looking for the casket, and found it in the middle drawer. He hesitated, as the casket looked strangely distorted.

A group of unicorns appeared, Hudlath turned round and saw them, and only he could see them, for they were still connected with the Atlantean golden age period, and did not materialise into other time periods. He checked the casket all over with his crystal. The unicorns surround the area with a brilliant light, which had Hudlath almost squinting with its intensity, and then beyond that light, some beings appeared in the room. Hudlath realised that they were some of the renegades who originated from within the Orion constellation, for they had the well-known characteristics of outcasts, their faces were wide, with dark grey eyes and yellow flecks in them, which had an unseeing quality to them and expressionless. He drew his crystal wand swiftly, of which the crystal itself was six inches long, and he brought a shield of light to bear between himself and the renegades. The unicorns helped by sending energy from their horns to link with Hudlath's wand energy, unseen by the renegades. The renegades stopped in their tracks, but still stood their ground with a menacing air, and changed their shape constantly while retaining a humanoid appearance.

One of the renegades stepped forward and transformed to emulate an errant knight, sword in hand, and then he spoke.
"That casket is guarded; one small movement of the casket will prove fatal. We demand that you return the other caskets within the next few days!" he demanded in a deep penetrating voice that seemed to echo and resonate around the room and tried to do the same within Hudlath's head, but he stopped that from happening immediately with his crystal, for he knew such things, if unchecked, could resonate inside people's head for a long time.

The unicorns impressed on Hudlath's mind non-verbally that these beings couldn't harm him, though they would do if he had been without his wand, but that they were also bluffing a little.
"The caskets are staying where they are!" retorted Hudlath emphatically, "and there will be three altogether in our hands as soon as possible."
He stood in a resolute stance, his eyes began to glow a little, and the energy from his wand emanated very strongly as he steadily projected his attention on it. The renegades stepped back a little as the light intensified, and a fiery energy surrounded Hudlath and the whole room. Hudlath now saw his chance to seize the casket and he swiftly departed with it back to his time period.

He sat down on a chair in his private quarters in the temple and used his crystal by his own personal altar space to contact Rhianah.

"Rhianah, I have found the third casket and successfully retrieved it, but will examine it to ensure that it's safe," explained Hudlath, "before returning it to where?"

"Hudlath, I think you'd better look after it for a while until the group at Oswestry are strong enough, for the renegades would surely come looking for it, and the advantage of it staying in your time is, as you know, that your time is still in the golden age, and that is where they cannot go!" explained Rhianah.

"Well, all right, I shall look after it myself for the time being, we mustn't burden the group with too much responsibility, even though we know it has been something they've chosen to do, and is therefore part of their destiny, for as long as some representatives of humanity are there to aid us and to repair the past, then redemption can take place, so, as long as this group can do what they can towards this, then all will be well, won't it?" commented Hudlath, "I'll contact Anchorin and the space beings, and then report back once I've inspected the casket, farewell for now!"

"Yes Hudlath, I'll await your call, unless Anchorin will let me know first, may the powers that be guide you on your way," answered Rhianah.

Hudlath laid the casket inside a small cabinet in his study area, and made to contact Anchorin when he heard a noise coming from the casket. He spun round and re-opened the cabinet. The casket had changed shape and looked like a large stone, and Hudlath's eyebrows rose in response.

'Oh, it still has some kind of charm on it,' he thought, and pointed his crystal at it, summoning powers of heaven and earth, and the crystal itself to cut through this illusion. The appearance of the stone peeled away like a burning layer of paper to reveal the casket again.

'I'll have to keep an eye on this object, to ensure it's totally free of these layers,' he thought, 'I'll tell Anchorin and the others meanwhile.

He resumed to setting up his communication with Anchorin and within the glowing end of his crystal wand he could see Anchorin's face.

"Greetings Anchorin!" he said cheerfully, "I have to tell you the good news, that I have the third casket here in the temple!" and Anchorin looked pleased, "unfortunately at present, the renegades have put many layers of deception over it, which I am presently removing, and won't open the box until I know for sure that it is clear, or else I may find myself in trouble."

"Oh yes, be careful Hudlath, don't open it until you are sure, it may be best if, when you think it's safe to open, you do it while I'm watching to ensure that your safety, unless you will have people at the temple who can help you," advised Anchorin.

"I suppose I could," he replied, "I hadn't involved anyone else up to now, as it seemed easier just to keep it to myself, besides, I'm always travelling around, and once I've returned I shall only wish to carry out the duties of the temple high priest, without anyone knowing about the casket situation, for that job is demanding enough! So I will contact you when the appropriate time comes!"

"I accept your point of view wholeheartedly Hudlath," said Anchorin, "probably wiser to keep the matter secret, and I will await your call in due course."

"Can you tell Zanadar and the others what is going on?" asked Hudlath.

"Yes, don't worry, I can do that. I've just been talking to them recently about the group and the casket situation. I'll tell them all that we've discussed," replied Anchorin.

"Thank you Anchorin," replied Hudlath and they waved to each other and his image faded as contact was closed.

There was another noise from the cabinet and it began to shake vigorously. Hudlath, eyes alert, drew his crystal wand and pointed it immediately towards the cabinet and asked for the casket to still itself, which it did. Hudlath peered cautiously inside to see that the casket was looking like a large insect. He didn't stop to see any further details of the variety and slammed the cabinet door shut, and then he concentrated on the crystal as he did before to burn off the next layer of the charm, which happened successfully as a small plume of smoke filtered out between the cabinet doors. Then he looked inside the cabinet and saw that the casket had reverted to its original shape again.

"You are a tricky little object!" he said to it in an admonishing tone. He closed the door on it again and surrounded the casket in a light filled bubble to control its further activities until he returned later, and he decided to lock the cabinet doors as well.

CHAPTER 11 – SELF-DEFENCE & THE GARDEN OF EDEN

Jadeir's crystal started glowing and he made that fact known to Karin, Sarah and Alyssia.

"That crystal is almost uncomfortable once it starts glowing girls!" he said loudly as he held one hand at his waist and speedily extracted the crystal from its bag with the other. "I'd better see who it is," and he activated the crystal, "Ah, it's Rhianah! She says that Hudlath has picked up the third casket, and apparently it was a tricky situation involving the renegades and their shape shifting charms they had placed upon the casket, and he's keeping it under surveillance. She will contact us once she's found any sign of any of the bases belonging to those characters," and then he put his crystal away in his pouch.

"That's good news about the casket," remarked Sarah, sewing her velvet bags as usual, "but I'm so glad Hudlath was there to cope with defending it."

"Yes, we're not quite up to that standard yet," echoed Karin.

"Do you know how to defend yourself against renegades Jadeir?" asked Alyssia, stopping a moment from her painting.

"I can do it, indeed," replied Jadeir, "but then it's easier for our kind to defend ourselves, for we can move so much quicker, and we have more power generally than humans, and can make our crystals very potent," explained Jadeir.

"It's nearly lunchtime folks," said Karin, getting up to prepare some food. "Jadeir, could you give us all a lesson in self defence once the others come up and we've had lunch?"

"That's a good idea," replied Jadeir, "that I shall do!"

The familiar sounds of footsteps from the shop grew louder and more distinct as Karin finished preparing lunch. Kenny and Maraya entered and sat down.

"I have been asked to give you all a lesson in self defence, because we may have to travel back to Rhianah's time," explained Jadeir.

"Has she found out where those people are based?" asked Kenny.

"Not yet, but I have a hunch she'll find them soon," answered Jadeir.

"The third casket's been found and brought back by Hudlath!" exclaimed Karin to Kenny and Maraya, and they looked delighted.

"Only that Hudlath is looking after it because the renegades from the colonies had put layers of charms on it, so it's being guarded until further notice."
"That sounds tricky," said Kenny, "how do you deal with charms, and were they common in Atlantis in the last days, Jadeir?"
"Yes, quite a lot to be found unfortunately," replied Jadeir, "if you ever see an object that looks as if its shape shifting, that is, the edges of it look a little dense and start forming into other shapes, then it has been charmed. You point your crystal at it and while using a circular motion; you send your good energy to surround the object in question. This increase in energy heightens its intensity, and you must continue, until the entity lifts up from the object or just dissolves. There may be layers on the object, in which case you may need to wrap the object in a protective bubble of light until you have had time to finish the job or continue when you can."
"That sounds very much like a sci-fi movie!" exclaimed Sarah, "and now for the self defence, as long as we don't have to fly through the air doing cartwheels!"
"No, you can let your crystals use that kind of energy," laughed Jadeir.

They finished lunch and then Jadeir gave his instructions.
"You have to bring good energy into your crystal and project it out steadily towards the being who is bothering you in order to place a seal between both of you. At the same time, encircle yourself with a mass of light. If you can sense any weak spots on the individual send some sharp energy there to put him off balance. The quicker you can do this to catch him out, the better, because he or she is going to be doing the same to you and will be well seasoned in self defence. The force that is returned by him or her may well be fierce and so expect that. If you have done any judo, think of the joints in the body, and so energy sent to them to destabilise the person will be effective, as long as the person isn't expecting it or doing the same to you!

"Is that the lesson finished Jadeir?" asked Sarah.
"Yes, that's the basic information, though there's one big snag involved, you'll need some practice," responded Jadeir, "so I've invited some friends of mine to come over and we can all practice somewhere together, maybe out near a hill fort?"
"We can go to the place where we first travelled to Atlantis," said Karin, "just outside Oswestry Jadeir."

"When you are in Atlantis, it is easier to defend yourself because, naturally, you are larger and have taken your amaranth and elixir potions, so you'll have an advantage there. Also, your crystals work much better there as a result," commented Jadeir, "but the difficulty lies in when you aren't in Atlantis, in case renegades come here," and Jadeir looked at them seriously, "so you must learn a few techniques."
"Jadeir," said Alyssia, "was it the prevalence of the amaranth and elixir plants which made Atlanteans so tall?"
"Oh yes!" replied Jadeir, "they thrived on it. On Sirius the amaranth and elixir were native, and on the Pleiades the withering plant and blue mist plant were native, but as these two traded with each other, they both exchanged their plants, so the Pleiadeans became tall, like the Sirians. Now, who's done some kung fu or judo before?"
"I did a bit of judo several years ago," said Alyssia, "but everyone kept on catching me out, so I left! Sorry, that's not very encouraging!"
"It sounds like your teacher wasn't doing the job properly, as everyone should manage it well if they're shown how, and have a minimum capacity for dexterity of movement," answered Jadeir.
Jadeir explained the basics about self-defence, with a view to where to point their crystals and use them effectively.

They exercised together, and Jadeir placed entities, which looked like rounded black objects with lots of small legs, around a log. He asked everyone to practice removing them with their crystals until they felt confident.

Suddenly a group of elves, fairies and gnomes appeared.
"We've been missing the fun!" they exclaimed.
"You're late!" said Jadeir firmly, "still, you could tackle this group now, they're getting quite good!"
With that, a pile of the rounded black objects landed near Jadeir's feet. The elves and other nature spirits gave a look of surprise.
"We got held up, too many vital jobs to do, to make sure everything is secure before winter comes," a gnome explained.
Jadeir smiled, "let me introduce you to our human friends. Everyone, the gnomes here are called – Garalph, Ganor, Staloph and Gemalon. The elves are Gadair, Cyaphon, Seilon and Kanas. The fauns are Kavanos and Kyphos. The group of fairies are Leannah, Philone, Phairos and Alynda. Jadeir, in turn, introduced the nature spirits to Kenny and the others. By the end of the session in the woodlands they were all laughing and joking

with one another. The nature spirits had a wonderful way of lifting everyone's spirits. Finally, they were all on the point of leaving the woods together.

"We have enjoyed ourselves a great deal and have been so glad to meet you all," said Sarah, and the others echoed their agreements.
"We might need your help on our trips to the end times of Atlantis," commented Kenny.
"Well, in that case, we would be most glad to oblige," gestured Garalph the gnome.
"We would be very grateful for your help," said Maraya, "would you all come or just a few of you?"
Immediately four of them stepped forwards, and they were Garalph the gnome, Leannah the fairy, Kavanos the faun and Gadair the elf.
"We shall be happy to oblige, and the others will stay and continue to look after the earth, but they can link to us when we are in Atlantis on occasions," explained Garalph.
Jadeir smiled, "unknown to you all," he said, looking at Sarah, Maraya and the others, "I arranged for them to come over, knowing that they would accompany you to Atlantis."
"Thank you, we're most grateful," said Sarah, and Alyssia, Karin, Kenny and Maraya repeated the sentence together.

"Perhaps we should form some kind of council," gestured Kenny, "though I suppose we more or less have done that now, having linked with Rhianah, Anchorin and Hudlath."
"Yes, though I think we must have a bit more stratagem," said Sarah, "that is, we must know exactly our plans of action, or else we may be letting ourselves into a lot of difficulty."
"A good point Sarah," agreed Kenny, "we do need to know exactly what is going on before we take action."
"At present Rhianah is our scout for the renegade's time period, and once we know what she can find, then we can plan some kind of action there," said Jadeir, "and Hudlath found the casket in the Yucatan, where the renegades had set up their portal there, as well as others in various parts of the world."
"Yes, they had one in Morocco as you know, but I wasn't aware of anything in Britain so far, though since they had been seen in Cornwall, they must have something in the country," said Maraya, "unfortunately, portals can pop up without anyone noticing that much is going on."

"Presumably more likely in urban settings," commented Sarah.

"Yes, much more likely," replied Maraya.

"We can find out," said Garalph, "as our communication system is much better than humans', and we could know by this evening what is going on in the country."

"Please do find out," said Karin.

The nature spirits meditated together, linking with others of their kind, and silently asked for them to investigate any portals. Everyone returned to the flat in Oswestry, and the all of the nature spirits decided to return to Pistyl Rhaeadr.

"Maraya," asked Sarah, "have you heard from your Moroccan friends recently?"

"I haven't actually, and have been a bit worried about them," admitted Maraya, "but since they don't have a casket, maybe they're not under too much of a threat."

"Maybe not Maraya," replied Sarah, "but these people obviously took them to get at us!"

"I've tried not to think about it too much," replied Maraya, "and I've asked them if they wanted to come up here several times. I guess they've hesitated due to the expense of moving such a distance."

"Perhaps we could find some work for them then?" gestured Sarah, "what do they do?"

"They work in electronics and computer generated projects generally," answered Maraya, "but I'm sure that kind of work would be more than easy to get over here," and Maraya shrugged her shoulders, "I'm just making guesses about them. I really don't know why they haven't considered coming, nor have I heard from them since I arrived in England, except once when I was in Somerset, which is a contrast with all the correspondence and phone calls I've made. Perhaps they went to Atlantis and are now searching for Costillo themselves."

Maraya looked worried and gave Sarah a fleeting glance.

"Maraya, we could get Rhianah, Anchorin and Hudlath to look out for them too," said Sarah consolingly.

Maraya gave Sarah a smile.

"I should have mentioned it sooner," answered Maraya, "but I just kept on putting it to the back of my mind. The thought of all three of them gone is too much to consider."

With that, tears started trickling down Maraya's face. Sarah put her hand on Maraya's shoulder, and the others crowded round Maraya with serious expressions. Jadeir immediately contacted Rhianah and told her to look out for the other two of the Moroccan group, Danuel and Sagario.
"I'll contact Anchorin and Hudlath, Jadeir!" said Rhianah.
"Yes, Anchorin may have information on them that Zanadar and the group know about," replied Jadeir.

"I don't think I can stay here any longer," stated Maraya, "I must go and find out what is going on, and where they all are. This concerns me, and it's not fair to ask you all to get involved in trying to rescue my friends."
Maraya got up from her chair and started walking to the door.
"I must do this on my own now," she said.
Jadeir rushed in front of her immediately.
"You'll do no such thing Maraya! I understand how you feel, but we must stick together, and that way, we'll manage to get things achieved. I think we ought to go as a group to Rhianah's when she has found some clues, and then we can really get to work. It's not easy waiting to take action, and we tend to feel helpless, but that is what we must do at present," he said.
Jadeir gently led Maraya back to her chair and the others said encouraging words until she agreed to stay with them all and work as a group. Jadeir's crystal began to glow once they'd sat down.
"Ah!" he said, "that could be our nature spirits. Yes right; one in St Ives, two in London, one on the south coast near Brighton, one in Birmingham, another in Bristol. Any more? Right, another in Manchester, but nothing around Oswestry, no? Good! Thank you Garalph."

Alyssia stirred in the night. She was wide-awake and opened her eyes. She was aware of something stirring in the air above her and watched to see what it was. Images of Danuel and Sagario hovered overhead and that of Costillo as well. Their faces were serious, and their eyes were full of concern, but they looked fairly healthy, Alyssia thought.
'Where are you?' said Alyssia mentally, 'can you tell me?'
'On the Colonies, and we travelled through the vortex from Huanca,' they said.
'How can you come here tonight?' asked Alyssia.
'We are asleep and managed to break free to speak to you, for they take charge twenty four hours a day here. We are being treated as well as

expected. We wait for any possible moment to escape, though extremely difficult,' replied Sagario.
Alyssia knew their chances were slim by their expressions.
'We'll do what we can as we have priests in Atlantis working with us, as well as nature spirits. I'll tell the others and then we can make plans!' answered Alyssia.
'Thank you, I hope you can,' answered Costillo, 'I wish to send Maraya my love, and that I'm alright, but don't worry if it's going to be too upsetting for her.'
'I understand,' replied Alyssia.
There was a flurry in the air and the three faces disappeared. Alyssia then drifted off to sleep again.

Next morning saw them all round the breakfast table. Jadeir was the only nature spirit present, and the group of four at Pistyl Rhaeadr were ready to return when action required their presence.
Alyssia told the others about her vision of Costillo, Sagario and Danuel, and that they had been taken off the planet.
"I'm glad Maraya isn't here at present, "but I can find a suitable time to tell her in private at some point," said Sarah, "and we'll have to tell Anchorin and Rhianah."
"No sooner said than done!" stated Kenny, who was getting his crystal out, but Jadeir was quicker and was already in touch by the time Kenny was just preparing, "well, of all the cheek!" he exclaimed, giving Jadeir his humorous penetrating stare.
Jadeir just turned and gave a sweet smile, and everyone chuckled.

Anchorin knew it was time to visit the Garden of Eden. Hudlath was with him in the mountain temple, when they had heard from Rhianah about Alyssia's communication with the Moroccan group, now on the colonies.
"I'll have to go alone Hudlath, as you know," said Anchorin, as he picked up his bag of food and drink, "I shall be in touch about what happens next, for it has been unheard of to need to enter the Garden. As you know, there are no records about entering the place."
"I shall await your summons, Anchorin, if need be," answered Hudlath, as he held his crystal, and disappeared back to his own time period.
Anchorin took the little buggy down the mountain, and he stopped briefly by the waterfall to refresh himself, as he wasn't really used to the hot lowland air.

He trekked northwards on foot, for though he was the chief high priest of Atlantis, he, like his culture in that time period, believed it necessary to stay humble and not have a life style superior to everyone else. The whole populace thought it essential that all people had an equal share of belongings, though some may be more skilled than others, but those who were more talented would be more than happy to share their skills selflessly.

Anchorin did have the skill to levitate for short distances, which he decided to make use of while he was adjusting to the lowland temperature.
'I think I'll levitate over to that horizon,' he thought.
He sped forwards, rising about ten feet above ground, and he glided along. 'Ah, good! I can see the northern mountain range, and just make out those green hills in front, that's where I want to be!'

As he approached the green hills, he could see the edge of a deep forest, which he knew was the Garden of Eden's borderlands. The forest was tucked between three hills and showed beautiful multi-coloured leaves in various pastel shades. Each leaf had a gold-tinged glimmer of light around it. Anchorin stopped beside the branches and savoured the colours of the leaves.
'Such beauty, but I must proceed,' he thought, with an expression of resolve.
He moved through the trees slowly, watching for clues. He sensed he had to turn right, passing through the trees at a diagonal. He found a large standing stone; it was thin and tall, with spiral markings on at its base, and diamonds at the top.
'Perhaps I should ask the stone where the Garden's entrance lies,' he thought, and he linked with the stone.
He could see the stone giving him an image of the Garden in plan formation. He saw the three hills together; their edges were a little concave. Within the centre of the hills lay the Garden, which was a triangular shape. He was also shown that he had entered over the side of one of the hills, and had to go diagonally because the main entrance lay in the middle of one of the sides of the triangular garden, and he was standing nearer one of the corners.

Anchorin thanked the stone and proceeded through the wood. There were many fairy folk all around, but that was nothing new, because there were so many all over Atlantis, and he had greeted, as many as possible, the ones he saw on his journey to the Garden. In fact, not many people went on long journeys because there were so many friendly people and fairy folk to talk to, that they'd probably not get very far, unless, like Anchorin, they had an urgent mission to complete. This thought made Anchorin chuckle a little despite the seriousness of the occasion.

Anchorin soon stopped in surprise, for he had come to the entrance, but how would he get inside? Just then, a tall female being appeared, surrounded by a pearly glow, and she wore a pale green dress.
"I wish to enter please, I am Anchorin, high priest of Chalidocea, and sent by Zanadar," and Anchorin bowed humbly.
The being smiled, "I am Arwena and I guard the entrance to the Garden."
Her voice had both high and deep tones simultaneously, and she came and studied Anchorin's face with her bright emerald eyes.
"I can see that you are truly genuine. I know of you Anchorin, of course, but it is part of our rules, that I must examine everyone's soul and spirit, to see their natures, for only those with the deepest maturity can enter. Just as I expected, so now you can enter too!" and she smiled and opened the doors, which were carved oak, yet Anchorin realised that they were actually alive still. Anchorin looked in wonderment, but then he had to go through without finding out anything further about them.

The most beautiful scents filled the air and he breathed them in, and immediately felt a glowing sensation rushing through his body. He looked at his arms and the rest of his body, and could see that the pearlescent glow was all around him too, just like Arwena. He took a few steps forward, a bit hesitantly as he couldn't see anything except a large sward of green, without being able to see the boundaries, for the greenery just seemed to fade out around the edges.
'Where is the Garden?' he thought, and a puzzled look gradually permeated his face, 'I suppose I must keep walking and hopefully I'll find out!'
"He started walking and saw nothing more than the green grass all around until he thought 'maybe I'm not concentrating properly,' so he prayed and projected light to the garden and linked to his temple, where prayers surround it constantly, and he brought that energy into the place.

With that, tall Sentinel beings appeared, their eyes were large and clear, and they approached Anchorin. A group of unicorns also appeared and came nearby.

"Welcome to our domain Anchorin. You needed to concentrate in order to reach to the heart of our garden," they said in unison, and they communicated telepathically, just like everyone else on Atlantis in the Golden Age.

"I can see the hills in the distance from the temple, and can just about see the huge dome of pearly light, which I can see radiating energy over the land to encourage everything to grow much easier. I did notice how much more luxuriant everything is here, as I approached, and had thought that Atlantis was pretty luxuriant already," replied Anchorin, smiling gently.

"You know why, don't you?" asked the Sentinel group.

"It must be more than the spiritual energy of the place," remarked Anchorin. Something in the nature of the place seemed to seep the answer through his whole being. "Of course! Because there is no winter at all here, the plants thrive all the time. The sun here is not too hot and the moisture comes from the strange mists."

Just then a gentle melody seemed to arise from a mass of flower-covered bushes, and a new branch emerged from one of the bushes, with large buds on it, and then a chord of music sounded accompanied by pale pink light, and then the buds gently started to open.

"How beautiful!" said Anchorin, watching with amazement.

"Sometimes the plants do this in front of strangers, just to impress them!" laughed the Sentinel.

"It's a wonderful place," remarked Anchorin, "but how will the Garden feel once I've left? Will it recuperate?"

"Don't worry," said the Sentinel reassuringly, "it may cast a subdued energy over the Garden as well as the world at large, but it will recover at a later date."

"How much later?" asked Anchorin with a serious expression.

"Up to fifteen thousand years, it depends," said the Sentinel, "but we spread the load by our own methods, so that the loss doesn't serious affect the planet. Energy is being stored all the time for when it is necessary."

"Does this time period take us through to the next Golden Age?" asked Anchorin.

"That is true!" replied the sentinel, "and it shall re-appear then. Nothing is truly lost Anchorin."

Anchorin then knew that he must approach the centre and receive the grail cup of the Garden of Eden. He began walking and the sentinels accompanied him, with the unicorns flanking them all. Anchorin could see their horns glowing a little, and realised he hadn't noticed that detail before.

They had walked in silence for at least a quarter of a mile, and a faint background of dreamy music could be heard periodically, with a movement of paler shades of colours around them all, and now it was getting louder. Anchorin noticed that the unicorns' horns were definitely getting brighter still.

"We must be approaching the centre," he thought to himself, yet of course, all of the sentinel beings and unicorns could hear.

"Yes Anchorin. Now we must fly over the top of that mass of plants over there in order to reach the centre," the sentinel explained.

They all rose up and glided gracefully over the top of more of the flower bushes they'd seen before. When they landed again, Anchorin could see the centre of the Garden. There was a temple of white marble, except that the base of the temple had a pinkish tinge, and the domed apex had a purplish tinge, and the whole structure had a burnished golden sheen. The temple was situated on a small island in the centre of a large lake, and the waters were still and glassy, and the temple's reflection was clearly visible.

This is where we leave you Anchorin, until you are ready to depart," instructed the Sentinel, "the unicorns will guide you a little further, however."

"Thank you everyone. I should have asked your individual names," exclaimed Anchorin, "but this garden is so beautiful, and the scents too; so my mind isn't working as well as it might. Probably it's also to do with this matter of taking something from the Garden, I suppose."

"It is predominantly the effect of the Garden, as the scents in the air induce a kind of trance state if you aren't used to it," explained the Sentinel, "and it is a place which overlaps many time zones too. As far as our names are concerned, we don't have individual names, and it hasn't caused any problems so far!"

The Sentinel gave a parting wave to Anchorin as he approached the water's edge. The seven unicorns surrounded him and he was glad that they would come over to the temple with him. They indicated for him to look into the water. As he did so, it was as if he could see the energy of the place reflected there in rainbows of bright light.   Anchorin lifted himself up and rose over the water's surface, and the unicorns hovered over it too, and then they all flew over to the temple.   He could see a filigree of gold decoration painted all over the surface of the dome now that he was closer.   He went to the door and turned to look at the unicorns, and they indicated for him to enter now, and they'd be there when he came out again.

The temple had a beautifully calm interior, and Anchorin walked slowly through an antechamber, noticing all the details of the intricate carved and painted relief work and patterns surfaces, and then he entered into a small room where he approached the centre.   "Do you wish to help the earth for all time?" came a voice.
"Are your motives completely selfless?" came another.
"Are you strong enough?" echoed a third.
"Yes, I believe so!" stated Anchorin boldly, "for I am the high priest of Atlantis and know I can be trusted.   It is not my position, but my responsibility that is foremost in my answer.   Please ask the divine source if you wish."
"We can see that you can be trusted, please enter through the open door," said the voices in unison, and a previously unseen door materialised, and Anchorin went through.

This room was dark and cold, but not oppressive, but Anchorin had not encountered such cold and discomfort before.
"What must I do now?" asked Anchorin, anticipating the voices reply again.
An image appeared on the far wall.   It was an image of the renegades. They were moving around and hitting people; Anchorin noticed that these people were not renegades and were obviously enslaved.
"This is the renegade's wish for planet earth, and it will become like this if we don't hurry!"
"How can I help?" asked Anchorin.
"Be willing to take the essence, let there be no doubts, and then you can move forward," came the answer.

Anchorin saw another image of renegades attacking and destroying the earth, the way they had done so with other planets, for he was shown fleeting images of the other destroyed planets.

"I understand and realise what I must do, and I accept the essence for good use and to safeguard our planet," he affirmed out loud.
Immediately the darkness and cold lifted away, and Anchorin found himself now inside a large pearl-coloured room filled with gentle music. In the centre stood a circular pedestal table, of about four feet in diameter and made of white marble, with gold coloured edging. Upon it stood a large container, also made of marble, which was also circular. Anchorin was encouraged to lift the lid. Inside was the strongest light Anchorin had ever seen, and he had to close his eyes.
"Only take the marble lid off. The inner container is the one you must take," instructed the voice again.
Anchorin lifted the inner casket of essence out of its marble casing.
"Now, before you place it inside your bag," said the voice, "it will be advantageous if I could place a small portion of it on your forehead, as that will strengthen you very much indeed," said the voice again.
Anchorin waited, as the lid rose gently and a small portion of the contents floated towards his forehead and he could feel an invisible finger rubbing it into his skin. He felt a rushing feeling, and saw a mass of colours swirling around him. Immediately he could see the group of beings in the room, who had been communicating with him all the while. He felt a sense of deeper timelessness, and could see what was going on in his mountain temple and other parts of Atlantis most clearly. Usually he had to meditate on it to know.
"Greetings Anchorin," said the friendly female beings. "I am Anui," said one, "I am Deanu," said the second, "and I am Giana," said the third.
"I am glad to meet you," replied Anchorin.
The three female beings came up close and stood facing Anchorin.
"Do you know us?" they asked in unison, and their three voices together seemed to form a chord in Anchorin's mind. It was a chord, which echoed back in time, and he could see visions of a fair, mountainous land, with countless waterfalls, like the one at the base of his temple mountain, where oracular priests and priestesses intuited and advised. There were no cities and people lived either in small villages or wandered and lived in caves or under trees. He could see people and animals sharing their lives together in harmony, and communicating with one another, including nature spirits, with the greatest of ease, and no one needed to eat much either. Anchorin felt himself part of that time period, and then he saw these three beings there too, in a sacred place by a mossy area, surrounded by waterfalls. Their chord-like songs were continuously

playing, and it was as if they had been singing throughout the annals of time, for all of earth's time period.

"You are the Mother Beings of the earth, closely working with Gaia and others, and have been singing throughout all time. You are the fulcrum of the planet, the sacred goddess energy at the source of life on earth," stated Anchorin.
"You perceive correctly," they said in unison, "we advise you to use the essence as you have just done whenever needed. Others must use it too, for you will all need it to be strong and perceptive, and it will link you with us and that is important, so we can advise too."
"How can a small thing like this take the strength away from the Garden?" asked Anchorin.
"It is very concentrated energy, and holds such a powerful essence, as it has a huge amount of life's energy poured into that casket, from the earth, ourselves and many other spirits, trees, rocks etc. Although we can regain our own basic energy reasonably quickly, it is the energy of all time's cycles, which have to accumulate here; that takes up the time. To regain the energy of the Garden itself, which droops and dies off until the phial in the casket is returned here again, and then the slow greening process begins to reappear. Now you must go!"

Anchorin thanked them, and as he moved out of the temple to the water's edge the unicorns accompanied him again, their horns glowing. As they all took off over the water and landed on the other side, Anchorin was aware of a slight fading of the golden energy around the dome of the temple. There was also the faintest hint of an autumnal chill beginning to permeate the Garden. It made him shiver a little, and he turned to look at the temple again, and could hear the chord-like singing grow stronger as the turning of the leaves on all the surrounding trees increased. Anchorin could feel a lump gathering in his throat, but the unicorns looked at him with a deep sense of peace and loving energy, which glowed from their eyes, that he felt better about what was happening, and could move back to the gate with some composure.

As he reached those living carved gates, he said farewell to the unicorns and they all looked at him for several minutes, their minds and hearts linking and it was as if their essence went into him, strengthening their support for Anchorin and the tasks he and the others would need to do in order to retrieve the disks to complete the three caskets, and seal the doors to the renegade's world.

Once through the gates, there was Arwena. Her tall pale green form, and her green eyes, that looked into Anchorin's. He sensed the powerful sense of vision that she was portraying to him.
"Look to what lies beyond what appears to be happening now, towards the final outcome, and all time periods after that. It's all for a good reason, think of that, and we encourage you to tell others about what you've experienced. We shall all be with you in your mission," explained Arwena, her viridian eyes looked like little green crystals.
Anchorin smiled, "I shall, Arwena, I'll tell many folk about the whole experience."
They said goodbye and Anchorin made his way back across the land, flying swiftly to return as soon as possible.

CHAPTER 12 - THE SUMMONS TO ATLANTIS

Anchorin used his crystal link to contact Rhianah and Hudlath.

"Call everyone over, they need to sample the essence, including yourselves!" he stated to them both simultaneously, "we've got to get going on this. Have you found any leads yet Rhianah?"

"I think I've found one or two places to check, and have asked others to scout around, but it is so difficult as those characters come and go so quickly. Perhaps they'll just have to come over, wait here and take those characters by surprise, I don't know!"

"Yes, it sounds difficult, but I seem to recall that each casket has a clue to where the disc can be found," said Anchorin.

"Yes indeed, at one time that was the case Anchorin," answered Rhianah, "though I did get my scouts to check up on those places, but they found nothing, so those clues mustn't be relevant any more. Though they have been looking in other places as well, of course, but no clues at present there either."

"Oh dear, that doesn't sound good," said Anchorin, "just when I wanted some action, as I have the essence, which means that the source of that energy has been taken from the Golden Age, and so in turn, it will affect the time periods nearest to it, and so on. So it's imperative that we take action as soon as we can, somehow."

"Maybe the essence will help us in finding what we seek?" suggested Rhianah.

"Yes, we must focus on that," answered Anchorin, "I have taken some already and have felt the benefits, and now know the basics of what is happening to all people all over Atlantis in the present time. It is easier in the Golden Age, and will be harder in the darker time periods, but since it is a good tool, we must use it now, so let's get everyone over to my temple as soon as they can travel."

"I shall arrange it immediately and get them all over within the next hour, and I'll let you know," replied Rhianah.

"It's a call from Rhianah I think," announced Jadeir, and he pulled the scrying crystal from his pouch and activated it.

"Gather round!" he called out.

They had just finished their evening meal, and pushed a few utensils aside as the others hurried over to Jadeir.

"Rhianah, what's happening, we're all here?" asked Jadeir.

"I've been asked by Anchorin to summon you all over to a meeting at his temple as soon as possible. He went to the Garden of Eden to collect the essence. It has such a strong energy that it will make us all much more perceptive in our search," she explained, "and we can elaborate on this discussion once you are all over there. Can you come now?"
"I don't see why not," replied Jadeir, and he looked around at everyone, "is that ok with you all?"
Everyone agreed, and so they all arranged to set off immediately.
"We'll see you there at Anchorin's temple, Rhianah, within half an hour," concluded Jadeir.

They all scurried around, preparing themselves and gathering clothing and some provisions into their hold-alls, in case they stayed longer than the meeting time, since the element of surprise was often present! Karin piled all the dishes into the sink to soak, and then went into the bedroom. Kenny got everyone's supplies of elixir, amaranth and blue mist tinctures together and ensured that they put it in their bags. Maraya and Sarah also ensured that the caskets were safely hidden and undetectable in Sarah's room. Jadeir called his nature spirit friends, Garalph the gnome, Leannah the fairy, Kavanos the faun, and Gadair the elf to come as soon as possible, and explained why.

Once they had finished getting ready, everyone gathered together in the sitting room with their bags, and then they all went downstairs. Jadeir was the first down, and he heard a few knocks on the back door.
"It's probably the Rhaeadr group!" he announced cheerfully, and of course it was, and they entered the healing room with the others.
"Hey! There won't be enough space once this lot expand in size, outside!" shouted Jadeir, ushering the eager nature spirits out of the door!
Maraya, Sarah, Alyssia and Karin took the lead in disappearing first, having expanded beforehand. Kenny and the nature spirits followed on swiftly, though only he needed to take the blue mist plant, for the others could just think themselves invisible.

"Where are the others?" said Kenny to Jadeir and his friends, "we only followed them by a few minutes."
They looked around in the mountain mists, and finally got onto a path.
"Oh look! There's the temple! We're on track after all!" announced Jadeir.

They all arrived at the temple door and went inside, and there they saw Maraya, Alyssia and the others, and behind them, Rhianah and Hudlath, and they all greeted one another. Anchorin arrived and ushered them all inside to his discussion room, where he had talked to Zanadar and the group not too long ago.

There in the centre of the table stood the marble casket containing the essence. It was circular and smaller than the hexagonal caskets, but it had a beautiful glow to it, which made everyone stop to look at it.
"This is the casket of essence everyone," said Anchorin, gesturing over to it, "now that it has been taken from the Garden of Eden, the energy levels all over Atlantis are waning. As you've been told, the essence will enhance your powers of perception, but for those who are not genuine and kind, they will not get any benefits, and in fact, they would at least, be very ill."
"That would be a compensation if it would be so unfortunate as to land in the renegades' hands," said Rhianah.
"Well, it's staying here for the foreseeable future," said Anchorin firmly, "as, by taking the essence three times at least, then you won't need to take any more after that, so, please stay for a day in order to take those doses."

"Anchorin," ventured Maraya, hesitantly, "did you know about the Moroccan group?" she said, trying not to show her feelings.
Anchorin looked at her with a concerned expression, "I've just read from you Maraya, that you now know they are all on the Colonies, and I shall tell Zanadar and the others immediately." He kept it quiet that he knew about the Moroccans already, but with his many duties on Atlantis, he hadn't contacted the Council of Twelve yet.
Maraya looked a little relieved that she didn't have to verbalise a reply. Anchorin then began to contact them. In the corner of the room a light appeared, and Zanadar's face became visible.
"Any news Anchorin?" he asked.
Anchorin told him what had happened with the Moroccan group, and that everyone else was present to take the essence.
"We'll do what we can to pinpoint their whereabouts," said Zanadar, "unfortunately we cannot go ourselves for our vibrations are too high to materialise, but can give details of what is going on, and the layout of everything for those who will be going."

"Well, do your best Zanadar, my friend," said Anchorin, and as he turned around to face everyone as the light and Zanadar's face disappeared.

"Help yourself to the essence everyone," announced Anchorin, "you just put a little on your forehead with your forefinger."

He opened the little marble casket and held it as he went around, offering it to the group, who helped themselves to their portions.

There were quite a few moved expressions amongst the Oswestry people for a short while as their perception began to expand and their awareness of activities and thoughts all over Atlantis came into their consciousness. Anchorin nodded approvingly and smiled.

"Now you know what it can do for us," he said.

"I can sense what those guardians of the essence looked like, Anchorin, and I can see that place in ancient times before Atlantis, where they lived, and it fits your description," remarked Hudlath, "they are here with us, not bodily of course," and he looked upwards into the centre of the room.

"I see them too Hudlath," said Anchorin, "welcome to our temple," and he paused, as if listening to them, "they are telling us that they will watch over and encourage us with our task. Thank you," and Hudlath looked up to thank them as well.

Of course, Jadeir and the others were aware of the beings, but now had a better perception of everything else taking place on the planet and were instantly aware of the other nature spirits in all parts of Atlantis.

"I've just greeted my friends at home!" said Jadeir cheerfully, and everyone smiled.

"Once we are topped up with the essence doses, I'll take everyone to my time period, Anchorin, if you think that's the best course of action at present," said Rhianah.

"No, I've just had a thought!" replied Anchorin, "they could access the vortex from here and travel to the colonies directly, and then go back to that time period from there, it would be a bit safer initially."

"Yes, of course," agreed Rhianah, "as long as they haven't made it inaccessible, in which case, there would be nowhere to land on in that time period, and they'd be rejected back to their destination."

"Yes," replied Anchorin and pondered a moment, "would anyone be willing to investigate and see if this is the case?"

"I'll go!" said the delicate voice of Leannah, "I'm so small, no one will notice me, and I can become invisible, and move around more effectively than humans!"

"Thank you Leannah, I'm sure you won't be detected," answered Anchorin, "and if you are sent backwards, just recount the details of your return destination swiftly and you'll come straight here," and he noticed questioning expressions on many of the Oswestry group's faces, "and if you do go astray somewhere, just redo the return details again and you will come back safely."

Soon enough, Leannah disappeared to investigate, while the others were having their second lot of doses of essence, and were helping around the temple doing various practical tasks.
"I still feel a little concerned about a tiny fairy going over to the Colonies," said Sarah with a slightly troubled look.
"Don't trouble yourself Sarah," replied Jadeir, "despite appearances, she has more strength in proportion to her size than any human!

The group gathered in Anchorin's meeting room again that evening after their meal and had their third dose of the essence.
"What is this spiral design on your table Anchorin?" asked Sarah, "It doesn't look entirely like a decoration with these metallic objects at either end."
"Well spotted Sarah!" answered Anchorin, "it's a device to reach the higher realms using sound. Here, I'll show you."
Anchorin got up from his seat and went to the table. He scored along the line with a pen-shaped tool he took from a tiny drawer from the underside of the table. Immediately a beautiful choral song emitted with sounds of musical instruments like flutes and gongs. Everyone had images of the dawning light, with bright stars above, which they told each other afterwards. Once the last chords of the music had quietened down, Anchorin spoke.
"This links you to those levels and affects all the cells in your body, so that it is strongly attuned to spiritual levels. This will help you in dealing with the difficulties that will lie ahead."
Everyone was quiet for a while, as if absorbing the nature of the music and the essence, savouring it to remember it all, the better.

The corner of the room lit up and Zanadar's face appeared, and Anchorin spun round in his seat.
"I didn't expect to hear from you so quickly Zanadar!" said Anchorin, "what's going on?"

"We've spotted the three Moroccans as well as others on Colony Y, and unfortunately those who are naturally smaller have reduced in size, which includes the Moroccans, and therefore they are much weaker than the Atlantean sized renegades," explained Zanadar, "also, we saw those two characters that accosted the Moroccan group and Sarah. It could be very dangerous going out to the Colonies, as their portal from Atlantis is manned heavily."
"Yes, thank you for that, and it gives us something definite to work from. One of our fairies has gone to check out the portal route from this time period," explained Anchorin, "also, did you see anything of the disks?"
"Not yet, but we'll keep on looking," replied Zanadar, and he vanished.

"Well, we're a bit further on with our investigations," commented Anchorin, "let's hope that we can find out where the disks are."
"Describe to us what the renegades' Colony planets are like, and where they are in relation to earth, please Anchorin," asked Sarah.
"Hudlath has been there in disguise, so he'll tell you," answered Anchorin with a slight twinkle in his eye.
"Yes I did investigate the Colonies some years ago, because I had heard from Rhianah that people were just going missing from her time period, and despite the help from her scouts, they couldn't find them anywhere. So I suggested going to the Colonies," said Hudlath, "they tried to talk me out of it, but I said that I could hold my own against the renegades, and the people had to be found. Also, it would be a valuable exercise to know what the renegades' planets looked like. So yes, to answer your question Sarah! These Colonies are quite some distance away, near Antares; but no distance for the Council of Twelve, who surveyed it beforehand. There are three planets, and in order of distance from us they tend to be called X, Y and Z. I was able to go straight to the relevant planet of X and take the renegades by surprise, and I brought the missing people back to safety."
"What do the planets look like Hudlath?" asked Alyssia, "are the conditions difficult?"
"Well, yes they are unpleasant really," explained Hudlath, "for it is cold, dark and devoid of vegetation on all three planets. You'll need to take whatever provisions you'd need with you, including elixir, lots of amaranth to sustain you, and plenty of blue mist plant!"
"Do they have all of those plants in your time Rhianah?" asked Karin.
"They are still around in our time, but only just. Us high priestesses have our system of keeping the plants alive and circulating to those who come

for them," said Rhianah, "of course the authorities had stopped any such thing from taking place, and the average size of people has dwindled very slightly during my time period as a result of doing without the amaranth and elixir plants, but it's not too noticeable for those who continue to take it, but we can adjust our size as you know. We have to grow it swiftly, remove the seeds, and be ready to dispose of the plants carefully should we intuit the need for secrecy. I immediately chop up the leaves and stems finely and make a tea from them."

Leannah then returned, for her face peered around the door and everyone greeted her enthusiastically.
"I'm afraid that I got rebuffed backwards, which means no going that way!" said Leannah gravely, "sorry to cause an anticlimax."
"We'll have to go via Rhianah's time period then," said Karin, looking around at everybody who all exchanged rather concerned glances.
"I'll come with you all," said Hudlath, "I know the geography and various methods of escapology, but first we must know what is happening with those disks."

"Everyone!" announced Anchorin, "since you will have to encounter those dark times, come to the violet healing room, for I have another technique to guard you on your way."
The whole group followed Anchorin to the healing room, which was quite small and circular, and in the centre stood a chalice with a lid on top, which sat upon a pedestal, which was carved from the rock. Anchorin ushered everyone to stand around the chalice.
"This is the fount of the violet flame," said Anchorin in a half whisper, "just repeat what I say and follow what I do."
Anchorin began praying, so everyone joined in. Then he went to the chalice and lifted the lid, and a vigorous column of violet flames welled up and out of its centre, which were surrounded by blue and white light, and the Oswestry group looked on, amazed. Anchorin beckoned for people to come forward, as he filled a goblet with the fiery flames.
"Drink this, for protection against the dark forces out there," he instructed. Each person and nature spirit took some, and the Oswestry group all said afterwards that the goblet's fire felt hot without burning, and that it was cleansing to the whole body, without being unpleasant.
They stood for a while until each one noticed that the violet flames surrounded them, and then Anchorin closed the ceremony and they all returned to the meeting room.

"Well everyone! I will stay up to watch out for any further messages from Zanadar about the disks. If anyone wishes to retire to the sleeping quarters, perhaps Rhianah, you could show them where they are?" suggested Anchorin.
"Certainly!" smiled Rhianah, and the Oswestry group got up from their chairs to depart.
"The air here is so pure, we need to adjust to it!" said Alyssia to Anchorin, and the others responded and smiled in agreement.

They exited the room, and Rhianah turned left and continued down the corridor past a few rooms, and then walked into a room on the right.
"Us females can share this room," said Rhianah, and then pointed to the room on the other side of the corridor, just opposite, "and that's the men's room, and the nature spirits will share our rooms too."
"Good night Kenny," they all said, as they each chose a bed, and Kenny gave Karin a big hug, gave everyone a wave, and then departed for his room. He found a spare bed and dropped into it and fell asleep instantly. He didn't hear Jadeir and the others coming in later on after further talks with Anchorin and Zanadar.

Zanadar then communicated with Anchorin, Hudlath and the nature spirits, once the Oswestry group had gone to bed.
"I have to tell you that we spotted the three disks in one building all together, and are inside an object like a round casket, within a cabinet. I can show you a plan view of the building," explained Zanadar, and where the relevant piece of furniture is," and he held it up, and Anchorin used a laser-like device which could identify with the image and transpose it onto a sheet of paper.
"I'll make a few copies of this for everyone tomorrow, thank you Zanadar, and I have to tell you that everyone will have to travel through the vortex via Rhianah's time, since Leannah found the way blocked in my time period," said Anchorin.
"I'm sure it will work, for we know where the disks and the Moroccan group are now," replied Zanadar, "and you all can communicate telepathically, and usually the renegades can't! "I shall watch over the group when they arrive on the Colony, and I shall probably bring Melkior and Aurion with me."
"Wonderful," replied Anchorin, and everyone looked pleased.

"I think we ought to set off tomorrow as soon as we can," said Jadeir, "as once everyone knows about this, they won't want to be waiting and thinking about it all."
"Yes, I'm sure," answered Anchorin, "they can take another extra dose in the morning. I know a fourth dose is above requirements, but I've had affirmation from the Garden that it won't harm, and will be an extra boost for difficult circumstances. It also helps when in combat with the renegades, as it will strengthen their powers of determination, and also the energy coming from their crystals."

As everyone was taking some breakfast and then their fourth dose, Anchorin told them all about Zanadar's news.
"Zanadar and the group found the discs on planet Y too, so at least everything is on one planet," commented Anchorin.
"It'll be hard to get both the disks and the Moroccans from there," said Sarah, looking anxious.
"It's going to be very tricky to gain access," commented Kenny, with his eyes downcast, and looking very serious.
"Remember that I have been there before, everyone!" announced Hudlath, "and I shall be accompanying you. Though it's a daunting prospect, it's not impossible, and we have the plan view of the complex on the second planet where the Moroccan group are held, and Zanadar, Melkior and Aurion will be helping."
"What about the other prisoners there?" asked Karin, "shouldn't we help them to escape too?"
"That is a point to consider," said Hudlath, "because they would be trapped there indefinitely should we manage to obtain the disks, and when we seal up the portal on return. If the people are willing to be cooperative, they could be a great help. Let's see when we get there."
"Here is a detailed map of Colony Y, everyone!" announced Anchorin, and he handed copies around, "Rhianah, I think we ought to keep in communication as long as possible. Just let me know where you are at critical stages of your journey to the portal."
"Yes Anchorin," replied Rhianah, "I'll contact when we are about to leave my house, and will try to at Guyana's flat or near the portal."
"Kenny," said Anchorin, "I'd advise you and Jadeir to return to the flat," and then Kenny started protesting.
"I can't leave the others," Kenny retorted, "they're predominantly women, and my wife too!!"

"Yes, I know Kenny," replied Anchorin, "please don't worry so much, for the combating is done via the crystals, remember, and once the others go through the portal, you will need all your strength to master things from the flat. You will have Jadeir with you and he knows what to do."
"But how can it be more dangerous at home?" asked Kenny.
"The renegades are obsessed with searching for the origins of opposing forces to them, and can often overlook what is happening under their noses. Except for Hudlath's experience with the casket in the Yucatan, for there they were forced to confront Hudlath there and then," explained Anchorin.

"Ok then, should Jadeir and I depart now?" said Kenny with a resigned air, looking at Karin.
"Wait until they depart for Rhianah's," said Anchorin, "her place is safe enough and they'll all be invisible en route."
"It will only take a few moments Kenny," reassured Rhianah, "and then we can re-appear to you once we are there."
"Ok then," replied Kenny.
The Oswestry group congregated together. Kenny hugged Karin firmly, and then gave each of the others brief hugs. Rhianah, Hudlath, Maraya and the Rhaeadr group came over to stand by the Oswestry group, and Kenny withdrew and went over to Jadeir. Hudlath looked over at Kenny.
"I'll look after the ladies, don't worry Kenny," Hudlath said emphatically, and Kenny smiled.
"Bye love," said Karin, "I'll see you soon, I know it!"
"Bye love," replied Kenny.

The departing group, except the nature spirits, took a dose of the blue mist plant and they all promptly disappeared, and departed from the room.
Jadeir got Kenny to sit down, as he was beginning to pace the room restlessly without realising.
"I have to explain in full your role of doorkeeper, Kenny," explained Anchorin, "as I've decided to keep it confidential for security purposes, in case of any bother for the mission at the other end," and Kenny listened to Anchorin intently.

Just then, the corner of the room lit up, and there the faces of Rhianah, Hudlath, the Oswestry group and the Rhaeadr group appeared. They all waved to each other animatedly, and it reassured Kenny a little.

"We'll do the same from Guyanah's flat," said Rhianah, "it probably will be tomorrow night, with any luck."

The screen images faded and Anchorin resumed his instructions.
"You see Kenny, "explained Anchorin, "once you start the real job of doorkeeper, you must concentrate on your crystal as often as possible, to link in to your friends, for while you are doing that, you can link up and get a gist of what is going on for them, but to do this more effectively, you have to put a lot of energy in, in order to keep them well protected and become connected to them. It's like a force field that the doorkeeper crystal you have is capable of creating, and it only becomes fully useable once the people you are helping are on a definite mission. You see, crystals know that and become strong catalysts, for they can sense things far better than humans. Jadeir can help to keep the momentum going with his crystal while you rest."
"It sounds quite a tiring job," remarked Kenny, "requiring a lot of energy and concentration." He paused in thought a moment, and then looked up and glanced at the corner of the room where they had last seen Rhianah and the group, and he looked concerned again, "wasn't Costillo a doorkeeper?"
"Yes Kenny, he was," answered Anchorin, giving Kenny a perceptive look, "but he unfortunately fell asleep at a critical moment, and the renegades' accomplices broke through easily, as they already knew where they lived. But in your case, I doubt if they know where you live, and there are two of you to keep watch, so all will be well there, I'm sure."
"They may have monitored Sarah's escape route from Cornwall," said Kenny, with a hint of concern.
"Perhaps they're waiting for a moment to strike?" answered Anchorin, "well it may be the case, but since the casket has been closed since Sarah came north, they won't know where it is."
Anchorin paused a moment as if looking for the right words.
"Kenny, there is a certain amount of risk in sending out the energy, as it comes from somewhere and runs in a line to it's destination, and the renegades can latch onto that," Anchorin explained, "I shall do my part in sending out energy to you and the others with Rhianah, but I won't attract attention, as I have other sources which can give you that energy, as and when you need it. Don't ask me, but it will be apparent at the given moment! Don't forget the violet flame, and the note chanting to rebuff any renegades! Well, that's all I can tell you! You can both go now."
"Thank you Anchorin," answered Kenny, "come on Jadeir!"

"It is I who really needs to thank you all, for without you, we'd have little chance of getting anything to happen," replied Anchorin.
"Can I ask you, if, when we return home, how we can synchronise with Rhianah's time period Anchorin?" asked Kenny.
"Don't worry about that, for each time period is different and I find Rhianah's time period runs a bit slower than mine, but just ask the crystals to synchronise to her time, and they'll adjust accordingly."

Kenny took a dose of his blue mist plant tincture, and said farewell before they both disappeared, and then reappeared in the healing room at Plas Myrddin.
"I haven't thought of an explanation to Bertha yet!" remarked Kenny, and they darted upstairs.
"You might not have to if they set their return time for today!" remarked Jadeir with a mischievous look.
"Yes Jadeir, but we won't be able to watch everything they do if they aren't there," answered Kenny, "it still seems unimaginable how they can return so much sooner than the allotted time they've spent elsewhere!"
"They might return in time to see what they did?" replied Jadeir, "though I think they won't return like that somehow. They'll just return chronologically."

Everything looked the same as they had left it. Kenny and Jadeir had returned to the time period just an hour or two after they left for Anchorin's. Kenny glanced at the washing up bowl full of dishes and he immediately thought of Karin.
"It seems strange without the others," he said a bit gloomily.
"Come on Kenny, let's get the crystals set up and we can go through what we have to do," said Jadeir, "can I use your laptop?"
"Yes, certainly," replied Kenny, "I'll make us a cup of tea while you're preparing, Jadeir."
He busied himself around the sink, washing the pots while waiting for the kettle to boil, reaching for the biscuit box afterwards, and brought everything to the table.

"Here Kenny, I've just got Rhianah here!" said Jadeir.
Kenny came over quickly and saw Karin, Rhianah and the others on the computer screen.
"We're just about to set off now Kenny," said Karin, looking intently at Kenny.

"What are the natives like there?" asked Kenny.
"Not as polite as in the past, and glad they didn't see us, many behave like a milder form of renegade," replied Karin.
"Well, go carefully dear, and don't forget to use the crystal chant," advised Kenny, "I wish I was there to look after you!"
"Hudlath is very efficient, don't worry," Karin said, "but we are setting off now, dear."
Rhianah's face reappeared in front of Jadeir's crystal again.
"You may not see much of us because of the blue mist, but we will send telepathic insights when you tune in," said Rhianah, "and you shall know by my glowing crystal, when we can show it, that we are doing fine. May the divine energy be with you."
"And with you all. We'll continue to link in, and will send the energy continually," replied Kenny and Jadeir together.
"We are intending to keep looking in on you all the time and send our crystals' energy," commented Jadeir, "but will switch off a moment initially, to ensure we've chosen the best place for our communication's in the flat."

"Shall we keep this communication set up here or in another room Kenny?" asked Jadeir, having ceased communications with Rhianah.
"If we have to keep an eye on it all the time, maybe the best place is here," said Kenny, "where we can eat, sit and do what's necessary. I don't think I'd want to be stuck in the bedroom at length."
"Right!" said Jadeir, "I'll just leave it here, facing the door, so we're ready for anyone entering the flat, and they'd just see the computer screen and not the crystals behind it, which we'll cover up!"
"Good thinking, Jadeir!" replied Kenny.

Rhianah, Hudlath, Alyssia, Karin, Sarah and the four nature spirits bundled up a good supply of food each to last them a couple of days, as well as the generous supply of the amaranth, elixir and blue mist tinctures, and they also had plenty of amaranth leaves and seeds to take, to eke out the food supply longer and serve as a healer if required.
Rhianah beckoned everyone to gather round in her temple room.

Once invisible, they set off together, venturing from the house. "Under no circumstances must we get separated," said Hudlath emphatically, "it will get too complicated and dangerous."

"We must try to get onto some form of transport," said Rhianah, "how about the transseater, as we're past the rush hour?"
"Let's go then!" agreed Hudlath swiftly, "where do you get it from, and will it go all the way to our destination?"
"No unfortunately," replied Rhianah, "we will have to change to another just over half way. We can get it across the street and around to the left."

Unlike Rhianah's house, most houses were unkempt, grey buildings, with what looked like a layer of cement over the whole surface and small windows. Most had their gardens concreted over, unlike Rhianah, who had a high hawthorn hedge, behind which, she grew herbs, vegetables, and of course all the neighbours thought she was odd, but she was polite and friendly with them all despite that.
Rhianah and the group all had clothing appropriate to this time period, which was totally different from Anchorin's time. They had to wear dark grey tunics and trousers or skirts, with a black cloak down to just past the knees. Many wore their hair mid length, just down to the shoulders and often tied back. This was the time period when control by crystals was beginning to manifest. The priests had headbands with quartz crystals on, programmed to control others. When there were wars or skirmishes, they would don helmets like those that Karin, Alyssia and Sarah had seen in the scrying crystal when they first opened the casket.

"It's a relief that we are invisible and can communicate without being heard," said Karin to Sarah.
"It certainly is," replied Sarah, "and that we can all see each other while we are invisible to others. It's a great advantage."
"The transseater should be here any time now," said Rhianah, instinctively looking around to check no one was going to bump into them.
Suddenly a vehicle appeared; it was a bit larger than a hoverbuggy, though it was running along the ground. It careered around a corner further up the road, and hurtled speedily down towards them.
"Get out of the way quick!" shouted Rhianah telepathically; "they drive crazy around here!"
Everyone jumped out of the way in time and the nature spirits had simply flown upwards; Sarah and Karin picked themselves up off the ground.
"I just hope someone gets off the transseater here," said Rhianah, "we'll all have to cram on somehow and it could be tricky. If it doesn't work and we all can't get on together, whoever got on must try to get off at the next stop and we'll catch you up."

"Don't worry, I'll jam my staff in front of the door!" said Hudlath with a mischievous glint in his eyes, which made everyone smile.
"Oh look! Here comes a transseater now, let's hope it stops!" said Rhianah.
The vehicle did stop and it opened its doors. Luckily the person who wanted to get off was lame and hobbled slowly to the door. However, Hudlath placed his staff by the door while the others in the group leapt on silently and found empty seats, and he followed.
"It's great getting something for free for a change," said Sarah with a chuckle, and they all exchanged a grin.

Hudlath gave Rhianah a nudge after several stops, because two people had got on who had an inquisitive air. They approached the seats of Rhianah's group and everyone was poised ready to move, in case the people chose their seats to sit on. The two people stared intently towards the group and then went to sit down behind them.
Hudlath, Rhianah and the others looked at each other suspiciously. Hudlath emulated a zipped up mouth and cast his eyes backwards, so everyone kept silent for the rest of the journey.

On approaching the last but one stop, a number of people rose to get off, and as the two suspicious people didn't move, Rhianah motioned for the group to quickly alight too.
"Phew! I'm glad to get off that transseater!" said Rhianah, "those men were making me feel very uncomfortable. I'm sure they sensed us."
"I think so too, so we'll have to be very careful," agreed Hudlath, "there are a few priests and their followers who still use their psychic powers."
"As I don't travel far from home, I haven't seen such activities first hand," commented Rhianah, "Guyanah told me that those who were psychic are employed by the authorities, and were infiltrating people's lives increasingly, so freedom is being constantly curtailed. As well as that, Guyanah told me that crystals are beginning to be implanted into people on a regular basis where she lives, now."
The others looked at her with concern, and mutually understood that things would inevitably worsen.

They walked on down some streets, and the houses and apartments were all the same dull grey colour, with small windows. They turned off down a small side alley so that Rhianah could contact her friend. She activated her crystal and it lit up, and immediately after that Hudlath warned her he could see those two men passing the end of the alley, and she hid the crystal again. Rhianah indicated a detour that would take them around the two men and in the direction that they wanted to go. They all tiptoed along as quietly and as speedily as they could, down a winding lane with those dark grey buildings looming closely either side; even Leannah and her group looked around apprehensively. Sarah had an uneasy feeling and tried to catch Rhianah's attention without sending verbal thoughts, and Alyssia brought out her crystal, for she'd seen a group of renegades and knew they could easily be discovered.

Rhianah turned to look and saw their urgent expressions, and immediately knew their thoughts. She pointed to her crystal and then her mouth. Everyone understood its meaning, to do the disappearing chant. They all duly chanted the notes and disappeared swiftly. In their wake, waves of energy moved like ripples folding in on themselves, rather than dispersing, which lessened their chance of being detected. They linked with the violet flame, as it meant that Anchorin would perceive the group, and their progress, and he could tell Zanadar. Kenny and Jadeir would still be sending out energy to the group via the crystals, and the group could perceive that energy from their crystals periodically.

The travellers could now move around trouble free, and boarded another transseater until the designated stopping point. They alighted, knowing that Guyanah's flat was only streets away, and saw a group of renegades directly ahead of them.
"Don't attract their attention," advised Hudlath, "because sometimes the chant's protection can stop working, and 'just when you thought you were safe', as they say in your time period," he said, looking directly at Sarah, Alyssia and Karin, "you find you aren't! I witnessed someone who was safely invisible who shouted something rude at a group of renegades. He reappeared before them, and with the shock, he couldn't defend himself quickly enough."

"Guyanah's flat is further along this road," instructed Rhianah, and they followed her until she stopped to cross the road.
The road traffic increased rather than lessened in intensity.
"Remember that you can't be seen!" reminded Hudlath with a wry smile, "can anyone in the Rhaeadr group hover? I know the nature spirits and Rhianah can do it."
They indicated that they couldn't, so Hudlath began to explain how.

"Right! You must concentrate on your crystals. Point them towards the ground and ask to be lifted."
Everyone pointed their crystals downwards, and saw beams of light coming from the crystals towards the ground. Hudlath, Rhianah and the Rhaeadr group lifted up immediately. The Oswestry group also concentrated hard and began to lift up too. Once they were all about eight feet high Hudlath instructed again.
"Picture the crystal propelling you forwards while pointing it down," he said.
They were all able to move across over the mass of moving vehicles, and safely landed on the other side of the road, and Hudlath smiled happily.
"It's up this small lane!" announced Rhianah.
They began to walk up the steep winding route, until they could hear voices further ahead, and they all glanced at each other again. They soon stopped in their tracks, as another group of renegades were visible ahead of them.
"I hope they haven't gone to Guyanah's flat," said Rhianah anxiously.
They walked to where the flat stood. Renegades were everywhere. The group squeezed past them and walked inside the flat and went upstairs. To Rhianah's horror, the door was wide open and the belongings inside were strewn around. They entered to the chaotic interior.
"She's been taken!" said Rhianah, looking at Hudlath.
"Let's see if there's any clues," said Hudlath, "anything that would give her away, or even a coded message for us to interpret."
They searched around and found nothing. Guyanah was well able to disguise her identity as a priestess, and was very able to operate without too many gadgets and accessories.
"It's serious if they've found her out, at least on one count," said Rhianah sadly.
"It was always risky living very close to the portal," replied Hudlath, "ideally, she should have operated a bit further away."
"But it has been very necessary, for without her help, the passage to the colonies wouldn't have been possible," commented Rhianah, "she said she had a micro plan of some renegade top secrets."
Rhianah began rummaging through all of Guyanah's belongings.
Hudlath told everyone to focus upon where this micro plan was.
"It's under a piece of furniture, stuck to the underside!" said Alyssia.
"You're right!" agreed Rhianah, "now I can see that too," and the nature spirits confirmed that as well.

They all hunted around for the appropriate piece of furniture, and all
gravitated in the bedroom, towards a chest of drawers, which was shaped
like half a hexagon in plan view.

"As we can't move objects in our present state, except what we are
carrying," commented Hudlath, "I'll record the evidence!"

He got out a gadget, which was rectangular with an extending arm, and it
had a dial on the end of it. He slid the device under the chest of drawers
and manoeuvred it around until a purple light glowed, and then he
pressed a purple button on the dial and the device clicked, and then he
brought the gadget out and put it away.

"There we are! My trusty spying eye machine never fails!" said Hudlath
with a half smile.

"Can we remove the evidence from the chest of drawers, so it can't be
found?" asked Rhianah.

"Yes I can," replied Garalph, "are you ready for the blast?" and he looked
at Hudlath and Rhianah, who nodded, and Garalph went ahead. There
was a small puff of smoke and some black fragments descended from the
underside of the chest, but they were soon dissolved.

Immediately, they heard footsteps returning up the stairs, and they all
looked at each other and ran out of the bedroom. It was too late, for a
couple of renegades with suspicious expressions had re-entered the flat
and were searching around intently. They came straight to the bedroom.
Hudlath and the others pressed their backs against the wall, stock still and
barely breathing. The renegades came extremely close to where Alyssia
and Karin stood, and they paused there, within inches of the two women.
The renegades were listening for movements. They wandered over to the
corner where Hudlath and everyone had been standing a moment ago,
which then gave the group a chance to escape.

There was a frustrated cry from one of the renegades as they had
discovered the chest of drawers with the burnt area underneath, still
slightly warm. Meanwhile, Hudlath and the others had reached the
bottom of the lane, and were heading towards the portal.

"We'll be able to see it after a few more streets, as it's just over the brow
of that hill," explained Rhianah.

"By the way, what's the micro plan about?" asked Hudlath, with a quizzical
look.

"It includes a code to enter the portal," explained Rhianah, "we have to
know it by heart and visualise it strongly, but very quickly, so that we
aren't detected by the renegades while we are saying it."

As they approached the brow of the hill, they were able to see the huge wall around the portal, which had a pyramid structure straddling the whole of the walled off area. It housed a vast energy field, which rose vertically, right out into deep space, and was about half a mile wide. The pyramid originally had a translucent cover on it but was eventually replaced by a dense, grey material, not unlike a cross between slate and concrete, Hudlath told the others later, when transiting through the vortex.

"There are four gates, with a group of renegade guards at each," explained Rhianah, "but we have added advantages."
"That we can fly over the walls, as well as be invisible!" responded Alyssia.
"When do we use the code?" asked Karin.
"When we approach the portal itself," explained Rhianah, "because usually people are checked in are tagged, but as we aren't, then we need to use the code. The only serious drawback is that we must reverse the chant before we go over the portal wall, as our bodies won't be compatible with the energy system of the portal."
Everyone looked concerned, except Hudlath, who knew about it already, having been acquainted with the Colonies.
"Can we sit down a moment, I need to eat something," said Karin.
"There's a seat over there in an alcove," said Maraya, "we can stop here and do everything that's necessary."
"It's a good spot, and we'll practice the code too," agreed Rhianah. They all sat down, except the nature spirits, who flew up to the tops of nearby buildings and kept watch there.
"The easiest way to learn," said Hudlath, getting his photographic device out, "is to get out your crystal, hold it in your left hand, as that will enhance your intuitive capacities. Point the crystal to my device here, and then ask for the crystal to send the information to your mind, and it will do so rapidly. You will find that you know it!"
The nature spirits zoomed to ground level to join in with the exercise, and all looked happily at each other. They all achieved that task, and then ate some food.
"I'll send a message to Jadeir," said Rhianah.
"I suppose we'd better, even though the present turn of events will be an extra worry," commented Hudlath.
"I'll just say that we're going over the wall, and not mention about Guyanah's disappearance," replied Rhianah, and Hudlath winked in agreement.

Rhianah activated her crystal after instinctively looking around. She spoke to Jadeir, informing him of their imminent intent to travel through the vortex. He wished them luck and to contact them when they returned.

"We shall do our chanting now," said Rhianah, "and then walk down to the vortex wall, recite the code and use the crystals to levitate us over the top."

"Once we are over the top," continued Hudlath, "we need to look out for a transship, which will take us to the relevant Colony Y, the ship will have a large Y printed on the side of it."

They chanted the necessary notes in reverse, and the stirring in the atmosphere came as a result. The humans took more blue mist plant as the others didn't need to, and all set off, and the timing was fortunate as three people were approaching the seat.

As they walked downhill together Hudlath glanced over to the distant hills that were now visible. The others followed suit, and they saw a familiar sight. There stood a mountain, with its summit immersed in clouds, and they all felt a strangely nostalgic feeling, which also seemed unreal.

"I'm afraid it isn't as it used to be," said Hudlath, a little grimly, and the others looked at him and understood, finding no words to say. It was Leannah who nudged them all, beckoning them to come, which broke their reverie, and kept them moving onwards.

Near the base of the hill, there was a convenient group of buildings, and they stopped there to survey the wall at close quarters. They looked at each other and agreed silently. Each of them recited their codes quietly, and then pointed their crystals downwards without taking them out of their pockets, and rose effortlessly upwards and began to float towards the wall. As they were almost over the wall, a large beast appeared out of a hole at the base of the wall and proceeded to leap upwards by about ten feet. Everyone had to rise upwards accordingly to miss the burning breath it projected, and afterwards the others perceived a faint thought-image of burnt toast around Hudlath's head that he conveyed to them, which humoured everyone. They all then flew through an open doorway in the side of the pyramid structure into the complex.

What greeted them the other side was a huge rabble of renegades, and their ally Atlanteans who worked with them. Hudlath looked at Rhianah, and then all the others. They realised then, that Hudlath was wordlessly informing them all that the renegades were organising another group to go to the colonies. They could see a crowd of people herded together ahead of them. The group all landed gently where they could find a space, and headed for the group going to Colony Y.

There was a lot of panicky jostling, of people trying to avoid being accosted by the renegades and their Atlantean 'servants', which was a polite term, but they were usually called 'the Allegiance of Lethe' or 'Lethe Lackeys'. Rhianah craned her neck, looking around intently. Hudlath knew she was searching for Guyanah, and eyed the group knowingly. There were sudden movements in the crowd as the renegades were pushing people towards a transship, which had opened its doors now. Rhianah and the others tried to avoid being squashed, and had to levitate themselves over the heads of the crowd most of the time to avoid being crushed, and then swoop into the craft deftly during that time, or else they would have had the doors shut in their faces. They found a corner to crouch in during the flight.

The engines pounded, and the ship took off vertically at speed, and they all felt the G force effects initially for about a minute. Then the energy of the vortex took over and there was a huge rush of energy, and realised that the ship was moving along at vast speeds without anyone feeling any effects whatsoever, which astonished most of the group. Maraya had her eyes closed for about half an hour, and when she opened them again she spoke telepathically.
"Guyanah is on this vessel!" she whispered, "on the deck below."
Rhianah looked at Maraya approvingly and indicated that they'll look for her when they would arrive, by thought impression.
"We'll have to be quick," advised Hudlath, "the renegades are extremely organised," and he impressed the idea into everyone's minds to give Guyanah some of the tinctures if they saw her, and to anyone else she'd met who would be interested, in order to escape.
Despite their brief exchanges conducted as subtly as possible, it attracted attention and the group heard the resolute footsteps of the renegades approaching. Everyone looked at each other and telepathically linked together that they should move very quickly! They walked briskly down the corridor to their left. It was tricky as renegades came from all angles.

Just when it looked like they would be found out, there were the sounds of a commotion downstairs, and some of the renegades departed. There was a loud noise coming from the other side of the remaining renegades, and they hurried off to investigate that. Meanwhile, the group safely departed, and they found another enclave on the far side of the ship. Hudlath looked very pleased with himself, and wordlessly implied something to Rhianah. She started smiling too, and so the thought impression circulated that Hudlath had developed a capacity for creating noisy diversion tactics, by conjuring up an invisible entity that could make loud noises, and he had subsequently dissipated the entity with another thought once the renegades had almost found it. They took it in turns to get some sleep, as once the group were on the Colony, resting would be the last thing on their minds.

Kenny now kept watch over lunchtime, while Jadeir made them something to eat. He was glad it was a day when Bertha took over in the afternoon. Kenny could see the group's movements easily, and even though he could see that they had taken the blue mist tincture, which made them invisible, he could see a fainter image of them, and it was the effect of the two crystals, enabling more visibility than usual. The group were now on the second trans-seater, travelling to their destination, secured by their invisibility. Kenny watched as the streaming energy from both his and Jadeir's crystals crossed through the barriers of time towards the group. It sustained a field of protective force for them as they progressed.

When Kenny's concentration flagged, Jadeir immediately took over, impressing his thought on the crystals to continue to project the good protective energy. Jadeir could also perceive that it surrounded them in a cushion, which would act as a catalyst to maintain the group's energy levels once on the colonies, where the environment was likely to drain their energy and transmission pretty effectively. Jadeir knew that the more the group absorbed now, they would be well prepared for what was to come, and contact would be less effective once they entered the vortex.

Jadeir brought the meal to the table, and handed a plate to Kenny, and they both began to eat. Kenny was still watching the screen and ate slowly. There was a clatter of a fork being dropped, and Jadeir turned to see Kenny's expression.
"There's loads of renegades around Guyanah's flat!" exclaimed Kenny, "it must be, as the group are entering the building now."
Jadeir came over swiftly to see, and they both sent out large amounts of the crystal's energy.
"Watch out Kenny!" warned Jadeir, "don't attract the renegades' attention!"

Kenny sent energy directly to the group as they entered the flat and they wandered around, and then especially when he saw renegades re-entering to search Guyanah's flat again. Jadeir joined in too now, and sent out his effervescent radiance, which contributed greatly, so that the group were able to escape totally undetected. Kenny lingered a split second to see what the renegades would do next and then returned to link with the group, when a strange contraction of the forces sent out started

happening. Kenny and Jadeir saw the familiar intense dark eyes of the character who had been pursuing Sarah and Maraya. The face manifested in the living room. Jadeir ran to confront the person and shot a green light at the man's face, and he cried out, and then disappeared.
"That'll stop him for a while," said Jadeir.
"Thanks Jadeir, I was way behind with that one!" replied Kenny, "trouble is, he and his mates know where we are now."
"Yes, but they have me to contend with!" responded Jadeir boldly.
"Do you mind if I finish my tea, Jadeir?" Kenny requested.
"All right my friend," smiled Jadeir, and he speedily came to the crystal and continued the distribution of energy again, while Kenny ate.
"Ah! It's Rhianah, Kenny," exclaimed Jadeir, and Kenny rushed over to see, chewing a last mouthful, "everyone over there is doing well."
"We are just about to fly over the portal wall," said Rhianah confidently, "and we are doing well here, and will be on Colony Y within about and hour or so after take off."
"Is Guyanah all right, as we saw the renegades at her flat?" asked Jadeir.
"We'll find her, don't worry, she may be on the ship!" Rhianah replied briskly.
Rhianah angled the crystal so that the rest of the group could see Kenny and Jadeir, and they waved to each other, and then Rhianah switched off her crystal.
"They're going now, and shall be ascending over the wall within about ten minutes I'd say," said Jadeir.
"Let me know when they're about to do it and I'll come and watch," replied Kenny, "I'm just going to wash up."

"They're going now Kenny!" shouted Jadeir, and Kenny rushed over.
"Hey, they're a bit more visible, you don't think they had to reverse the chant?" asked Kenny, looking quite anxious.
"It looks like it Kenny," responded Jadeir, "they must have done it after talking to us. It didn't seem to register with our crystals, that's funny."
"I wonder if Hudlath had anything to do with that?" said Kenny.
Jadeir eyed him, "you could be right there. Perhaps they wanted to avoid worrying us, but we found out anyway." Jadeir pondered a moment, "yes, they did it to enable them to travel in the portal."
"Look at that dragon! It's a monster all right!" cried Kenny, "and hey, there's that portal pyramid, it certainly doesn't look as good now!"
"They're over safely. Keep the energy going, crystals!" said Jadeir. They both watched the group hovering around until they found an entrance

within the pyramid's structure. They watched the group get onto the transship, and take off initially. The image went blurred as the ship took off, ascending into the path of the vortex's power, and then they both looked at each other sadly.

There was a polite knock at the door, and Kenny went to open it. There stood a figure attired with long robes.
"I hope you don't mind me calling," the man said politely, "Anchorin told me this crystal was left in the temple, and that it needed to be brought to a man called Kenny."
"I am Kenny, thank you. Won't you come in a minute?" he asked.
"I'd better return as there are many things to do, especially with the essence jar removed, for we have to maintain the equilibrium. I do know that this is a gatekeeper crystal, and will be of vital importance to you!"
"Thank you very much, it is much appreciated," answered Kenny, and he smiled cheerfully at the priest.
The priest smiled back and Kenny watched him vanish on the stairwell, as he descended to go. Kenny shut the door and brought the crystal to put with the others.
"Oh, Costillo's crystal," commented Jadeir, "my jewels of jade! It's a big one!" he said, turning the crystal over in his hand and then placed it with the other two again and activated it swiftly. It was soon transmitting good energy to the group as the other two were doing.

Kenny finished the washing up, and was just wiping his hands when there was a strange crashing sound, which echoed around the room. Jadeir's eyes became alert.
"Take over Kenny, it may be renegades!" cried Jadeir.
Kenny swapped positions with Jadeir just as three angry faces half materialised in the living room, and then two more by the door to the flat. Jadeir pointed towards the three and pelted them with the energy, and with a green crackling explosion they went, and then he did the same to the others just as they were advancing rapidly.
"They're going to be persistent, Kenny!" stated Jadeir.
"Maybe we'd better take turns in sleeping in here on the sofa," said Kenny.
"They hadn't reckoned on us having three crystals though!" smiled Jadeir, and Kenny gave a thumbs up. He went over to a cupboard and returned to the computer with a tin.
"Chocolate biscuits," said Jadeir, "what an idea!"

"A good one I'd say," remarked Kenny, "we'll need plenty of fodder to keep us going."
"I can continue watching if you want to sleep Kenny," suggested Jadeir, in-between munches.
"Ok, I feel quite tired. We could swap shifts every two to three hours?" suggested Kenny, and Jadeir gave an approving look, "as long as you don't nibble all my biscuits!"
"As if I would!" replied Jadeir, with an innocent expression.
Kenny went off to get a spare duvet from a cupboard in his and Karin's room, and also returned with the fairy gem he was given in Rhaeadr. He settled on the sofa with the gem in his pocket and was soon asleep.

The group watched as everyone was bundled off the transship, and they managed to squeeze their way past the other occupants. Karin accidentally stood on the foot of one of the renegades, who were standing by the exit door, but the individual didn't realise who it was in all the scuffle, and she had to suppress an urge to laugh despite the seriousness of the situation. Once free of the ship and exit area, the group could extricate themselves from the crush of the desperate minded people, who were now being herded forwards forcibly towards a group of towering dark grey buildings. Rhianah, Hudlath and the others looked at each other, and they all instantly knew that the buildings were factories and places of forced labour. They saw other slightly lower buildings and knew that they were the sleeping quarters.

Alyssia cast her eyes upwards and drew attention for the group to do the same, unsure as yet if any unguarded thoughts on the Colony would be instantly identified, and would attract unwanted attention. As the others did so, they saw Zanadar's face smiling at them, and also those of Melkior and Aurion accompanying him. They all received an intuitive flash that Zanadar and the others would tell them where the disks were held, and they became very attentive. The group then withdrew some distance away from the unfortunate Atlanteans who were being prodded and pushed around, and then goaded over to the factory building. The group could see that the atmosphere of the planet was deeply affecting the Atlanteans already and they looked tired and dull eyed. Zanadar pointed over to another large building to the left side of the factory, and indicated that the disks were at the back of it, and on the top floor.

Hudlath smiled, and everyone was of one mind to go and investigate immediately. Zanadar told them that the tranships ran frequently, and there would be one returning to Atlantis through the vortex in about five hours time.
The group sped over to the indicated building, knowing that they wouldn't be able to do the crystal chant again here, as it would draw attention to themselves, and they needed to be physically present to accomplish their tasks. The door to the building was locked, as expected, and only a key code system would allow entry. They decided to wait for someone to come and enter the building, so they could observe the code. Someone duly came, and then two renegades entered. Hudlath tried the code of the first person, pressing the symbolic buttons, and then the door unlocked and they all entered, except for Garalph, who decided to keep on lookout duty. He intended to conjure up energies to help delay any outcomes, should there be any threat involved.

The remaining group crept up the stairwell up to the top floor. Zanadar indicated to turn left down a long corridor past many rooms. The group could hear people talking inside various rooms, and behind one door there was a very heated discussion going on. Several renegades burst out of the door in a scuffle, which meant that the group had to press themselves against the wall and slip past as swiftly as possible, though one renegade had collided with Sarah and she felt as if something had dislocated in her shoulder, as her face was screwed up in pain. The nature spirits naturally cast a bright green light, unseen to the renegades in the dull atmosphere, which was a protection for them all.

They followed Zanadar's directions down another corridor and around to another door with a key coded system on it. Kavanos the faun approached Sarah and pressed his hand on her shoulder and let out some of that bright green light to heal it. Sarah's shoulder immediately healed and her face showed an expression of relief and amazement and Kavanos smiled. Hudlath banged on the door with his staff and an Atlantean came to the door with a suspicious look, as he peered through it and saw nothing there. The group rushed inside and the Atlantean felt himself being pushed aside, and he teetered against the door with astonishment. He then recovered his composure and started rushing towards an alarm button, but Hudlath anticipated that in time and pushed the man's arm away with his staff, and wrestled with him, the man swinging wild punches at invisibility, while Hudlath hit him until he had successfully knocked him out.

Zanadar pointed to the cabinet he had mentioned previously in Anchorin's temple meeting room, so Alyssia, Karin and Sarah rushed over to it, while Rhianah, Maraya and Hudlath kept guard, for there were other connecting doors off that room, other than the entrance door. The cabinet was locked, as only to be expected, but Melkior came forward as he knew about locking mechanisms on other planets. He indicated to pass a hand over the lock in a clockwise direction, with the index and second finger straight, and held together, and the third and fourth fingers curled up. They heard a whirring inside the cabinet and a tiny door they hadn't noticed before opened up. It had a tiny keypad inside it, and Melkior said the code changed every hour, and he gave the appropriate symbols for that occasion, and Karin pressed the keys and the door flew open. There were shelves of disks of varying sizes, and Melkior's expression was amazement at the sight. Aurion came and looked, he concentrated for a moment, as he was searching for the right disks. He indicated the right choice by encircling them with a silvery light. Alyssia picked them out and handed them to Sarah who put them in her bag.

They closed the cabinet doors and Melkior instructed how to reseal up the locks. They went over to Hudlath and the others, and then exited the building before the Atlantean guard began to recover. The group heard the alarm bell ringing as they ran off to look for the Moroccan group. Zanadar indicated to the factory and the group sped over to the door, and by this time Garalph was reunited with them again. Hudlath had turned to see him and smiled broadly when he noticed that Garalph had tripped up a couple of renegades as they'd ran out of the exit door of the building. The two of them were arguing with each other, each accusing the other of the tricky deed.

There was yet another keypad on the factory door and Gadair blasted it with some green light, making Hudlath start a little, and he gave Gadair a wry look. The door opened and they entered with ease. At first they thought it strange that no one had noticed their dramatic entrance, but the Atlanteans were hard at work making new tranships. There were endless conveyer belts, people compiling various parts of the ships, with plenty of cutting, welding and banging going on. The renegades were too busy fiercely shouting and goading everyone to work faster and harder, that the group realised now, that they couldn't have heard them at all, and a small explosion was as nothing to the entire deafening clamour in this factory. Gadair had already known that before they had entered the soundproofed building, even if the humans in the group were unaware.

The group were now looking intently for the Moroccans as well as Guyanah, and had to search through the whole factory, only to realise that they must be off duty, so they exited through where they entered and wandered over to the sleeping quarters. Yet more keypads and Hudlath restrained Gadair's enthusiasm for blasting it inactive this time. Melkior linked with Hudlath to give the relevant coding and they entered silently. They wondered at the lack of guards at the doors, but then realised why when they saw a couple of Atlanteans shuffling to the bathroom, for they looked very comatose as if drugged. The group knew it was the waters of Lethe that were administered regularly when they stopped for food and drink. Garalph stayed by the entrance door on lookout duty again.

The group hurried along, gently opening and shutting doors until Zanadar linked in to say which room he had found them in. The group opened the relevant door gently to see five beds in a row, as in all the rooms, with barely enough space to move. There lay the three Moroccans, their faces sunken and weary. They looked strangely small upon the Atlantean sized beds. Maraya had a few tears in her eyes, but went forward to Costillo with her elixir tincture in hand. She put her hand on his shoulder, and as he didn't rouse, she gave him quite a shake. He looked around, frowned, and opened his mouth to yawn, and Maraya whispered gently in his ear.
"It's Maraya here," she said and swiftly put some tincture in his mouth while he was yawning. "Elixir tincture Costillo," she continued, "for we are here to rescue you all."
Costillo looked puzzled and dazed, trying to rouse himself out of his trance state.
"Maraya?" he asked with a confused look, as if trying to remember.
"Have an amaranth leaf Costillo, it will help you to remember," she said, and encouraged him to take and eat it.
He started to chew, and as he did so, a tear rolled down his cheek as it began to counteract the drugged Lethe water. His body began to grow larger now, little by little, and his eyes began to look alert again. Meanwhile Sarah, Alyssia, Karin and Hudlath were administering the elixir tincture and amaranth leaves to the other four occupants.

Costillo now had full recall, as did the other four. Maraya reached for his hands and he caught hold of them, and they hugged each other even though Costillo and his fellow inmates couldn't see the group yet.

"We must save as many of the other people here as we can, because the vortex will close to the Colonies once we return home," whispered Maraya to Costillo and the others.

"We must hurry to get the tincture and amaranth leaves to everyone else in the block," added Hudlath.

"Hudlath is a high priest, and I have many friends with me," explained Maraya to Costillo and the others, you'll see them later once we give you the blue mist plant, but for now, could you give the others the herbs since you are all visible."

"Maraya dear, and others," said Costillo, and he looked briefly around him, "there would be others in the block who would betray us for they've been here too long, they're too drugged, it's risky. We do have some friends however, though we had all strangely forgotten about each other in this state," and he turned to look at the other occupants, "Danuel, you get Gario; Sagario, you get Petros and Stephano; Golilio, you get Kalaph and Salena; and Kenaph, you get your friends Ellaia and Kyrian. I'll get Feredino and Elania. Bring them here!" and they all rushed off swiftly with a bunch of amaranth leaves each, and left without a sound.

The group remained there, and the nature spirits created a green protective light around the building to secure it. Then the door to Costillo's room opened and the three Moroccans and the other two then returned with the other eight people.

"Those amaranth leaves are wonderful, it was as if I was awakening from a bad dream," said Feredino, "can we not save any more people?"

"It's risky my friend, it could jeopardise our escape!" responded Costillo.

An urgent thought from Garalph to act quickly was transmitted to the group, and soon after there was a sound at the entrance door.

"Oh no! A shift change already! Can we disappear?" asked Costillo quickly, "Maraya, blue mist plant!"

Maraya swiftly got out her tincture, as did the others, and they helped to give everyone a dose.

"We must get out when it's expedient, for the renegades will come in every room and get us up. If we aren't there, they'll be all over the place searching," explained Costillo anxiously.

"Best thing is to stand by the door and wait for them to pass by, and then escape out then," explained Sagario.

The group rushed for the door, and held themselves against the wall, though most were pressed into an alcove area.
"Get up, lazy bones!" yelled a renegade entering the door, and he turned to look in the group's direction with such deliberate concentration that Hudlath thought that they'd been identified, but then he moved on towards the sleeping quarters. Once people were found to be missing, then there was a commotion.

Meanwhile, all twenty-three of them managed to get out of the building undetected, to sounds of "search everywhere until they're found!" The renegades emptied the sleeping quarters, and the occupants were made to line up in rows awaiting inspection. Their garments had numerical identification, which was tattooed on the back and also on their forearms. The renegades would tick off these numbers, having wandered along looking at people's backs, and took great pleasure in creeping up behind someone, and bellowing at them when the poor unfortunate individual was least expecting anything. Some brave people in the row behind would shuffle their feet to indicate a warning, but the renegades caught on to that and stopped it with extra strong doses of Lethe water.

"The next flight leaves in about three hours according to Zanadar," whispered Rhianah, "and we must find Guyanah."
"Yes, also where those people went, who came off our ship," said Sarah, "somewhere in the factory's direction.
Aurion's shining silvery blue face with bird-like feathery fronds coming from the back of his head appeared in front of them and indicated that she had been taken to a building further on and behind the factory.
"Let's go!" said Hudlath, and they moved swiftly past the factory. There were extremely tall control tower buildings like sentinel posts. The group could see, from that vantage point that the whole of Colony Y would be totally under surveillance. Under the dark grey gloomy skies, the group wandered over to three buildings behind the factory. Aurion's face indicated to go into the furthest building. A group of renegades were talking in the entrance and so the group hovered silently nearby, waiting for them to move on.

Hudlath and the others realised that this was the reception building for newcomers. At a suitable moment when the renegades went back inside, Hudlath indicated for everyone to stay outside, and only himself, Rhianah and Maraya would go inside, since all three of them knew Guyanah. Karin, Alyssia and Sarah were to stay with the others, and their crystals would protect them. He also asked Gadair to accompany him, and for the other nature spirits to remain behind with the others.

Hudlath, the two women and Gadair swiftly went inside, whilst the remainder withdrew to an area nearby, where a building had become dilapidated and no one was likely to frequent that area. Once indoors, Hudlath, Rhianah, Maraya and Gadair looked around and at each other, for they all intuitively knew where Guyanah would be simultaneously. Aurion confirmed that they were going in the right direction. They wandered down endless corridors as fast as they could, until they came to a door, and Melkior linked in to give them the entry code. On entering, they saw a sea of faces ahead, ringed by renegades.
'Lethe water!' thought Hudlath, and looked at everyone intently.
Everyone realised that the first doses of Lethe water were being administered. They looked at each other with concern when they realised that the Atlantean hostages at the front of the room were being forced to take the water and then led forcibly out of another door to the side. The next group of ten would then step forward. They looked around swiftly to see if Guyanah was there.

The group waited until another ten people took their place at the front, hoping to spot Guyanah's face. Still, she wasn't apparent yet, but then finally, Rhianah saw her after two more rows. Suddenly Hudlath pointed his crystal at the far end of the room and created a loud explosive bang, and a few renegades rushed over to look. The group sprung into action and seized Guyanah, who looked a bit shocked by being dragged away whilst being unable to see anyone doing it. The renegades realised that the explosion was a hoax, and returned swiftly to barge in, and they pushed Guyanah back again. There was a tug of war as Hudlath intervened to pull Guyanah away again. He struck the attacking renegades with the end of his staff and then their group ran off with Guyanah. The bemused but angry renegades cried out, and their other comrades from an adjoining room entered and began the chase. Meanwhile, Rhianah tried to give Guyanah some blue mist plant while running down the corridor. Once they were around a corner, Guyanah

stopped to take a mouthful, and then handed the tincture bottle back to Rhianah and then they ran on again. Guyanah, meanwhile, was becoming rapidly invisible and was now able to see her four helpers.
Outside the building, they attracted the attention of the rest of the group, and hurried around to the square in front of the factory. By this time sirens were going.

The transship lay ahead of them, under the pyramid, which was a replica of the one on Atlantis, and it was obviously the next vehicle to go earthwards. The group hurried over to the pyramid, and found it was sealed up, for the entrance through the wall was closed and on ascending, Hudlath saw that the doors through the pyramid and onto the transship were sealed up too.

"Kenny!" said Jadeir, giving Kenny a gentle stirring; "it's over two and a half hours now."
Kenny turned over and murmured, before slowly emerging from under the duvet, and began a series of vigorous yawns.
"I'll be awake in a minute Jadeir!" said Kenny sonorously, and Jadeir returned to the computer to keep on sending energy until Kenny was ready to take over. He was soon sitting at the screen sending crystal energy out as much as he could, and was relieved to remind himself that nature spirits required much less sleep than humans.
'I wonder how Karin is now. Have they found Costillo and the other Moroccans, and Guyanah, and what about the disks?' He pictured himself on the grey planet searching about briefly, but stopped himself abruptly to continue concentrating on the immediate requirements of sending out the energy.

There was a loud crack, and suddenly the room was full of renegades. Kenny shouted to Jadeir, who began to stir. Kenny pointed a crystal at them and sent some green light, and one of them vanished. The other renegades were bearing down on him, and Jadeir hadn't woken properly yet. Kenny suddenly remembered his fairy gem and pulled it out of his pocket. He called on the fairy kingdom, and prayed hard for it to work. Then, it was as if a mass of fairies were in the room, and were all sending a very strong green light, which filled the whole room, and there was a burst of flames, roaring fiercely. The group of renegades, who were inches away from Kenny and Jadeir, were dramatically driven back by the fiery blaze and then they disappeared from view.

Kenny breathed a huge sigh of relief, and Jadeir, now fully awake looked over to Kenny questioningly.

"Anything happen while I was asleep Kenny?" he asked.

"No Jadeir, nothing much, you can go back to sleep again, old chum," said Kenny, with his comical stare.

Jadeir gave acknowledgement and turned over again.

"Well actually, Jadeir, we did have about ten renegades a moment ago," admitted Kenny, "but I used my fairy gem on them and it worked a treat!" and he gave it a little polish, while still concentrating on sending out the energy with the three crystals.

Jadeir turned back over again and looked at Kenny with surprise.

"You mean ten renegades, in here?" replied Jadeir, wide eyed with amazement, "and you didn't tell me."

"I tried to, it was all so quick," answered Kenny, "one moment they appeared, then almost touching us, and I grabbed the fairy gem just in time. There wasn't a moment to lose, not even to wake you properly, though I did shout at you!"

Jadeir looked concerned and felt in his pocket for something. He brought out a tiny pocket watch about the size of an average wristwatch. He concentrated by staring at it and the lid sprung open, and he pointed a finger at a button.

"Next time, just call 'Jadeir's jewels!' and this watch will activate a very high frequency level that will wake me instantly."

"Got it!" replied Kenny, and he turned around in his seat to give full concentration to sending the energy again.

"By the way, what actually happened when you activated the fairy gem, Kenny?" asked Jadeir, now sitting bolt upright, "I've never seen one in action."

"On bringing out the gem from my pocket, I simply prayed hard for help, and then calling on the fairy kingdom," commented Kenny, "and then it seemed as if there were a mass of fairies in the room, and they produced this mass of green light, which burst into flames, and all the renegades simply vanished. I'm surprised you didn't notice anything, it was so powerful!"

"Wonderful," replied Jadeir, "that's just how it has been described to me. I'm so glad you had the gem with you, but I'm so sorry that I slept through it, occasionally I do go into a deep sleep, and in fact I was linking back to Atlantis just then."

Jadeir looked pleased on hearing about the gem, but his expression held a little sadness for not being awake to defend Kenny at that moment; he sat there looking thoughtful for a moment.

"I just pray that this energy is reaching the group successfully," said Kenny, with a concerned expression.

"Don't you worry," replied Jadeir, glad for an opportunity to be of some assistance, "I'll have a look into the energy direction and locate their destination.

Jadeir's eyes narrowed slightly and he concentrated hard, while Kenny still sent out the energy. His inner vision could see the energy speeding swiftly across the time barrier via Atlantis and through the vortex to Colony Y, and he could see the energy going to the group.

"Kenny!" he shouted, "I can see the energy going to them and they are alive and making their way to the ship for the return journey. The Moroccans with their friends, and Guyanah are with them too!" and Jadeir turned to look at Kenny happily.

"That's amazing! Can you show me how to do it Jadeir, what do I do?" asked Kenny.

They both asked the crystals to keep sending out the energy on autopilot for a few minutes while Jadeir gave Kenny some instructions.

"Just focus on the crystal's energy, and ask to be shown the destination of that energy," explained Jadeir.

Kenny concentrated and looked at the energy for a few moments. He then looked at Jadeir and smiled.

"I saw them too! The energy whooshed me along through the vortex and then I could see the Colony, and soon found the group. There certainly are quite a crowd of them now," replied Kenny.

"Good, you are doing well," said Jadeir, "now that we've both linked to the group visually, we can now monitor their progress more effectively."

"Why couldn't we see them before?" asked Kenny.

Jadeir paused for thought.

"I think it's because of the build up of energy that has been sent to them, as well as the power of the essence," he replied, "and now it's time you had a rest, you deserve it!"

Kenny curled up on the sofa again and instantly fell asleep, while Jadeir continued sending energy throughout the rest of the night.

Hudlath speedily looked around the perimeter of the pyramid structure, hovering to examine it carefully for a few moments here and there, and

then he moved on until he'd circumnavigated the whole structure. He returned to Rhianah, Guyanah and the others with a serious expression.
"I'm not sure how we can get through this entrance to the vortex at present. There's nothing much to see around the edge in the way of latches, locks or doorways," he explained.
"We'll go and see what we can do," responded Gadair and Garalph, "us folk can usually get through anything."
They darted off, while the others looked in all directions, anticipating danger at any minute, for a group of renegades were visible, coming round the factory walls from Guyanah's hostage site, and other renegades were coming from out of the dormitories.

Hudlath looked more concerned now, and the group looked at each other, silently communicating the same message to each other wordlessly, that the renegades would soon sense their presence. On top of the surveillance tower they now witnessed an antenna extending upwards. A device at its apex was opening out. Hudlath looked positively agitated, as did Rhianah, Guyanah and the nature spirits. Hudlath immediately concentrated on linking with Zanadar, Aurion and Melkior.

Zanadar's concerned face appeared to them.
"I've told Aurion to retrieve the spaceship to airlift you all. I must confess that we haven't lessened the vibratory level of the spacecraft to enter three-dimensional space for quite some time. It must still be possible, however, and we'll do it, though I warn you that it would only last for a very short while!"
At this Hudlath gave Zanadar a pertinent look, which Zanadar instantly understood.
"Don't worry, it should last the journey to Anchorin's temple," Zanadar affirmed with a hint of positivity.

Meanwhile, the renegades were rapidly moving in their direction, and the structure on top of the antenna revolved around slowly, like a magic eye. It was making a thorough search of the Colony, and soon would be facing them. The group hurried around to the far side of the pyramid structure to evade being spotted. The renegades were almost up to the pyramid now, and the eye was looking over to them directly now and flashed. The group ran off madly, and Karin cried out mentally, 'Kenny! Kenny!'

Kenny could hear a voice calling him. He had been in a very deep sleep, and had to force himself to wake up.

"Kenny! Come here quickly!" shouted Jadeir, with a concerned look.

Kenny leapt to the three crystals, and Jadeir had managed to get them to project an image of the group on the Colony onto the computer monitor.

"What's happening?" cried Kenny as he looked at the screen.

"The renegades know that they are there, and are chasing the group!" replied Jadeir.

"I see that the vortex is inaccessible," said Kenny, "how on earth will they get back?"

"We'll send as much energy as we can, Kenny," responded Jadeir, and both of them did their utmost. Meanwhile, they heard Karin's call of desperation to Kenny. Kenny's expression looked calm, but inside he was almost desperate himself, but speedily thought of the essence, Anchorin, and all who were helping, and sent out the bold thought of 'HOLD ON KARIN!'

Despite sending as much energy as they could, Kenny and Jadeir could only watch the desperate scene of the group weaving their way around the building complex, for there was a huge impenetrable barricade surrounding the buildings on the Colony.

Hudlath brought out his crystal, indicating that if the renegades came around the corner, he would use it. He indicated for the others to get theirs ready too, for they had run into a cul-de-sac, and were considering whether to run back out of it. Fortune was in their favour, for in their hesitation, they remained in the best position, as sounds of renegades running swiftly grew increasingly louder, and it was only a matter of moments when they would be face to face with them.

The only slight advantage Hudlath and the group had was their invisibility, and the rescuers would have used their crystal chant to become more immaterial to the present scene, but of course they couldn't leave the others behind in a defenceless state. Those who had crystals stood in front, arms outstretched and pointing their crystals in readiness. The first of the renegades turned the corner and charged. Hudlath's crystal burst with fiery energy and knocked the renegade flying. Other renegades turned the corner and the others joined in and they fell too. More and more renegades turned the corner in an unending stream. Some were firing now, but the power of the crystals' energy fields managed to stave off much of the power of the renegades' atomic weaponry. Various members of the group were being burnt by the renegades' guns, but as fast as the members of the group were shot, Gadair did his best to give instant healing in return, while the other nature spirits defended.

Then a larger group of renegades amassed an attack from windows in an adjacent building, and all fired simultaneously. Many of the group holding crystals were hit, and a number of them fell and many times over, while Gadair rushed in all directions healing their wounds, until they could get their crystals again and resume attacking the renegades. Hudlath glanced skyward fleetingly in desperation, trying to attract Zanadar's attention.
"Help is here at last, don't give up!" cried Zanadar.
The spaceship approaching Colony Y hovered over the group and materialised into a three dimensional form effectively after a couple of attempts. A brilliant shaft of light descended to the group in an instant, and lifted them into the craft before any renegades could stop them. The group could hear cries of anger from below as they had disappeared inside the craft to safety.
Kenny and Jadeir looked at each other in profound relief when they witnessed the spaceship collecting the group, and both half collapsed onto the sofa, able to relax at last.
"Our job is finally done now Jadeir," said Kenny, running his hands through his hair and then stretched, "would you care to join me for breakfast?"
"I certainly would, Mr Kenton!" replied Jadeir, "I'll make the toast."
As they were finishing off their meal, Jadeir's crystal started glowing, and he reached over to retrieve and activate it.
"Anchorin here Jadeir and Kenny," announced the cheerful looking high priest, "everyone is here, safe and well now, so come over as soon as you can, and don't forget the caskets!"
"We're just finishing our breakfast, and will come over in a few minutes, Anchorin," replied Jadeir.

Kenny put the breakfast utensils in the sink and Jadeir picked up the three crystals and gave Kenny his crystal. Kenny picked out his potions from the cupboard and found his rucksack in the bedroom. They were about to go to the door of the flat when Kenny stopped in mid step.
"Oh, the caskets!" Kenny cried, "I'm so tired I nearly forgot them!"
"Where are they Kenny?" asked Jadeir.
"In Sarah's room I think," replied Kenny.

"I'll sense where they are easier than you, we'd better move fast!" said Jadeir.

He was already in Sarah's room by the end of the sentence, with Kenny giving him a puzzled look, wondering at the sudden urgency. Jadeir found the caskets and returned.

"I'll put them in your bag, Kenny," said Jadeir.

Jadeir put the two invisible objects into the rucksack, and Kenny slung it carefully onto his back, and they rushed downstairs to the healing room. There was a cracking sound from upstairs, and they both gave each other a concerned look.

"You go on ahead to Anchorin's, Kenny. I'll follow once I've dealt with them!" said Jadeir softly, not wishing to be heard.

Kenny looked concerned, gave a slight nod and continued to the healing room, "don't be long!" he whispered back.

As Kenny safely disappeared, Jadeir zapped at the renegades when he opened the door to the flat and they dispersed, and then he returned downstairs again. Increasing numbers of renegades appeared all around him, but he kept on zapping them, until they all eventually disappeared in a green fiery blaze. He then entered the healing room and transported himself to Anchorin's temple.

Kenny arrived outside the orichalcum dome and two of the resident monks beckoned him over, welcoming him cheerfully. Overhead, he could see the spaceship hovering. They went through the entrance door and Kenny followed the monks to the meeting room, and then they ushered him through the door.

Kenny saw the entire group who had returned from Colony Y, including Zanadar, Aurion and Melkior. He stood for a second, looking at them all in relief and then moved swiftly over to greet them all as they all approached to greet him. He spotted Karin and they gave each other an extra big hug. Anchorin came over to Kenny and shook his hand.
"Very glad to see you again, Kenny!" he said, smiling broadly, "we've all done our hugging before you came, as you can imagine. Did you bring the caskets in that bag?"
"Yes Anchorin, they are here," replied Kenny, and he removed the rucksack and carefully extracted the caskets from inside it and gave them to Anchorin.
Anchorin uncovered the caskets from the cloth covers, which Sarah and Maraya had wrapped them in before they left, and placed them on the centre table beside the alabaster pot of essence, and they promptly became visible again. Kenny then brought out the three gatekeeper crystals and placed them next to the caskets, and then went over to sit by Karin and the others. Hudlath stopped talking to Zanadar on noticing the caskets, and arose from his seat. He quietly walked over to Anchorin and started talking to him as he was still standing by the table examining the caskets.
"Here are the disks, Anchorin," said Hudlath, and he put them on the table beside the caskets. "Anchorin, I checked the third casket over a few times after I removed the portals which linked it to the renegades, but it may need to be re-examined."
"If you could return now, Hudlath, and when you bring it, take it to the healing room to check it," commented Anchorin, "it is vital that it is examined before making contact with the other caskets because..."
Hudlath quickly interjected, "because to do so if there was still a link between the renegades and the third casket, then the object could be swept away in the process, and possibly the others too!"
"Exactly!" replied Anchorin.

"I'll go now without further delay!" said Hudlath firmly, and he went out of the meeting room door to depart back to his time period.
There was a sound of voices in the corridor outside, which made everyone look over and then Jadeir entered.
"Greetings Jadeir!" cried Anchorin and everyone else joined in and he went round shaking hands with everyone, and then went over to sit with the other nature spirits and they began chatting animatedly together.

Hudlath took out his crystal and walked to Anchorin's office in order to return to what was his office in his time period. Once there, he disappeared instantly. There was the cabinet and he reached for the key inside a small pot, and opened it. The casket lay there quietly and he picked it up and placed it on the desk, still eyeing it closely. He locked the cabinet door, put the casket under his arm, and then focused on his crystal to return to Anchorin's time period. Once there, he looked at the casket. Immediately from within the casket something emanated and it looked like a star. Hudlath looked at it intently, for it shone beautifully for a few moments, but then it dulled gradually and rapidly began to turn into a dark looking eye. Hudlath had wasted no time in watching all of this and had cloaked the casket, while still seeing all this clairvoyantly, and sped out of the office calling Anchorin urgently and within seconds the door to the meeting room opened.
"Anchorin!" cried Hudlath, "the casket has the eye!"
Anchorin's face became set with determination, "into the healing room!"
They hurried inside and they both surrounded the casket in bright light. Anchorin removed the violet flame vessel from the central pedestal, and Hudlath placed the casket in its place. Anchorin called all the nature spirits to come through. There were seven crystals arranged in a circular formation, also on pedestals at the same height as the central one, and were all focused on the casket.
The nature spirits all entered, gathering around in a circle.
"What do you wish us to do Anchorin?" asked Gadair and Garalph.
"The casket has the eye on it," replied Anchorin, "we need your crystal power!"
The nature spirits all positioned themselves between the seven crystals. Anchorin stepped forwards, and as he stood by the casket, he looked at everyone intently, warning them to be ready. He swiftly lifted the covering material from the casket and stepped back into place with the others, and they all immediately activated their crystals sending energy towards the casket. The light from everyone's crystals increased in

intensity and the resistance from the eye increased also. It sent out a fierce energy in all directions, like black darts, and sinewy cords that wriggled and entwined around the crystals the nature spirits were holding. The group continued to send out their powerful green energy, which snapped the cords as they successively reappeared.
"Focus on the eye!" cried out Anchorin.
They all sent powerful fiery bursts of dazzling white energy directly at the eye so strongly for a period of time, and then everyone began to notice that the power of the eye was beginning to fade. It went dull and finally turned to dust and evaporated away.
"Well done everyone," cried Anchorin, "it took some overpowering!"
Hudlath went forward to look at the casket. He opened the lid and examined it carefully.
"It's pristine now!" he said, smiled happily and picked it up.
"Exellent!" replied Anchorin, "let's go through to the meeting room now."
They all returned and Hudlath placed the third casket beside the other two. Anchorin asked everyone to pay attention.
"I wish to re-assemble the caskets with all their components now, so please be aware of the effects that will follow from this," he explained.
He opened the lid of the Oswestry group's casket and replaced all the crystals and put a disk in its slot. Anchorin would know if it were the correct disk, for it would glow. Immediately there was a surge of energy, which emanated from the casket, and a bright light filled the room, which made everyone's eyes look brighter. Anchorin did the same with the Moroccan casket and the same surge of energy happened again. As Anchorin assembled the third casket the surge of energy was so powerful, everyone felt a tremendous sense of deep peace and began to understand the origins on planet Earth, see links to other planets, and also visions of life upon them, and the connections between them and Earth.

Once the visions and surges of energy quietened somewhat Anchorin arose from his chair to speak again.
"Now you know some of the power of the caskets my friends!" he stated, and he gave a brief smile and paused in thought. "My friends, you have all been so invaluable in helping with this mission, but as you know, once the caskets are reassembled then it becomes more difficult to cross the time barriers, so, my friends, it is time for those who wish to return to their time periods to depart. Before you go I wish to ask you to join me in another task, but you will do this when you return home. I ask you to link with us all here when I take the alabaster pot back, by praying and

sending out good energy. This is to hopefully shorten the time period when the essence in the pot reawakens again," and everyone murmured agreement, "and now you must go!"

Rhianah spoke first, "Guyanah and I are committed in helping in our time period despite how things are there and the consequences that lie ahead, so we must go. Feredino, will you and your friends return with us?"

"Yes, it is decided that we will, and help you," Feredino replied amidst affirmations from the others.

"Yes, so you must," replied Anchorin, "we all have our duties to do. Does anyone else wish to return?"

Hudlath spoke next, "yes, I must return too, I have my responsibilities as a high priest."

Sarah spoke for the Oswestry group, "we need to return also, don't we?" she said, looking around, and everyone agreed.

Maraya spoke for the Moroccan group, "we wish to stay Anchorin, if that is all right with you."

"You are welcome to stay with us," he said, smiling, "let us all share some refreshments before we say goodbye to each other, there is time before the links between the time periods close up."

Anchorin called some of his monks to bring some food and the vital spring water.

Kenny went over to Jadeir and asked him if he wished to come and stay with them in Oswestry.

"My friend, I would really like to stay with you, but my true home is here in Atlantis, but I will miss you and your friends," said Jadeir, giving Kenny a hearty hug.

Having eaten and drank, everyone began to gradually get up and have last talks with each other. The Oswestry group went around saying goodbye to Rhianah, Guyanah, and those from Colony Y, the space beings, Jadeir and the Moroccan group.

Anchorin went out of the room briefly and returned within a few minutes with a rectangular casket and placed it on the central table.

"Everyone!" he said in a loud voice, "I have brought some crystals for everyone; it is your reward if you like, and also because you travellers will need them to return home with!" With that he opened the box to reveal rows of quartz crystal wands with orichalcum handles inlaid with amethyst. "Come and help yourselves, and thank you again for helping us!"

Rhianah, Guyanah and the Colony Y group were the first to take their crystal wands, and announced that they would leave now. Everyone waved heartily to them until they vanished. Hudlath was next and took a wand and looked at everyone with a broad smile. "You know that we may all meet again!" gave an enigmatic look while radiating a bright warm energy to everyone and vanished.

"What does he mean that we may all meet again?" asked Kenny, looking puzzled.

Anchorin smiled, "Well, we know that the reassembly of the caskets closes the doors to time travel, but you are all going to have those crystal wands, and if your help is really needed then it could be arranged."

"Would it be possible quite soon?" asked Kenny.

"Not for a while, as the casket has to be returned to the Garden of Eden, and we have to see the reversal of procedures there for a while before the time portals can be opened," explained Anchorin.

"I suppose it is time we left, Anchorin," said Sarah, looking at Kenny's serious expression.

"We're coming back with you all too!" cried Leannah and the other Pistyll Rheaedr nature spirits, which cheered the Oswestry group.

"Well ok, we'd better go," said Kenny, "I must say that it seems a bit of an anticlimax having to leave here."

"I know Kenny," replied Anchorin gently, "but we all have our duties to do, wherever we have to be. Once you return and get immersed again, all will be well, believe me!" and he gave Kenny a kind smile.

Kenny said later to Karin that he could see something in Anchorin's eyes, like starlight with some kind of intuitive message which made him feel that although they were all going their separate ways, there was a deep sense of unity between them all, and that greatly comforted him.

The Oswestry group arose from their chairs and gathered together, along with the nature spirits. They all took a crystal wand each, and waved to everyone as they departed.

Zanadar, Aurion and Melkior stirred from their seats.

"We really ought to return to the spaceship now as we have work to do in some of the neighbouring universes, now that things are settled here," said Zanadar.

"Blessings to you!" said Zanadar, Aurion and Melkior and all three vanished, to reappear on their spaceship, which was still hovering overhead.

"I'll be seeing them again soon, no doubt!" said Anchorin to the Moroccan group.

Anchorin looked towards one of the walls with a piercing expression, with lids half closed.
"The climate out there is still wintry, but not quite as stormy since the caskets were assembled," said Anchorin, "it is time I returned the alabaster pot."
He made ready to set off, with the pot inside its little casket and placed it inside a shoulder bag, and then picked up his staff.
"Just make yourselves at home until I return, and then we can see where your destiny lies in Chalidocea," said Anchorin, "and don't forget to take your crystal wands too!"
"Thank you, Anchorin, we won't!" they cried.
Once Anchorin left, they helped themselves to the wands. One of the monks came in to clear away the plates and remaining refreshments.
"Excuse me please," asked Maraya, "we noticed that when we all took the crystal wands from this box, there were exactly the right amount. Did Anchorin know this beforehand?"
"Yes, he did," replied the monk, "he knew this when he realised that the caskets would disappear within the later time period. He had those wands made at least thirty years ago in your time!"
"That's amazing!" cried Costillo, "how could he know?"
"It is very possible when you are linked to universal time," said the monk with a smile, "anything can be known then!"
"Can you link to that universal time?" asked Sagario.
"I'm trying!" laughed the monk, "I can see some things, but need lots more practice," and the others smiled.
"By the way, if we are spending time here, we ought to know all the monks names, including yours!" said Maraya.
"My name is Uyindin, which means 'lapping the edges of the universe' in your language, not a bad name eh!" he said.
"That's beautiful," said Danuel, with a thoughtful look.
Maraya looked at Uyindin's eyes and saw that familiar bright glow in them, a prevalent characteristic on Atlantean soil, but for a fleeting moment, she saw a twinkle of a star in his eyes.
"I'll tell you the other monks' names as you meet them. Come, I'll introduce you to them," said Uyindin, and he picked up his tray.
"Let us help you with these dishes," said Maraya.

They picked up what they could and followed Uyindin to the kitchen, and he introduced the Moroccan group to some of the other monks.

Anchorin had travelled across the wintry white landscape, and had flown there despite being assailed by falling snow whipping against him as he progressed. It seemed a long journey to him this time, and he was relieved to arrive at the wooden gates to the Garden. A heavy mist hung over the trees and the gates had long since lost their leaves. Arwena's tall figure came into view; she had a dark green shawl around her, but her eyes still held that bright emerald green colour. She welcomed Anchorin inside the Garden again, and they greeted each other warmly. He hurried onwards, intent on reaching the temple as soon as he could. Through the mists and dank grass he saw the faded foliage and the lake beyond it. He rose and flew over the water, realising he was now accompanied by the unicorns and the Sentinel group. He landed gently on the temple's island, leaving footprints in the layer of snow as he approached the temple. Once inside, he called to the female guardians, Anui, Deanu and Giana, and they approached Anchorin.
"Here is the alabaster pot, my friends," said Anchorin, holding it out to them.
"Thank you Anchorin, just place it back on the table, please," they said.
He did so and a faint glow began to emanate from it, and started to increase in strength, lightening the surroundings. Anchorin prayed that the return of this pot could, with the prayers of his and all other Atlantean temples during the time of the pot's absence from the Garden, somehow hasten the return to the sublime state it was in previously.
"Link to your temple now," advised the group, "and ask them to contact every temple in Poseidia to continue sending good energy and prayers this way and it will truly help."
"Anchorin brought out his crystal and contacted the monks there. Uyindin answered, "I will inform everyone here and spread the message across the country immediately!"
Anchorin waited patiently. In his heart he would know when the country had been informed; meanwhile he watched how the glow of the pot increased and it was now getting quite bright, casting some warmth around the room.
Anchorin sensed images of people in prayer and nature spirits sending good energy too, so he knew all was now in progress. He even sensed those in the other time periods in prayer, and he began to join in with his prayers and energy sending. Intent in prayer, the thought suddenly

passed through his mind if all was being effective, and immediately he was told by Anui to continue for several more hours.

As time progressed he could feel the brightness increase. He briefly thought of Hudlath, Rhianah and the Oswestry group and their efforts and whether it could penetrate the time barriers and be of value too. Somehow a glowing feeling came to him on considering this, and he knew within him that their endeavours were working.

Finally, after those hours of praying and projecting energy, Anchorin sprinkled some ground amaranth seeds and elixir powder over the casket and he sent a heartfelt plea for the lands to be restored. The thought of waiting for fifteen thousand years for everything to revert back to normal would be a very gloomy prospect indeed.

"We have been in touch with the forces in the depths of our planet and they have decided to help us in overturning this ruling, and have also been in touch with the Council of Twelve," said Anui, Deanu and Giana, "now extra strength will be given to the essence."

With that, and immense burst of energy surged upwards out of the earth and into the pot, and a beam of light and energy rushed downward into the pot also. The radiance that exuded from the essence as a result filled the whole room and warmed it. Anchorin now knew this radiance was spreading outwards throughout the Garden of Eden and beyond. A smile of relief spread over his face and he cried out with joy, and the female guardians smiled happily.

"Now you can leave, knowing your land is restored, Anchorin," they said, "thank you so much to you and your friends for all your help." "Thank you so much too, for ensuring that the time span was shortened considerably," replied Anchorin.

He walked out of the temple to see the bright sunlight and summery foliage, now with flowers unfurling and he could smell the beautiful scents. The unicorns looked at Anchorin, their eyes brightly filled with a starry light. They looked at Anchorin as if to say 'we told you everything would work out.'

He knew then that anything was possible and even the most impossible barriers melt before heartfelt intent. He smiled at them happily and they approached gently, encircling him, and Anchorin put his arms around two of the unicorn's necks and felt suffused by such a glowing love for all life, far more than he usually felt. After several moments the unicorns gently

withdrew and Anchorin gave them all a wave as he departed towards the wooden gates, and he could see new saplings growing out of them now.
"I'm so glad to see the spring again Arwena," said Anchorin, and there were tears in his eyes.
Arwena gave him a hug and bright spring green light radiated from her and surrounded Anchorin.
"You are truly linked to us here now," she said with a smile, and several fairies landed on her shoulders, and a group of elves came to stand beside them both.
Anchorin bade farewell to them all and flew off back to the temple, appreciating the sunny warmth on his face.

Kenny, Karin, Sarah and Alyssia had also just finished their prayer time. It was early evening by that time.
"I feel such a beautiful glow in my heart having done the prayers and energy transmitting," commented Karin.
"I feel the same way too," said Sarah, and the others agreed.
"You know," said Alyssia, "I'm getting images. It's as if there's something happening somewhere. All I can see is the colour of green."
"Do you think it could be coming from Atlantis?" asked Kenny excitedly, "the greening of the land could be happening right now!"
"Look!" cried Sarah, "the crystal wands are glowing!"
"It must be!" echoed Karin, "how wonderful."
"Anchorin and Hudlath could be right after all, do you think?" asked Kenny, "that we may all meet up again."
Sarah went to peer out of the south-facing window in Karin and Kenny's room.
"Come and look at this cloud over the moon!" cried Sarah. Everyone went to look. It was a unicorn's head in profile. Just then, there was the familiar sound of an elixir plant seed head dropping off and everyone looked at each other and laughed.
Kenny put his arm around Karin's shoulder.
"It's not just coincidence. We are definitely being told that all is well in Atlantis, and it will be possible to go back in time again some day," he said.

* 9 7 8 1 9 0 7 0 4 2 2 4 9 *